Saint Bride and Her Book

Birgitta of Sweden's Revelations

Translated from Middle English,
with Introduction, Notes,
and Interpretative Essay

This book is published by Focus Information Group, Inc., PO Box 369, Newburyport MA, 01950.

Saint Bride and Her Book

Birgitta of Sweden's Revelations

**Translated from Middle English,
with Introduction, Notes,
and Interpretative Essay**

Julia Bolton Holloway

Focus Texts
Newburyport Massachusetts

Frontispiece: Diptych, Saints Birgitta and Catherine of Sweden
Veckhom, Uppland. Antikvarisk-Topografiska Arkivet, Stockholm, Sweden

Table of Contents

Illustrations

Cover Andrea da Firenze, *via Veritatis*, Spanish Chapel, Santa Maria Novella, Pope, Emperor, Kind Peter of Cyprus, possibly Saints Birgitta and Catherine of Sweden. Fratelli Alinari, Florence, Italy

Frontispiece Diptych, Saints Birgitta and Catherine of Sweden, Veckholm, Uppland, Antikvarisk-topografdiska, Stockholm, Sweden.

Woodblocks From *Revelationes Sanctae Brigittae* (Lubeck: Ghotan, 1492). *Editio princeps* first edition.   vii, 1,3,32,33, 120,121

To
James N. Corbridge, Jr.,
Chancellor,
The University Of Colorado At Boulder,
Because He Aided This Book,
And To The Memory Of
Alva Myrdal,
Sweden's Minister of Disarmament,
For Her Work For Peace

Preface

 Saint Birgitta's Life, her *vita*, and her Book, the *Revelations*, exist in countless documents and manuscripts, in many languages. In this book's chronology, map, and texts, we see her, in time and space, attaining power and influence. St. Birgitta wrote of herself as Christ's bride, his *sponsa*. English writers therefore often called her Saint Bride, as well as Byrgitt or, more rarely, Bridget, among them Margery Kempe using the punning form of her name, "Saint Bride."

Because Birgitta and her daughter Catherine were considered for canonization as saints within their own century, careful written accounts were compiled about both women. Paradoxically, when a saint is canonized by the church, that individual, though dead, undergoes a *processus*, a trial, much in the same manner as does a living person about to be convicted or acquitted of a crime. The canonization process likewise consists of the telling of tales by witnesses; indeed the *Acta et Processus*, the *Deeds and Trial*, becomes a collection of biographical stories, out of sequence, but compellingly narrated, as authenticating anecdotes and examples of sanctity, as if they were *The Ring and the Book* in reverse. These documents survive. A *vita* was also created, both for the canonization and using these canonization documents.

These documents concerning the life of Saint Bride largely survive because Birgitta herself had already written books and letters setting forth her visions from Christ, the Virgin, and Saints to Popes, Emperors, and Kings. These books included her eight-volume *Revelations*, her *Rule* for her Order of the Holy Saviour and Saint Birgitta, and her *Sermo Angelicus*, the *Conversation with the Angel*, dictated to her by an angel, and *Cantus Sororum*, the *Sisters' Songs*, giving the Offices for her nuns and monks to sing. This book attempts to present, edit, and translate some of these writings.

Besides such texts are her wonder-working relics, parts of her body, and also her garments and possessions, such as her patchwork quilt of a mantle cobbled together from a wornout dress. These objects are treasured in the double monasteries founded as daughter houses throughout Europe from her mother house, the Abbey in Vadstena, Sweden, in the same places as were her manuscripts to be found. It is possible to patch together again the "Book of Saint Bride," as if it were a cloak fashioned from a robe, through using her own words from the autobiographical *Revelations*, and from others' accounts of her in the trial for canonization. It was, indeed, in that manner that books by her and about her were written in the Middle Ages. We even have an example of her own writing, preserved in Stockholm, where she has penned Swedish words upon Italian paper, sewing two sheets together in order not to waste them.

This volume consists of an introduction giving the life–the *vita*–of Saint Birgitta from a Latin document preserved in Florence, Italy, but written out in Vadstena, Sweden, by Johannes Johannis of Kalmar, in 1397, soon after her canonization. Then the text of Princeton University's Garrett manuscript of her *Revelations* follows. I chose to translate this particular version of the extant *Revelations* because it stresses the prophetic visionary quality of her writings, because it presents her *Revelations* in an already appropriately edited medieval version, and because its second part is focused on women. The manuscript is likely written out by two English Brigittine monastics, one, perhaps, male, the other possibly a nun, who translate and digest into Middle English Saint Birgitta's far lengthier eight-volume work recorded in Latin by male priests, the Swedish Master Mathias, the two Peter Olavis, of Alvastra and of Skenninge, and the Spanish Alfonso of Jaen, her appointed confessors. Last in the volume is given an interpretive essay discussing Bride's use of textuality as a woman in order to gain access to power and to influence the rulers of Christendom, in the manner of the Sibyls and the Prophets, and the adoption of that textuality by other women both within and outside of her monastic communities. Throughout, the texts generated by Bride's community are themselves presented as evidence for this book's arguments. The footnotes to the Text are for the use of undergraduate readers; the endnotes to the Introduction and the Interpretative Essay document the research carried out in Sweden, Italy, Germany and England amongst manuscripts and books usually not in English (it is suggested that the undergraduate student ignore these); the bibliography, or Suggestions for Further Reading, only lists those works concerning Birgitta of Sweden, studies on women, monasticism and pilgrimage related to this book, the Brigittine presence in England, and works on Julian of Norwich and Margery Kempe, whom she influenced, that would be accessible and useful to undergraduate students.

In the translation and in the essays, Birgitta is either called such or given the form "Bride," as she is called in some Middle English manuscripts, such as British Library MS Claudius BI, MS Julius FII, and the *Book of Margery Kempe*, in obvious reference to Christ speaking of her as his *"sponsa,"* his Bride. In the Princeton, Garrett Collection, manuscript translated here she is "seynte Byrgitte" or "saynt Birgytt," that spelling being more correct and true to the Swedish form of her name. This book avoids the Irish form, Bridget. The Garrett manuscript text uses "ghost," rather than "Spirit," "maker," rather than "Creator," "ayan-byer" ("again-buyer"), rather than "Redeemer," "righteousness" rather than "Justice," and so forth, forms of words which are closer to their original meaning in English but for which today's customary usage is in alienating Latin. Medieval texts used little capitalization in connection with God. Some, but not all, of the modern printing conventions in this area are adopted, generally nouns only being capitalized. Roman and arabic numbers in square brackets following the manuscript's rubrics (parts emphasized by being written in red, here in bold), refer to book and chapter divisions in *Revelationes Sanctae Brigittae* (Rome: Grignani, 1628). A facsimile edition is greatly needed of the fine Lübeck 1492 *editio princeps*, or first edition, for scholarly use.

One section of this Middle English manuscript, on the "Doom of Kings," was previously translated into Modern English by Patrick O'Moore and published in 1982 in an edition limited to 40 copies, followed by a translation of *Revelations* V and VII and other materials from the Latin texts, in *Birgitta of Sweden: Life and Selected Writings*, edited by Marguerite Tjader Harris, Albert Ryle Kezel, and Tore Nyberg, published by the Paulist Press in 1990. Several books have been written in English about Saint Birgitta of Sweden. But there is still a great need to position Birgitta in the gallery of portraits of major women writers. She had been placed in the canon of saints in 1391, the Emperor Charles of Bohemia, Chaucer's Queen Anne of Bohemia's father, several Popes, Queens Joan of Naples, Eleanor of Cyprus, and Margaret of Sweden and even the Grand Inquisitor, Torquemada, vouching for her sanctity. In 1492, celebrating the centenary of her canonization, her *Revelations* was printed, instead of handwritten, for the first time. It is fitting that this book should appear, six centuries after her canonization, in 1991.

Much of this book's material I learned from my colleagues, Professors

John Fleming, Gail McMurray Gibson, Julian Jaynes, William Jordan, Jean Preston, Princeton University, Jeanne Krochalis, Pennsylvania State University, David Anderson, University of Tübingen (who noted Vauchez' work on canonization materials as a mode for conveying history), Clifford and Audrey Davidson, University of Western Michigan, Anthony Luttrell, Bath, Amy Vandersall, University of Colorado, Boulder, and Judson Boyce Allen, all of whom have taught me to love medieval justice, medieval manuscripts and medieval archives. Also greatly deserving of thanks is Professor Jane Chance of Rice University who commissioned this book, and who has stimulated and supported the work of fellow women scholars, so that they may in turn shape a generation of women readers believing in ourselves, a major example being this series in the Focus Library. My sister-in-law, Maria Antonia Bandres y Bolton, will remember our visit together to the monastery of Farfa because my brother, Richard Rothwell Bolton, had found in its library our father's book on Pope John XXIII. Princeton University allowed me to teach a seminar on Medieval Pilgrimage and Literature, where I first really encountered this tiny, intrepid woman saint and pilgrim. My student, John Wheaton, then pilgrimaged to Sweden. Next, Joan Bechtold incorporated Birgitta of Sweden into her Master's Thesis, along with Matilda of Tuscany and Catherine of Siena, on the three women who dialogued with Popes and Emperors. John Wheaton became a journalist. Joan is becoming a lawyer. As an undergraduate student, Lancia Chadwick carefully read this book's manuscript and made suggestions for similar readers.

A separate book on the Life of Saint Birgitta, translated from the complete text by Birger Gregersson and, perhaps, Thomas Gascoigne, and which gives a more complete bibliography, is published by Peregrina Publishing, Toronto, Canada. An article, "Bride, Julian, Margery and Alice: Birgitta of Sweden's Textual Community in Medieval England," listing Brigittine, Julian and Margery manuscripts and incunabula, is appearing in a book of essays on Margery Kempe, edited by Professor Sandra McEntire, and published by Garland Press, New York. The Latin text of the Florentine Paradiso document is being published in connection with the 1991 Brigittine Congress in Rome.

Thanks are due to the Graduate Committee on Research and Creative Work of the University of Colorado at Boulder and the College of Arts and Sciences for travel grants enabling me to visit libraries in Sweden, England, France, Italy and the Vatican on a pilgrimage quest amidst Brigittine manuscripts and books, as well as to the Interlibrary Loan Service of my university's Norlin Library. I thank Father Leonard Boyle at the Vatican Library, and likewise Florentine librarians, at the Biblioteca Nazionale, the

Laurentian and the Riccardian, and the archivists at the Archivio di Stato; also librarians and scholars in England, especially the Bodleian and the British Library, Bavaria, Paris, and Sweden, including Birger Bergh, Esbjörne Belfrage and Arne Jönsson of Lund University. I am grateful to Father Michael Maclean of Norwich Cathedral for his information about Julian and Margery and Father John E. Halborg for reading this book in manuscript. Thanks are due too to Christopher de Hamel of Sothebys, London, and to Julian Plante of the Hill Monastic Library, for information on the whereabouts of several Syon and Brigittine manuscripts. I also wish to thank those who gave hospitality to this pilgrim writer, the Community of the Holy Family, Ingrid de Hevesy Rådman, Diana Leap, Giorgio Nencetti, Jeremy DuQuesnay Adams and Bonnie Wheeler. The woodblocks in this book are taken from Andreas Lindblom, *Den Heliga Birgitta bildverk i skulptur och måleri från sveriges medeltid* (Stockholm: P.A. Norstedt, 1918), who in turn reproduced them from the first edition of Birgitta's *Revelations*, her Life and Writings, printed in Lübeck in 1492. The engravings, as much as does the text, stress the importance of Saint Bride and her Book. Above all, I wish to thank the Lady Abbess of Syon, the Prioress and Father Bachbauer of Altomünster, and Sister Patricia of Vadstena, for their great kindness. I had not expected, when I started this quest, to find that women throughout Europe can still live the Rule Birgitta wrote. Nor had I expected to find such a wealth of medieval manuscripts written by, for and about women.

Last, and most, of all, I wish to thank Saint Bride and her Book for shaping this mirroring textuality and even my life of flesh and blood with her words and books these many centuries later. The concluding verse was written in 1374 by Bishop Nicholas Hermansson of Linköping, who had been Birgitta's sons' Latin teacher.

Rosa, rorans bonitatem,
Stella, stillans claritatem,
Birgitta, vas gratiae,

Rose, bedewed with goodness,
Star, shining with clearness,
Birgitta, vessel of grace.

St. Bride's Day, 1990
Paradiso, Florence

Chronology of Saint Bride's Life, Times and Influence

1296 King Birger Magnusson asks Birger Persson to emend laws.
1303 Ingeborg, pregnant with Bridget, shipwecked, saved by Duke Eric. Birgitta born, Finsta.
1310 Ingeborg's death. Birgitta raised by Aunt Catherine of Apenäs.
1311 Birgitta's first Revelation. Virgin crowns Birgitta.
1316 Birgitta marries Ulf Gudmarson.
1330 Ulf, Lawman of Närke, or Nericia. Birgitta taught Latin with her sons by Nicholas Hermansson, later Bishop of Linköping. Birger Persson, Gudmar Ulfsson die. Ingeborg Ulfsdotter enters convent.
1332 Catherine Ulfsdotter born. Master Peter Olavi, Birgitta's tutor.
1335 King Magnus marries Blanche of Namur, Birgitta her governess.
1341 Virgin tells Birgitta she will see Christ in Jerusalem.
1342 Ulf and Birgitta make pilgrimage to Compostela. Ulf's illness in Arras. Nicholas Acciaiuoli founds Carthusian Certosa, Florence. Queen Joan of Naples, at 16, marries Andrew of Hungary.
1343 Julian of Norwich born.
1344 Ulf's death, burial at Alvastra. God makes Birgitta his Bride. Master Mathias her adviser.
1344-46 Rule of Order of Holy Saviour composed.
1345 Master Mathias, at Bride's request, translates Pentateuch into Swedish. Joan has her husband killed.
1346 Christ tells Bride to go to Rome. Magnus gives Vadstena to Bride.
1347 Bride tells the prophecy of Christ as Ploughman bringing Black Death. Queen Joan remarries, to Louis of Taranto, at instigation of Nicholas Acciaiuoli, her lover and his tutor.
1349 Bride leaves Sweden. Black Death outbreak, prophesied to King Magnus by Bride.
1350 Magister Mathias' death. Bride makes pilgrimage to Rome in Jubilee Year. Lodges in Cardinal's palace by Saint Lawrence in Damaso. Travels to Farfa. Catherine leaves for Rome.
1351 Bride tells Pope Clement VI to leave Avignon for Rome. Catherine prepares to return to Sweden. Eggert, her husband, dies. She decides to stay with Bride.
1352 Whitsunday, Coronation of Joan and Louis of Naples. December 2, lightning strikes bells of St. Peters' and melts them. Christ had told Bride this would be sign of Pope Clement's death. Bride starts writing *Sermo Angelicus* [*Conversation with the Angel*].

1354 Bride's household evicted from Cardinal's palace, moves to Francesca Papazuri's palace, which becomes Casa di Santa Brigida.
1355 Bride tells Emperor Charles of Bohemia to reform the Empire. April 2, he comes to Rome as pilgrim, April 5, is crowned in St. Peter's. October 15, Pope sends Birger and Catherine 400 gold florins.
1358-60 King Magnus under papal interdict.
1360 Cecilia Ulfsdotter abducted by brother Charles from convent of St. Ingrid in Skenninge and married to knight.
1363 Israel Birgersson, Bride's brother, refuses crown of Sweden, dies on crusade in Riga.
1364 King Magnus captured in war, imprisoned. Albert elected king. Cecilia Ulfsdotter marries a second time.
1365-1367 Bride in Naples, cures Lapa Acciaiuoli Buondelmonte's son, Esau, from terminal tuberculosis, crippling.
1366 Bride orders Pope Urban V and Emperor Charles to improve their rule. Birger Ulfsson starts building Vadstena Abbey. Bride and Queen Joan of Naples meet. Death of Nicholas Acciaiuoli, predicted by Bride.
1367 Tax imposed on every Swedish citizen to build Vadstena Abbey. April 30, Pope Urban V leaves Avignon for Rome. Bride raises Roman nobleman's son from the dead, Gentile Orsini, by placing her cloak over his corpse.
1368 October 21, Pope and Emperor in Rome. Alfonso of Jaen resigns bishopric, becomes Hieronomyte hermit. Crucifix speaks to Bride at St. Paul's Outside the Walls, Rome. Julian of Norwich writes First Text of *Revelations*, Westminster Cathedral manuscript.
1369 Bride predicts Pope's death if he returns to Avignon. June 16, passport issued to Bride's family to travel to Bari.
1370 August 4, Montefiascone, Urban V's Bull grants Augustinian Rule, Rule of the Holy Saviour as supplement, no indulgence for Vadstena. Bride asks the new Pope, Gregory XI, to come to Rome. Thomas Stubbs, Richard Lavenham at Oxford, acquire *Revelations*.
1372 Bride begins pilgrimage to Jerusalem, Charles Ulfsson dying in Naples. March 11, Naples, March 14, sails to Messina from Naples, reaching Messina, March 19, Cyprus, March 26, Cephalonia, March 30, in great tempest going to Cos, April 1-4, greeted by Master of the Order of St John Hospitaller, April 8, Cyprus, Paphos, then, with a good wind, Famagusta. Birger Ulfsson dubbed a knight in Holy Sepulchre. Bride receives many Revelations on Calvary and in Bethlehem as she had been promised by the Virgin when in Sweden.

1373 May 13, 4:00 a.m., Julian of Norwich's Revelation. July 23, Bride dies in Papazuri house near Campo dei Fiori, body brought to Saint Lawrence in Panisperna and laid in marble sarcophagus. Francesca Papazuri places painting of Crucifixion in room of Bride's death.

1374 Bones of right arm left in Panisperna. July 4, Catherine and Birger bring Bride's remains to Vadstena. Catherine, head of nuns, Petrus Olavi, of monks. *Revelations* and other writings edited and published as manuscripts. King Magnus' death at sea. Catherine of Siena examined by Inquisition. Pope sends her Alphonse of Jaen.

1375 Pope Gregory returns to Rome. Catherine, at the King of Sweden's request, comes to Rome to negotiate Bride's canonization.

1376 Pope Gregory proposes Bride's canonization to Cardinals.

1377 Pope Gregory's death.

1378 Pope Urban VI unwilling to canonize Bride. Codex Saint Lawrence in Panisperna.

1379 Catherine stops Tiber from flooding Rome. December 3, Pope Urban VI establishes Brigittine Rule, canonization process begun.

1380 Catherine receives Bull from Pope permitting Bride's remains to be enshrined, returns to Sweden.

1381 Master Peter Olavi's and Catherine's deaths. Peasants' Revolt, Wyclif's first complete Bible. Richard Rolle's canonization proposed.

1383 December 8, Francesca Papazuri's Deed of Gift of Casa di Santa Brigida to Vadstena.

1384 October 23, 21 monks, 46 nuns enclosed at Vadstena by Bishop Nicholas Hermansson.

1385 Three Vadstena monks go to Rome for canonization process.

1386 Cardinal Adam Easton of England, Benedictine monk of Norwich Priory, vows to work for Bride's canonization if he is saved from execution for conspiracy against Pope.

1388 Vadstena rebuilt in stone after fire.

1389 Cardinal Adam reinstated by Pope.

1391 Birger Ulfsson dies, August 26. Cecilia Ulfsdotter dies. Bride canonized, October 7. Boniface IX's bull, October 9, canonization, indulgence. Nuns of Saint Lawrence in Panisperna enshrine relic.

1392 Julian of Norwich completes longer version, *Revelations*.

1418 Birgitta Karlsdotter, Bride's great granddaughter, when dying has vision of Bride and wild strawberries, buried at Vadstena.

1419 April, Pope Martin V approves Rule.

1434 Margery Kempe visits Sheen, Syon Abbey.

1436 *Book of Margery Kempe.*

Map of Saint Bride's Pilgrimages and Brigittine Convents

Introduction: Saint Bride: Flesh and Blood Made Word and Book

 Birgitta of Sweden, commonly known as Brigida in Italy, Bride or Bridget in England, a noblewoman of that northernmost country who lived from 1303 to 1373, was a mother of eight children, traveled as a pilgrim throughout Europe and to Jerusalem, and spoke and wrote as an equal to popes and emperors. She was acknowledged by almost all as God's Ambassador, his Bride and his *canale* or channel of communication (pp. 33-35).[1]

In the fourteenth century, Europe was shifting from the Middle Ages to the Renaissance. But Bride's own northern kingdom of Sweden would remain stylistically in the Middle Ages for centuries and had only recently with great fervor shifted from paganism to Christianity, its people filled with the desire to perform arduous pilgrimages, journeys to distant, sacred shrines generally situated in Romance and Mediterranean regions, Compostela, Rome and Jerusalem. Bride herself would travel from the north to the west, the south, and the east upon such pilgrimages, crisscrossing all of continental Europe and reaching Jerusalem in Asia.

Medieval Europe was supposedly governed by the Pope and the Emperor but in actual fact feudal kingdoms, dukedoms, and counties allowed for much autonomy. Bride would go to the top, communicating with the Pope, the Emperor and the kings of Europe, not realizing the initial inefficacy of her action. Medieval Europe saw itself as divided into categories, such as Knight, Monk and Ploughman for men, Virgin, Bride and Widow for women. It forgot about the new presence of the Merchant.[2] When Bride would speak about a merchant he would symbolize for her the temptations of the World, the Flesh and the Devil, and especially of her desire to remain with her children, rather than enter the monastic life of abnegation.[3]

Medieval Europe believed when calamities occurred, such as the Black Death following in the wake of malnutrition brought about by climate changes and crop failures, that God was punishing man for his sinfulness.[4] Medieval Europe was bound to a code and economy of interdependence formulated upon religious and philosophical ethics.[5] Bride made use of this pseudo-causal perception, of prophecy, to obtain political and religious power and she largely succeeded because she and others fully believed in such concepts.

This is the story of a woman and her book. Women, even more so than do men, die unnamed and unknown. Because of women's almost universal apartheid from education and power, which excluded us also from textuality and its monuments, our names are generally not inscribed on brass, stone, parchment or paper. But Saint Bride left to us tangible monuments and relics of herself, parts of her body in her shrine at Vadstena and its daughter houses throughout Europe,[6] and even the artifacts and relics of the pilgrim staff and wooden bowl inscribed with Latin words in Cyrillic letters: the board upon which she wrote her books, upon which she ate, and upon which, according to the tradition, she may have even died, the hair shirt, and the ancient patched mantle in which she begged for the keep of her household.[7] Likewise throughout Europe, and even in America, precious manuscript books which were written by her and her amanuenses,[8] then copied out by others, including the nuns in her convents, as well as copies of the process or trial for canonization as a saint, are to be found. André Vauchez has ably argued for the need to study such archival documents as a means to historical study.[9] In this book about her book we shall use these monuments, especially manuscripts, some of which in turn were written by medieval English men and perhaps women, to tell her tale.

Her success came about because, as the daughter of one Lawman, Birger Persson, and the wife of another, Ulf Gudmarsson, Bride saw how to use the power of the written word. Therefore, let us first begin with Birgitta's family, and then of her childhood. Birgitta's father, Birger Persson, became Lawman, *legifer*, of Uppland, rewriting, in collaboration with others, the new law to replace the old heathen one. He began it with a preface speaking of Moses as "the first Lawman," stating further, "the Law shall be the honor of the just and wise, but shall chastise the wrong-doers and the unwise," "If all men were just no Law would be needed."[10] Iceland preserved this form of parliament, the All Thing, and the office of the Lawman, who recited orally to the assembled group the formulae of the Law.[11] Birger Persson's work is divided into sections, on inheritance, "May God so let us divide the inheritance, that we may inherit the kingdom of heaven"; on land, "The land shall be built upon the Law and not upon violence, for the state of a land is best when the Law is followed," "God lets us so desire land that we may obtain heaven"; on peace, "This is said of peace. May God give peace to all who come hither with the will to peace, to be here and to fare forth from here. Peace be to our king, our land and Lawman, and to all those who have listened to the saying of the Law."[12] Birger Persson's Uppland Law was confirmed by King Birger Magnusson in 1296, a few years before the birth of Birger's daughter, Birgitta.[13]

I. Bride as Virgin

For the narration of Bride's life, beginning with her childhood, let us use a document in Florence once kept in a former Brigittine abbey, the Paradiso, and written out in Sweden in 1397 by Johannes Johannis of Kalmar, a son of a goldsmith, who later became a Brigittine brother.[14] Its text is based in turn upon the Latin text authorized by the Swedish Archbishop of Uppsala, Birger Gregersson, in 1376, three years following Bride's death, from material compiled and written by Bishop Alfonso of Jaen, Petrus Olavi, and Bishop Nicholas Hermansson of Linköping, and which is often used to preface Saint Bride's own writings, the *Revelations*.[15] It presents to us an official and authorized life of Bride as a Saint, though it, as legend, is not entirely to be trusted. It is patched together much like her mantle, from the canonization materials, giving anecdotes and stories told by her friends, associates and relatives, and from her own autobiographical *Revelations*, or *Showings* as Julian of Norwich would title her *Revelations* written in imitation of those of Bride. In narrating Bride's life, the *Acta Sanctorum* or *Acts of the Saints* in turn speaks of her first as Virgin, then as Wife, lastly as Widow, categories she herself stressed in her visions. Each of these texts, her own autobiographical *Revelations*, the legal testimonies of the canonization trial, and this *vita* created from these other two texts, deals with a woman of flesh and blood, while each imposes expectations from doctrine and from saints' legends, allowing fiction to embroider fact.

 Truly, this glorious woman by her father Birger and her mother Ingeborg[16] was born of the royal stock and lineage of the kings of Sweden, noted for their religious faith and constancy in virtue, whose nobility was clear from the beginning. Her mother while pregnant when crossing the sea was shipwrecked in a storm in which many, both men and women, died, but she came safely to shore and the next night in a vision a person stood by her, dressed in marvelous shining clothes and concerning the so greatly venerated widow said without pronouncing outwardly, "You are saved because of the goodness that is in your womb. Therefore, nurture it with the love of

God as it is a gift given to you from God."[17]

When the girl Birgitta was just born, the priest in the nearby parish church, noted for his perfect life, while resting from praying in the night, saw in a vision the Virgin sitting in a shining cloud, having a book in her hand, saying to him, "A daughter is born to Birger, whose voice will be heard through the world with admiration."[18]

But from her birth until she was three years old, it was as if she was mute. Then, against the nature of children, she did not stammer or make gestures but she was heard and seen to speak in complete and shaped sentences.[19]

During her childhood her devotion was noted, she prayed and fasted and performed other good works.

III. Bride as Wife

Inexorably, however, the family insisted upon a new chapter in her life, that of Bride as Wife. Bride sought to reconcile sainthood and marriage. She especially loved the story of Saint Cecilia's chaste marriage to Valerianus,[20] and, when she was wed to Ulf Gudmarsson, she made him make a similar vow of chastity.[21]

She wished to serve God in the state of virginity, but her parents compelled her to marry Ulf Gudhmarson,[22] a most noble and Christian prince of Nericia. And when it was fitting they were wed, the husband being eighteen and his wife thirteen, yet they chose to live a whole year in abstinence, imitating the young Thobias and Sarah, daughter of Raguel, humbly praying to God, and when they loved, it was without sin and in order for God to grant them progeny to serve him. And when they did come together in fear of God and trembling, it was not lust but in order to have children. During this time the devout wife fasted and prayed and carried out other pious and customary works. And she was especially devoted to the Virgin, so that one time when she was in childbirth and the midwives and women with her despaired of her life, an imperious, unknown woman dressed in white silk garments was seen to enter her room and assist by the bed, touching each of her limbs. Then the woman disappeared and immediately she gave birth without more pain and completely recovered. And with this the said couple being still young and recently married, the husband was persuaded by the admonitions of his happy sainted wife. For the courage of a man does not need to be stripped when he returns good and not evil all the days of his life, the wife speaking to him often that they should observe chastity and no young couple were more devout being always most fervent in the fear of God, and the love of their neighbor. They made a vow of pilgrimage to visit the shrine of blessed James the Apostle in Compostela.[23] And on returning, by common consent, both entered different monasteries, the said prince in that resolve dying in the Lord.[24]

Medieval society–in the world of time–was rigidly hierarchical and structured, representing the Three Orders, Monk, Knight and Ploughman. But in eternity, in religion and on pilgrimage, instead, all could theologically be equal. Women, for this reason, especially made use of pilgrimages in particular and religion in general in order to attain access to power normally denied to us by male legal encoding. In Bride's day the legal and religious abolition of thralldom, serfdom or slavery was an important issue. For, as well as law, the family's background stressed religion, monasticism and pilgrimage. Birger Persson's first wife, Kristina (+1295), was related to Ingrid Elof's daughter, who, in 1270, had founded the convent for nuns at Skenninge, near Vadstena, upon her return from pilgrimage to the Holy Land. Many of Bride's relatives had made pilgrimages,[25] participating in that liberating and liminal state outside of hierarchies.[26]

Contextually, beside marriage and parenting and the making of pilgrimages to St. Olav's shrine at Trondheim and St. James' shrine at Compostela, Bride had assumed grave responsibilities at court. The young King Magnus Smek ("Caress") of Sweden, was married to Blanche, or Blanka, de Namur in 1335, the same year that he had extended the Uppland law forbidding the buying and selling of thralls to other sections of Sweden, "To the glory of God and the Virgin Mary, for in as much as God delivered us from heathendom he has made us all free."[27] Birger Persson wrote that law. Birger Persson's daughter was entrusted with the education of the very young queen and king, at one time rescuing the relics of Saint Louis, King Louis IX of France, in their ivory casket which Blanka had carelessly left lying about in a castle corridor.[28] Bride took her educational materials from Franciscan materials, from Saint Louis's testament to his son[29] and from the Norwegian *Mirror for Kings*, creating of these eventually her own *Liber Coelestis Imperatoris ad Reges*, or *Book of the Heavenly Emperor to the Kings of the Earth*, to be culled from her writings by Alfonso of Jaen and containing ten commandments. St. Francis had written to Brother Leo, "*Scribo tibi sicut mater,*" "I write to you as would a mother." So did Bride, who was only three years older than he, write to Magnus. She had earlier taught her husband to read and use the Franciscan Little Office of the Blessed Virgin Mary. Now she taught these to the royal couple.[30] Later, she would have horrific visions warning King Magnus against his excesses (pp. 37-38, 67-97).

III. Bride as Widow

This section of the vita, in all its versions, muddles together the categories of wife and widow, in its quest to present Bride as a head of a household, stressing her religiosity as wife and as widow, discussing her behavior both in Sweden and in Rome.

But the holy widow who had dedicated her life to God from her youth fasted and prayed. Like a chartered ship carrying its bread a great distance, she was told by the holy Spirit, on leaving her country and knowing she was going to Germany, that she would come to Jerusalem to the actual places where our Redeemer, Jesus Christ, was announced, born, educated, baptized, where he preached, performed miracles, was crucified and buried, and ascended into heaven, seing these with great devotion and veneration. Whether in Rome when she returned there or before or in her own country and the parts around it or in Germany or in Spain or in Italy or in other lands around the sea or holy places or saints' relics beyond the sea, on hearing of relics she would rest little but they would be hastily and personally visited by the said holy widow, in each town quickly traveling to its shrine.

But after her husband's death out of reverence for the holy Trinity, she tightly tied around her naked flesh a hemp rope fastening it with many knots. And she tied it similarly around each shin and knee. And even when she was ill, she used no linen except on her head, dressing in a hair shirt next to her flesh, above it wearing clothes not according to the condition of her person, but which were very humble and abject. And she observed not only those vigils and fasts which holy mother church stipulated, she even added many others beyond those ordered by mother church, four weekly fasts and similarly four in the weeks while her husband still lived, and after his death continually until a few years before her happy passing, she slept in her clothes on a carpet without a straw mattress or feather pillow or anything else like that placed on the earth or floor, holding her body in prayer, abstinence and for divine work, and restoring herself with little sleep. Each Friday in the memory of the most sacred passion of our lord Jesus Christ, she contented herself with fasting on bread and water, and on many other days in memory of diverse saints she similarly passed in abstinence. And whether she abstained from fasting or sat at table, she always rose from that meal most soberly, not satiated, but refreshed.[31] And each Friday she took a burning candle of wax letting it drop while it burned on her nude flesh so that the wounds continually remained.

And she always kept gentian which is a most bitter herb or root in her mouth.[32]

Coming to Rome, neither caring about the harshness and rigor of the cold nor the heat of summer nor the impediment of muddy roads, nor rain, nor snow, nor hail, she visited all the various stations ordained by holy church and other holy saints' churches, and though she could have used a horse for making it easer for herself, she greatly taxed her body by going on foot each day. She kneeled for so long that her knees became as hard, it could be said, as a camel's. She was of such admirable and splendid meekness that often she sat unknown with destitute pilgrims at the Poor Clare monastery of Saint Lawrence in Panisperna in the city of Rome and there took alms with them and kissed them in thanks. And frequently with her own hands and out of reverence for God she repaired the beggars' clothing. She tenaciously observed obedience to her priests and superiors and confessors, such that she dared not lift up her eyes from the ground even if she had leave of the spiritual father. While her husband was alive she made her confession every Friday, and after his death she made a true confession even each day with great contrition and with such bitterness as if from the most grave sins, yet there was nothing in her words, habits, thoughts or deeds that could have been considered blameworthy. The words of God said by preachers which men ignored, she adhered to assiduously and intently. Each Sunday and feast day she received the venerated sacramental body of Christ with devotion and tears. The path to her house was not the bread of idleness, her hands being open to work and her palms extended to the poor, her works of charity being inexaustible to the sick, infirm and lowly persons in her unwearied exercising of the revering of God. Now while her husband was alive, each day she fed twelve paupers, conserving in her own house what was appropriate and necessary to feed them. And every Thursday in memory of our Lord's supper, with her own hands she washed their feet. Out of her own resources she repaired many ruined hospitals in her region and piously, kindly, mercifully, and diligently ministered to them, with pity visiting them and handling, washing, binding and warming their sores without horror or distaste.[33]

And in Vadstena in the Diocese of Linköping out of her own resources she had the venerated canonical monastery built, for sixty nuns living in an enclosed cloister, and twenty-five brothers of the Order of Saint Augustine called the Holy Saviour, for which nuns and brothers the holy widow wrote certain constitutions herself and later had them approved by the Apostolic See to be held and observed, endowing the monastery sufficiently that no one need support it.

Admirable patience flourished in her that she tolerated most patiently, even when infirm in her own body, or with the shocks of the deaths of her husband and her son Charles, and other adversities, without murmuring, without complaining, with humble submissiveness blessing God, being always restrained, constant in faith, superior in hope, true in charity, daring in justice, delighting above all in equity. She despised carnal lusts and vain alluring depravity and arrogance, pomp and inane glorying and great curiosity. Of her singular continence and modesty enough has been said above. But what was found was she was most prudent with the best discretion from her youth until her last hour, laying down human fragility, hesitating to judge, not saying good was evil, nor evil good, not holding light to be shadows nor shadows, light. Whatever sacred works, without ceasing, this generous widow brought about, many of them being thoughts and intimate affections and most secret acts made manifest and her visions and various revelations seen and heard and spiritual prophecy preached by her to many of which not all were completely effected, but are described here and there in her many volumes of revelations.

The end of her life was foretold five days beforehand. And this came about in her seventieth year. And not until then her son Birger and her daughter Catherine were summoned in fear and strongly urged above all in fear of God and love of neighbor and the saints, to persevere in her works. She made her last confession, as she ought, receiving the last rites and supreme unction, then just as her soul was leaving her, while her mind was still intact, having received communion and after adoring the body of Christ, her eyes raised to the heavens, saying "Into your hands, I commend my spirit," that blessed soul returned to its Creator.

For it was as Widow that Bride could truly enter her vocation as Writer and Prophet. From other sources than this official life we learn of her great business during this period of her life. Two years following Ulf's death, in 1346, King Magnus and Queen Blanka were persuaded to donate their castle of Vadstena to Bride for her monastery of the Order of the Holy Saviour. Bride herself, reacting against the corruption in the realm wrought by a homosexual king, sought to achieve rights for women and salvation for Sweden through manipulating popes and emperors, through visions and pilgrimages, through the writing of books, and through founding a religious order, *"Per mulieres primum et principaliter,"* "for women, first and foremost," at Vadstena, to be paid for by the tax throughout the realm of "Our Lady's Penny."[34]

Birgitta took her father's and husband's legalism to the highest spheres, harnessing writing to the services of religion and theology. The biography stresses her self-punishing asceticism, which is behavior used by those who lack power.[35] This official and male text does not note the visual elements of her visions, her revelations, relying instead on words rather than images, and especially on the oral testimony of witnesses written down during the curial process or legal trial for her canonization as saint and which were used to establish her official sanctity in the eyes of the Church. But even her own book comes to us through the filter of her male confessors, Master Mathias,[36] the two Peter Olavis, one of them the Prior of Alvastra, and later, Alfonso of Jaen, a bishop from Spain, who all oversaw her writings and her visions. Then that book, in turn, was to be translated and written out by her Brigittine monks and nuns in England and elsewhere in the fifteenth century, giving to themselves paradigms of a severe and sweet freedom.

Bride's tutor, the Dominican Master Mathias, had had himself an excellent and difficult education in theology, which he imparted to her. He had studied the Bible in Paris, where Nicholas Lyra, a Jewish convert, lectured upon these gathered texts of the Vulgate and its commentaries, both Jewish and Christian. On his return to Sweden, Master Mathias continued these studies, giving to Birgitta a Swedish Pentateuch as well as reading saints' legends and lives to her. He was often tortured with religious doubts, Bride praying for him. He even had serious doubts about Bride herself, speaking of these as being similar to those of Simon the Pharisee towards Mary Magdalen. Once, "it seemed to Mathias as if all the heretics stood before him and said, as if with one mouth: 'We are the truth!'" He labored with the commentary on the Bible, and a commentary on the Apocalypse which influenced Saint Bernardino of Siena. His Bible has Genesis begin: "In the beginning God created heaven and earth, not of Himself as the Father begot the Son, not of another matter as a smith makes an axe. The earth was then still void, empty and dark; void, because nothing grew upon it; empty, because neither man nor beast had been created; dark, because there were neither sun nor stars." He then wrote the Prologue to the *Revelations*, which begins, "Stupor et mirabilia audita sunt in terra nostra . . . . " [Stupendous and marvelous things are heard in our land . . . .], which was actually the letter of credence taken to the Pope in Avignon in 1347 by Bride's emmissaries.[37]

Her book, the *Revelations*, commenced in Sweden and continued throughout the remainder of her life in Italy, begins with God's words, "*Ego sum Creator omnium*," "I am the Creator of all," mirroring those of St. John in the Gospel and the Apocalypse of the Bible. It quarries male theology for women's use. It describes her visions, written down by the two Peter Olavis,[38] of Mary and Christ, in which the Virgin is not unlike the vision in the *Seventh Seal* experienced by Jof the juggler where she epitomizes Gothic courtliness. The Virgin and Christ together encourage Bride with the concept of the religious Order she desired to found for women—*per mulieres primum et principaliter*," "For women first and principally"—and its Rule, Christ telling her to have Peter Olavi (or Olavsson) of Alvastra write it out without adding to or subtracting anything from the spirit of those words spoken by him to Bride.[39]

Such convents, where women lived together, having made vows of chastity, poverty and obedience, were common in the Middle Ages—though not as successful as were the abbeys and priories founded by and for men. Early monasticism had been shaped by sixth-century St. Benedict and his Rule, then reformed by twelfth-century St. Bernard, these two Orders being of the black-garbed Benedictine and the white-garbed Cistercian monks. Then St. Francis and St. Dominic in the thirteenth century founded their Orders of wandering, begging and preaching Friars, the Franciscans and the Dominicans. It was also possible for women to be Benedictine, Cistercian, Franciscan (Poor Clares or Clarissans after St. Clare, friend of St. Francis) and Dominican nuns.

Bride's convent, her Rule states, is to be governed by an Abbess, who in her turn represents the Virgin, the Queen of the Apostles, all her nuns being as Brides of Christ, who is their Bridegroom.[40] In the Rule, Christ spoke to Bride saying, "I am like a most powerful king, who plants his vines and makes the best wine," and telling her that with her he would be planting a "New Vine."[41] Bride envisioned the convent at Vadstena both allegorically and physically, as having four walls, of justice, wisdom, protection and mercy, and a door for pilgrims, called the forgiveness of sins. It was so built in reality. Its north wall facing the convent has apertures by means of which the nuns made their confession and received communion, including the chalice of water and wine along with the consecrated bread.[42] Nuns, as brides of Christ, were widows, their bridegroom being dead. In this manner they were free from sexuality, being a Christian version of the Amazon state. For Bride's nuns were severely sequestered and cloistered from the outside world by their own choice.

Within the convent a grave was always open at which they prayed the *De profundis*, "Out of the depths," Psalm 130's prayer for the dead, daily, and at the door from the convent to the church a bier with a little earth upon it was placed—to remind the nuns of their own deaths.[43] In several chapters

Bride described the nuns' garb, emphasizing the headdress as a white wimple, or head covering, covered with a black veil, fastened with three pins, then a crown of white linen placed over the black veil on which are "sewn five small pieces of red cloth like five drops of blood–the first over the forehead, the second at the back of the neck, the third and fourth by the ears, the fifth on the top of the head, as on the middle of a cross," signifying the Crown of Thorns and the Five Wounds of Christ.[44]

The Rule, the *Regula Sancti Salvatoris*, the *Rule of the Holy Saviour*, contains twenty-eight chapters carefully legislating the details of the Brigittine monastic life. It stresses the Franciscan, Poor Clare-like, poverty of the Brigittine nuns, who could not even possess a thimble of their own. At times Bride used the Franciscan term of "Brother Ass" for the body.[45] The Rule also incorporates Benedictine and Cistercian liturgical practices, centering these upon the Virgin.[46] The Chapters of the Rule would be read in Chapter each Thursday by the nuns. Bride dictated these to Master Mathias and Petrus Olavi of Alvastra between the years 1344-1346.[47] In 1349, Bishop Hemming of Äbo in Finland and Prior Petrus of Alvastra took the Rule to Avignon to have it approved by Pope Clement–and failed.[48] King Magnus had already given to Bride the royal castle at Vadstena for her convent. Later–capriciously–he would have that edifice torn down. What remained was the royal banqueting hall, the former scene of drunken orgies, above which are built the nuns' cells.

The *Liber Celestis* or *Heavenly Book*, another title for the *Revelations*, like a child in the womb, was constantly shifting and growing. Its first, second, and fifth of the eight books were written in Sweden, between 1344 to 1349. The fifth book deals with Master Mathias' religious doubts in the setting of a vision of a monk on a ladder discoursing with Christ and the Virgin. The third book dealt with visions concerning ecclesiasts, the fourth book, the visions in Italy, the sixth being an appendix to the rest, the seventh, a travel diary of the pilgrimage to the Holy Land, and the eighth, Alfonso de Jaen's compilation from Bride's political writings, the *Liber coelestis Imperatores ad Reges* or *Book of the Celestial Emperor to the Kings*. With these were also the *Sermo Angelicus* or *Conversation with the Angel*, the Brigittine Office[49] and finally a supplement, compiled by Prior Petrus from his notes, especially including the material left behind in Sweden, called the *Extravagantes* or Appendices. By 1378, at the time of Bride's canonization as a saint, Alfonso de Jaen could write to Archbishop Birger of Uppsala, the compiler of the *vita* or biography of Saint Bride given in this Introduction, noting that the Brigittine books (*libri celestes*) were being read in Spain, in the two Sicilies and Italy.[50]

Bride entered the arena of international affairs. She had already sent Bishop Hemming of Äbo to Clement VI and to the kings of France and England, strongly advocating that there be peace between King Philip of France and King Edward of England in the Pope's name, espousing the concept of the Respublica Christiana, in her attempt to avert what would become the Hundred Years' War.[51] Now she heard a voice telling her to go to Rome for the Jubilee year of 1350 and bring together the Pope and the Emperor in that city where the streets are paved with gold and the purple blood of martyrs.[52] Her dream was to have the Pope and the Emperor both present in that ancient, ruined city of which the great aquaducts were now broken and where malaria held sway. But the Pope did not choose to leave Avignon for Rome, even for the Jubilee he had proclaimed for Christendom.[53] Bride wrote to Charles IV, assuming a *persona* or voice of power, the voice of God, "The Emperor Christ writes to the Emperor of Germany":

I am speaking words of justice and truth to a woman. Receive therefore the words which she has received from my lips and written in her books. . . And you, who are the lord of the empire, must therefore know that I, the Creator of all things, have dictated a Rule for nuns and have given this Rule to the woman who writes to you. Read the Rule therefore and speak to the Pope about this Rule which I have dictated with my own lips, and which I have approved.[54]

Both in Italy and in Sweden, and indeed throughout all Europe, the calamitous plague of the mid-century was to be indelibly impressed. On Bride's journey to Italy she met with the Black Death, the outbreak of bubonic plague, transmitted by fleas from rats, which ravaged Europe from 1348 to 1350, and which soon also reached her own Sweden, King Magnus Eriksson writing of this

. . . terrible news, that every Christian man and woman must sorely fear, for God, because of the sins of men, has sent a great plague upon the whole world, so that the greater part of the people who live in the lands lying to the west of our land, have died a swift death, and now this flying sickness is all over Norway . . . and will soon be here, and it takes such a hold that before they are sick people fall down and die without the sacraments, and wherever it comes there are not so many people left that they can bury the dead.[55]

They bitterly recalled Bride's prophecy made two years earlier, as Christ's channel, to King Magnus (pp. 37-38):

Thus says the Son of God: I will visit this kingdom . . . with wrath . . . I will rise up in all my power and will not spare either young or old, rich or poor, just or unjust. I will come with my plough and pull up the trees by the roots, so that where there before were a thousand people only a hundred will be left, and their houses shall stand empty.[56] Pilgrimage and plague were closely associated in the Middle Ages. In Birgitta's Uppland only a sixth of the population was left alive after the 1350 plague there, King Magnus summoning the clergy and ordering them to decree to the people that they enact their penitence through giving to the poor, dressing in woolen garments and walking barefoot, like pilgrims.[57] So had Bride herself traveled. To this day, her simple wooden pilgrim staff of juniper and bowl of maple can be seen at Altomünster, outside Munich in Bavaria, probably being given to the Brigittine house founded there later, but associated with the places Bride had visited on her journeys.[58] On their journeying they also visited Cologne in Germany with its shrine of the Three Kings[59] and the Sainte Baume in southern France, the place sacred to Mary Magdalen, her sister, Martha, and her brother, the leper, Lazarus. Bride liked to write about Mary Magdalen and Martha, having named one of her own daughters, Martha.

Bride reached Rome, lodging in a cardinal's palace by Saint Lawrence in Damaso, and took up her career again as writer. She customarily did her writing in a small chapel off its church.[60] An angel dictated to her the text that became the *Conversation with the Angel*.[61] And Peter came, saying,

Oh, my daughter, this city of Rome was in times past a city in which dwelt the warriors of Christ, its streets were strewn as if with gold and silver. But now all its precious sapphires are lying in the mire . . . . Toads and vipers build here.[62]

Politics, apocalypse and religion were inextricably intertwined in the fourteenth century. Usually such chiliastic politics, believing in the end of the world, were only in the male domain. Bride made politics also be woman's work. At Pentecost the Abbot Joachim had contemplated the Book of the Apocalypse, especially concerning the Woman Clothed with the Sun. At Pentecost, simiarly, in 1347, Cola di Rienzo had assumed the government of the City of Rome, as the Kingdom of the Holy Spirit, becoming Senator. Later, when he returned from exile first at the Emperor's court at Prague, then the Pope's prison at Avignon, and proclaimed, "Romans, I bring you peace, freedom, justice,"[63] he would meet with resistance and eventually be brutally murdered by the Roman crowd. Similarly, had the Roman Jubilee been proclaimed for the year 1300 in that pattern of apocalyptic chiliasm, the Hebrew Jubilee having been when all debts were to be forgiven, all slaves freed, and the land to lie fallow, the Christian one allowing for the forgiveness of sins if one journeyed to Rome, Dante setting his *Commedia* in that Jubilee year of 1300.[64] However, though Pope Clement proclaimed this 1350 Jubilee, he remained in Avignon, in Bride's view, thereby obviating its efficacy.[65] She was bitterly disappointed in him.

During Cola's Senatorship of Rome, Bride visited the shrine of Saint Agnes, erected by Constantine's daughter, Constantia. Bride was seeking models who were women, rather then men, upon whom she could pattern her life—and who could teach her the purest Latin that she so much needed to learn. St. Agnes in visions taught Bride her Latin, the Virgin having ordered her to learn that universal language of power.[66] Agnes, like Cecilia, was an early Christian martyr, who had remained chaste despite a marriage proposal, who had refused to sacrifice to idols, and who had been sent to a brothel, *juxta theatrum*, by the theatre, and then burnt at the stake. Her parents saw her in a vision with many other maidens, where she held a lamb. Agnes' *vita* or biography ends with the author's colophon: "But I, Ambrose, the servant of God, could not suffer that this should not be put into writing, and in her honor who was so dear a martyr, I have written of her deeds."[67] St. Agnes one day presented Bride a crown set with seven precious stones, jasper, sapphire, emerald, pearl, topaz, diamond, carbuncle, one for each great insult Bride had had to endure, the first of which had been given "by him who said that you would do better to stay at home and spin like other women than to dispute about the Holy Scriptures."[68]

Already, Bride's accurate prediction of the Black Death to King Magnus had made her prophetic powers awesome. Then, on December 2, 1352, lightning struck the bells of St. Peter's and melted them. Christ had already told Bride this would be the sign of Pope Clement's death.[69] Next, from Rome, Bride visited the great—and corrupt—monastery of Farfa, staying outside of it in a shed.[70] Vision followed vision, Master Peter having to write these down all night long. Christ spoke by Bride to Farfa's Abbot, chiding him who ought to be a mirror to his monks of perfection but who was instead lecherous and covetous, only giving to the already rich and never to the poor.[71] The Virgin asked Bride what faults she really saw, Bride answering that his dress was not that of a monk. Fulfilling her prediction, the Abbot was to die suddenly, without being confessed of his sins.

Bride's pilgrimage had torn apart her family, separating her from Catherine, Charles and Birger. Peter Olavi returned to Rome, driven by inexplicable anxiety, to find Lady Catherine, Bride's daughter, there, meeting her by chance in the basilica of St. Peter's.[72] She had come to join her mother, leaving her chaste young husband, Eggert. At first her brother Charles had forbidden her pilgrimage but she had insisted.[73] There was the very real fear of rape because of her great beauty, St. Agnes sensibly noting,

"If this happened against her will, it cannot be accounted as a sin to her. The young girl must shake it off, as a swan shakes the water off its wings." Catherine had been depressed in Sweden. She was also depressed in Rome, wanting to mutilate the beauty of her face. When she was about to do so a stone fell on her, rendering her unconscious. She pleaded that Master Petrus beat her with olive branches–until finally she recognized that was enough, and her joy returned.[74] As Bride chose Saint Agnes, so did Catherine choose Saint Sebastian to guard her virginity, and we learn of her reading saints' legends and the Bible.[75] When one travels to Altomünster one sees there the image of Saint Catherine on the convent wall, a deer crouched at the beautiful woman's feet, from the legend that a deer hunted by her husband took refuge with her in this manner.

Paradoxically, another of Bride's daughters, Cecilia, unlike her namesake saint,[76] ran away, aided by her brother Charles, from the convent St. Ingrid founded at Skenninge on returning from Jerusalem. Cecilia would marry several times, her mother understanding this. A daughter of hers named Birgitta in turn was to become a nun at Vadstena. News had reached Bride of this running away in Rome, along with the information of the deaths of Catherine's Eggert, Master Mathias, Bride's daughter Ingeborg, her brother Israel Birgersson (who had almost been King of Sweden), and Archbishop Hemming of Uppsala.[77] Meanwhile Bride gained important contacts in Rome, especially with the princes of the Orsini family, one of whom, with his Humanist training, rewrote Bride's Rule in more scholarly Latin and later participated in the commencement of the canonization.[78]

Bride's household never had enough money. One day when Catherine was praying at St. Peter's, a Norwegian woman pilgrim in white robe, black cloak, a girdle around her waist and a white kerchief (the garb Bride herself is shown to have worn in Scandinavian paintings of her), asked Catherine to pray for the Lady Gisla, her brother Charles' wife, and then vanished. Soon news reached them of Gisla's death in Sweden and of her gift to them of her richly jewelled wedding crown.[79] Yet again, when funds were low, a Swedish tailor, on his pilgrimage to Jerusalem, visited them–and gave them all his savings for the journey, returning to Sweden to get his loan repaid by her son Charles, then journeying forth once more, this time reaching Jerusalem, and upon his return home becoming an industrious lay brother at Vadstena.[80] But that money ran out too.

In despair, Bride wondered whether she should borrow. The Virgin instead told her to beg. Which she did, standing amongst the church beggars outside Saint Lawrence in Panisperna, in the mornings, spending the rest of the day visiting the seven churches of the pilgrimage stations and indulgences, learning Latin grammar, saying prayers and writing.[81] Thus she supported her entourage, who came to include her two sons, Birger and Charles, her daughter Catherine, several friends, several servants, the two Peter Olavis, one a Master from Skenninge, the other a Cistercian Prior from Alvastra, and eventually even the Bishop turned Hieronomyte hermit, Alfonso de Jaen. In 1354, she had to move from the grand Cardinal's palace and live instead with a noble widow, Francesca Papazuri, in the Piazza Farnese, near the Campo de' Fiori.[82] Thus the Swedish noblewoman, whom the Italians spoke of as a *principessa*, a princess,[83] became a beggar. The theatricality of the act helped rather than hindered Bride.

Bride continued to write. Of the two men named Peter Olavi, it was Prior Peter of Alvastra who was best suited to writing down Bride's Swedish visions in Latin, Master Peter of Skenninge who could compose the hymns for the Brigittine Office, the *Cantus Sororum*, or *Sisters' Songs*, in a liturgy centered upon the Virgin Mary.[84] Every day she worked at these lessons to be read to the nuns. Finally the work was finished. "The robe for the Queen of Heaven is now cut out," said the angel, in an intensely feminine image, combining text and textile, "it is for you now to make it up."[85] (We remember that Bride's own beggar's cloak was patched together from a woman's robe. Later, in the *Revelations*, Bride will speak of Mary's cloak of mercy being similarly humble in its appearance [pp. 99-102].[86])

Bride combined poverty and royalty. Finally, in 1355, the Emperor Charles came from Prague, having been prepared for this event by Cola di Rienzo's mysticism. But Cola had just been killed by the savage Roman populace. The Emperor came dressed humbly as a pilgrim, then was crowned in St. Peter's on Easter Day by the Pope's delegate, the Pope being still in Avignon, and as hurriedly left, soon after issuing the "Golden Bull" of 1356, making Emperor and Pope independent of each other.[87] Next Bride visited Naples and its beautiful, lascivious Queen Joan. Joan's grandfather had been King Robert the Wise, who had collected seven thousand manuscripts and at whose court had lived Petrarch, Boccaccio and Acciaiuoli, Acciaiuoli continuing on at the court and coming to know Bride who would be present at his deathbed in 1366.[88] Bride had a vision of him she gave to his wife in which he lamented that he had ever known Joan and Lewis (pp. 54-62). Joan was said to have murdered her husband. She was to fall in love with Bride's son, Charles. The Emperor Charles and Queen Joan would strongly support Bride's canonization after her death.

Bride's dream of the coming of the Pope and the Emperor to Rome was furthered when, in 1367, Pope Urban V came to Rome. But Bride was concerned more for Vadstena than she was even for Rome. She wrote to him, as she had with previous Popes, at Christ's command, enclosing the copy of the Rule and begging for the papal indulgence for the convent at Vadstena, modeled on that which St. Francis requested for the Portiuncula. However, as with Saint Francis, Christ told her "If you cannot get the Pope's letter and seal for this indulgence, let my blessing suffice. I will confirm and establish my words and all the saints shall be my witnesses. My Mother be to you a seal, my Father a surety, and the holy Spirit shall comfort those who come to your convent," and in 1369 the cloister at Vadstena was commenced in earnest.[89] When the church was finished the Brigittine nuns placed these words, inscribed upon stone, at its door.[90] Later, Popes would grant to Vadstena the Saint Peter in Chains indulgence of the Portiuncula.[91] Popes Gregory XI, 1377, Urban VI, 1379, both upheld the decision not to grant the indulgence; Bride had requested indulgence granted to Francis' church of the Portiuncula; after her death, in 1391, the indulgence, same as that for the Chains of Peter in Rome, was granted to Vadstena.»

In 1368, the Emperor Charles with his fourth wife came to Rome to be crowned by the Pope, Pope Urban V and the Emperor meeting each other at the Castel Sant'Angelo on October 21, Bride likewise giving them a letter reminding them that Christ had approved of her Rule for an order of nuns.[92] Bride was a major architect of their historic encounter. In her voluntary poverty she had embodied the state of Rome as widowed of its Pope and Emperor, resonant with the lines from Jeremiah's Lamentations on Jerusalem, "How doth the city sit solitary, that was full of people! How she is become as a widow! She that was great among the nations, and princess among the provinces, How she is become tributary!" But now she had joined together the scattered parts of Christendom, headed by Pope and by Emperor, in the sacred city of Rome.

Bride and Catherine met Pope Urban at Montefiascone, June 12, 1369. Then Birger and Charles, her two sons, joined Bride in Rome, the Pope writing for them a passport, for "the lady Birgitta and her children Charles of Ulfasa, Birger and Catherine, who are travelling from Rome to St. Nicholas in Bari and to Sant' Angelo on Monte Gargano."[93] Bride journeyed as a poor pilgrim to Monte Gargano, sacred to St. Michael, and Bari, sacred to St. Nicholas, having already been to Compostela, sacred to St. James, thus beginning to fulfill the threefold pilgrimages of the Middle Ages of *Deus*, "God" (the tomb of Christ in Jerusalem); *Homo*, "Man" (the tombs of the Apostles in Rome and Compostela); *Angelus*, "Angel" (the shrine of St. Michael).[94] Songs are still sung in that region by women of St. Bride as the patron of those who are dying, in which the Saint is described as contemplating the crucifix, on her head a crown of thorns, in one hand a candle, the other holding the ever present book she reads and writes.[95] With them was also Alfonso of Jaen, who in 1368 had resigned his bishopric to become a hermit in the Order his brother founded named the Hieronymites after St. Jerome.[96] Bride chose Alfonso to cast the final version of her *Revelations* into good Latin.

Pope Urban V on August 5, 1370, at Montefiascone, refused to approve the Rule in its own right, allowing it only to be a supplement to the Augustinian Rule which he deemed as the most appropriate for her Order.[97] Incidentally, Augustine's Rule, used by Austin Canons—such as Chaucer's Pardoner—and claimed by them to predate Benedict's Rule, was originally written by Augustine in a letter addressed to his sister's convent.[98] Pope Urban did permit Bride to build the convent which she was never to see, but did not grant her the Portiuncula and Saint Peter in Chains indulgence she requested. This indulgence granting pilgrims remission from purgatorial punishment after their deaths for visiting Vadstena would have given the convent power, prestige and wealth. To punish Urban V, Bride had a vision in which the Virgin chided him for his sins.[99]

Bride's pilgrimages already had crisscrossed Europe. She had journeyed as a pilgrim to Assisi when St. Francis in a vision in a church in Trastevere told her to "Come to my chamber and eat and drink with me," only to find when she got there, that he meant the invitation spiritually, not physically.[100] We recall her earlier pilgrimages to Trondheim and Compostela, her others to Bari and Monte Gargano and elsewhere. In 1371, she set off for Jerusalem, in Asia, in her seventieth year, her son Charles becoming ill, likely with tuberculosis, and Queen Joan's lover, before his death,[101] her other son, Birger, being knighted in the Church of the Holy Sepulchre.[102] She was joined in the pilgrimage by William Williamson, an English knight, and a Franciscan, Martin of Aragon, who heard her preach of her intent on Cyprus.[103] This pilgrimage had been promised to Bride in vision after vision, year after year.[104]

A thousand years previously, Jerome had journeyed from Rome to Bethlehem, Paula, a great Roman lady, and her daughter, Eustochium, joining him there. Paula traveled about the Holy Land, intensely participating, mentally, in reenactments of the events on Calvary and at Bethlehem. As had Jerome's Paula before her,[105] Bride now in turn deeply experienced the events of the Crucifixion upon Golgotha, speaking of the bleeding from his head and his body, and of his Mother and John at his side, the Virgin and herself both pierced with the sword of grief. Then, after His death, "He was wounded all over and stained entirely with blood. His sorrowful Mother dried His whole body and all His wounds with a linen cloth and then they bore Him away in great grief and much weeping and laid Him in the grave." Pilgrims were bookish, even if they were illiterate, believing that their journey upon God's World, recreated his Word, the Bible, and seeking to record or have their pilgrimage be recorded. Bride immediately went to the pilgrim hostel, asked for pen and ink, and wrote down these words, describing her vision of the crucified Christ.[106] It was in Jerusalem, in the Church of the Holy Sepulchre, that Bride also had a marvelous vision of the Judgement of her now dead son Charles (pp. 113-119). It was in Jerusalem, too, that she wrote down Christ's words, "*Ego sum quasi aquila, que previdens in aere volentes*," "I am like the eagle who soaring in the air foresees the future," that would be copied out again and again in Florentine manuscripts of prophecies.[107]

After Golgotha, Bride visited Bethlehem and Jordan, again deeply experiencing herself the events that once had taken place. Her relationship with Mary and Christ in these visions is that of daughter-in-law and bride to a mother-in-law and fellow spouse and she uses the words "Sponsa . . . astat," "the bride stood."[108] Her description of her vision would profoundly influence Renaissance paintings. Johannes Jørgensen describes, in Denmark, in an old pilgrimage church, the scene of the birth of Christ, one of the participants being a woman pilgrim, with a staff in her hand and a bag over her shoulder. It is Bride as a pilgrim in the year 1372, revisioning the event, and the Virgin is as she described, kneeling before the Child who is placed upon her cloak upon the ground before her.[109] The same scene, in Florentine style, is to be found in Santa Maria Novella, just inside the great west door. In completing this pilgrimage Bride mirrored those of Saints Elin of Skövde and Ingrid of Skenninge, of Sigurd Jorsalafar ("Jerusalem journeyer"), and the Kings Canute of Denmark and Olav of Norway.[110]

Deeply concerned about the scandalous behavior she saw everywhere Bride fulminated in her texts, whether they were recorded visions or preached sermons. On her way back to Rome she had to preach in Naples, beginning her text there as she had her first Revelation, "*Ego sum Creator omnium*," "I am the Creator of all."[111] She preached as well on Cyprus and warned Famagusta of its impending conquest by Genoa.[112] She likewise prophesied to Queen Eleanor of Cyprus, widow of King Peter of Cyprus[113] and daughter of King Peter of Aragon, and the Prince of Antioch concerning the capture of Constantinople by the Turks to take place in 1453.[114] Alfonso of Jaen also gave vent, but more privately, to these concerns. Amongst his unpublished papers at his death was a bitter parodic Mass in honor of "Our Lady of Simony."[115] Bride sent Alfonso to Avignon to persuade Gregory XI to return to Rome. She died before that occurred. Queen Joan, in her own attempt to reform, had purchased and freed a slave woman, sending her to Bride too late, the woman next coming to Vadstena, dying there as Sister Catherine Magnus' daughter.[116] Bride died a failure. She immediately became a success.

IV. Bride as Saint

Excited by the death of the venerated widow, a great rumor went about the city, a crowd of people running together with great devotion and reverence to see the holy corpse, unanimously glorifying and praising God. At the abovesaid monastery of Saint Lawrence where she had indicated, her funeral procession was accompanied by such a crowd of people that for two days they were not able to bury her, and only then could they take her, praising God, to be interred.

Her body had not yet been carried to her sepulchre when a certain woman named Agnes de Comtessa in Rome, known from birth to have a huge and deformed goiter, ran with the others to venerate the body, and laid her own belt on the hand of Bride with devotion, making it touch that belt, then with similar devotion placed it around her own neck and shortly after the goiter shrank and was reduced to normal size owing to the divine miracle. Truly, Francesca de Sabella, a nun of the said monastery of Saint Lawrence, who for two years had been weakened and afflicted by a stomach disorder lay always ill in bed in her room and honoring the widow whose friend she was, now dragged her body with great difficulty through the cloister, coming to the iron grill and lying there all night praying to God that by the merit and prayers of the widow whose body lay there, she might have such healing of her long illness that she could be with her sisters at divine office and that she might when necessary go about the cloister without help from anyone, and she remained there until her health returned to her body and what she had prayed for was attained.[117]

Truly, blessed God showed the great merit of this beloved widow when Elsebi Snara, a women of the said Diocese of Linköping, gave birth with great pain to a dead infant and when she came to herself she prayed to God humbly that through the merits of the so-celebrated widow, the child might come to life. She prayed that if the baby would revive, she would visit the tomb of the holy widow with a wax image, and immediately the baby became warm and began to breathe, becoming full of life. The woman, full of devotion and joy, went to implement her vow.[118]

But what was remembered by most was that by the merits of this widow's soul with God's omnipotence deaf ears were opened, mute tongues untied, paralytic limbs had control restored to them, curved spines were straightened and invalids freed from their contractions, the blind had their sight restored, women in childbirth were freed from danger, and the incurably ill were healed. She led those laboring in shipwrecks and stormy waters safely to port. But the votive images and statues at the abovesaid monastery in Vadstena, to which the venerated body of the widow was translated, give ample testimony to the truth.

We find Francesca Papazuri, in 1374, writing to Lapa Acciaiuoli asking for permission to place paintings in the room where Bride had died of the Crucifixion and Saints John, James, Catherine of Alexandria, Mary Magdalene, Peter, Paul, Agnes, and John the Baptist.[119] Immediately a European-wide movement began in support of Bride's canonization as a saint and for the indulgence for Vadstena. Advocates were the Emperor Charles of Bohemia, father to Chaucer's Queen Anne of Bohemia, Queen Margaret of Norway, Queen Joan of Naples, Queen Eleanor of Cyprus, and later even the Grand Inquisitor, Torquemada. However, while Thomas Gascoigne, Chancellor of the University of Oxford, revered her, strangely enough Christine de Pizan's supporter, Jean Gerson, Chancellor of the University of Paris, attacked her validity.[120] In 1391, the tiny and intrepid prophet, princess and pilgrim, who had married and had had eight children, and who had bullied kings and emperors and bishops and popes, officially became Saint Bride. Likewise the indulgence for Vadstena was granted.

Not all of Bride's remains had gone to Vadstena. An arm bone was given as relic to to Poor Clare nuns of Saint Lawrence in Panisperna. Another would later be given to Altomünster. Another came to Syon, from whence most of that would be acquired by Thomas Gascoigne for the Oseney Abbey of Chaucer's Miller's Tale. What would be left in the Vadstena shrine would be her skull and Catherine's and a few other bones, the rest being replaced with the bones of other saints, among them one labeled "*de sto sigfrido*," "of St. Sigfrid." Thus Bride's body came to embrace all Europe.[121] Similarly did her texts proliferate throughout Christendom. And the Brigittine monasteries came to consist of numerous daughter houses spreading out from her mother house at Vadstena in Sweden.

Already, Bride had crisscrossed the map of Europe and beyond on her pilgrimages. Now the Abbey of Vadstena and the Casa di Santa Brigida, the little house on the Piazza Farnese where she had finished writing her *Conversation with the Angel* and the *Revelations*, became the two major connecting pivots between the Romance and Germanic language divisions of

Europe. Rapidly other houses were established, for instance, along the route upon which Catherine and Birger had brought her relics and also in such places as Florence, Pisa, Genoa and London. Already, Nicholas Acciaiuoli (1310-1365), the Florentine Seneschal for King Robert of Naples, had founded Certosa, a Carthusian abbey outside Florence, in 1364, and had had it richly endowed with treasures, amongst the relics being a letter written by Bride to his family.[122]

Next, Antonio degli Alberti (1356-1428) gave his land at Paradiso, near Certosa, for the Brigittines, the early nuns including his daughters, one of them even named Brigida.[123] Others came from all the distinguished families of Renaissance Florence and we find in the documents the names of Bardi, Benci, Antenori, Acciaiuoli, Benincasa, Corsini, Frescobaldi, Guicciardini, Medici, Macchiavelli, Neri, Ricasoli, Ruccellai, Soderini.[124] In Pisa we find the Dominican Chiara Gambacorte associated with Alfonso de Jaen in her *vita* or biography.[125] In Genoa, a daughter house was founded from Paradiso, called Scala Coelis.[126]

In Siena, St. Catherine of Siena (1347-1380, canonized 1461), to whom the Pope appointed Alfonso de Jaen as advisor following St. Bride's death, began to copy Bride's life in a far-reaching *imitatio Brigidae*, or imitation of Bride. She sought to outdo Bride. So not only did she become mystically married to Christ as his spouse, as his bride, but she even had the wedding ring be of Christ's foreskin, not a detail likely to have been conceived by Bride of Sweden. Also, she, as had Bride with Urban V, brought her Pope in turn back from the so-called Babylonian Captivity in France, causing Gregory XI, on September 13, 1376, to leave Avignon for Rome.[127] Catherine of Siena attempted to work with Catherine of Sweden to gain Queen Joan's influence. However, the Swedish Catherine, remembering the circumstances of her brother Charles' death, refused. Then, following Catherine of Siena's death, we find her secretary, Christopher Di Ganno, writing out a magnificent two volume manuscript of Birgitta's *Revelations*, still in Siena's city library.[128]

· Daughter houses came to be founded as well in England, Bavaria, Prussia, Holland, Denmark, Norway and Finland as in Italy and Sweden from the mother house at Vadstena (1384-1595, and present). They, likewise, were given the most beautiful names, Syon, in England (1415-presently in Devon, after exile in Lisbon); Paradiso, Florence (1394-17th century), Misericordia and Scala Coeli, Genoa, in Italy; Mariental, Tallin, in Estonia; Munkaliv, Bergen, Norway; Marienbrunn, Gdansk, (1396-1833),[129] and Stephanus Triumphans, Krakov, in Poland; Triumphus Mariae, Lublin, Marienwold, Lübeck (1415-1558), Marienfrucht, Kaldenkirch (1625-1802), Marienkron, Stralsund, and Marienmay, Maihingen (1472-1580),[130] in Germany;

Marienthron in Flanders; Mariensterre, Gouda, Marie Refugie, Uden (present), and Maria Hart, Weert (present), in Holland; Marienbo, Låland, in Denmark (1416-1556); several houses in France and Brussels dating from the seventeenth century, suppressed with the Revolution,[131] perhaps even Angelopolis in Mexico, and many others.[132] In these monasteries manuscripts were being written out of Bride's Book, her *Revelations*, her *Conversation with the Angel*, the *Sisters' Songs*, and a multitude of other texts. Our manuscript, translated here, was likely written out in Syon Abbey at Richmond. These abbeys flourished until the Reformation. The Brigittine double monasteries were, in fact, encouraged by Popes to counter the Schism, the split between Catholicism and Protestantism at the Reformation, which both Birgitta of Sweden and Catherine of Siena predicted would occur.[133] Half of their surviving manuscripts, generally those in the vernacular languages rather than in Latin, were written by women.

As a coda to this tale, Queen Christina of Sweden (1626-1689), who was raised a Lutheran, but who converted to Catholicism and abdicated her throne, in 1655 established her learned salon amidst her library of books, later to become part of the Vatican Library, in the Farnese Palace, adjacent to St. Bride's Church, in Rome. Then Emmanuel Swedenborg (1688-1772), son of a Lutheran minister, wrote his *Revelations*, which would influence William Blake (1757-1827) and his Lyrics and Prophecies and Elizabeth Barrett Browning (1806-1861) and her *Aurora Leigh*. In Swedish Swedenborg's *Revelations* are titled *Uppenbarelser*, the same title as is given to the Swedish text of Birgitta's *Revelations*. One finds copies of the two books side by side in Scandinavian bookshops. Birgitta of Sweden functioned in her day as Prophet and as Sibyl; she assumed classical and medieval paradigms of freedom and empowerment for women and men, queens and commoners, to follow.

Notes

1 Birger Gregersson, *Officium Sancte Birgitte*, ed. Carl-Gustaf Undhagen (Uppsala: Almquist and Wiksells, 1960), p. 209, *"tu eris sponsa mea et canale meum, et audies et videbis spiritualia, et spiritus meus remanebit tecum usque ad mortem,"* "you will be my bride and my channel, and will hear and see spiritually, and my spirit will remain with you until death."

2 Georges Duby, *The Three Orders: Feudal Society Imagined*, trans. Arthur Goldhammer (Chicago: University of Chicago Press, 1980).

3 Johannes Jørgensen, *Saint Bridget of Sweden*, trans. Ingeborg Lund (London: Longmans Green and Co.: 1954) 1:222; *Revelations* 2:24; *Extrav.* 95.

4 William J. Brandt, *The Shape of Medieval History: Studies in Modes of Perception* (New Haven: Yale University Press, 1966).

5 We see this in the great fresco cycle in the Town Hall of Siena, depicting Good and Bad Government, where on the south and east sides allegorical figures of the Virtues preside over peace and prosperity in the city and its hinterlands, while allegorical Vices preside on the north and west sides where the city and its surroundings are subjected to pillage, rape, battle, murder and sudden death in the midst of mercenary armies and general crop failure and famine. See Quentin Skinner, "Ambrogio Lorenzetti: The Artist as Political Philosopher," *Proceedings of the British Academy*, 19 February, 1986, pp. 1-56.

6 A. Bygdén, N.-G. Gejvall and C.-H. Hjortsjö, *Les reliques de Sainte Brigitte de Suède: Examen médico-anthropologique et historique* (Lund: C.W.K. Gleerup, 1954).

7 Thomas Gascoigne, Oxford, Bodleian MS Digby 172, fol. 37, Bride dying on the miserable board of poverty, covered by her ancient and mended mantle, *"coperta de super antiquo et emendato mantello"*; Aron Andersson and Anne Marie Franzén, *Birgittareliker* (Stockholm: Almquist and Wiksells, 1975), pp. 18-29,33-44; Jørgensen 2:311; mantle is today kept at Saint Lucy in Selci in Rome, being brought there by the Poor Clare nuns from Saint Lawrence in Panisperna when they gave up that convent.

8 *Amanuensis*, one who takes down a text in writing that is dictated to him, *"a manu,"* "by hand."

9 André Vauchez, *La sainteté en Occident aux derniers siècles du Moyen Age: d'aprés les procés de canonisation et les documents hagiographiques* (Rome: Ecole Francaise de Rome, Palais Farnese, 1981).

10 Jørgensen 1:15.

11 *Njal's Saga*, trans. Magnus Magnusson and Hermann Paulsson (Harmondsworth: Penguin, 1960), p. 64.

12 Jørgensen 1:15-16. Slavery was abolished out of reverence for the mercy of Christ who was sold by Judas.

13 *Acta Sanctorum*, Octobr. IV (henceforth *ASS* Oct 4) 4:377C, notes document in king's hand to Birger in King's Archives, Stockholm.

14 Archivio di Stato, Florence (henceforth *ASF*), Monastero Di Santa Brigida detto del Paradiso 79; Johannes Johannis Kalmarnensis, a Vadstena brother, 1362-1446, was in Reval, Estonia, in 1407 to help in establishing the Brigittine house of Mariendal; in London, England, 1416, to help in establishing the Brigittine abbey of Syon; he copied out major Brigittine manuscripts of the *Revalations* and spoke of the *Revelations* as equivalent to the Bible, Edmund Colledge, "Epistola solitarii ad reges: Alphonse of Pecha as Organizer of Birgittine and Urbanist Propaganda," *Mediaeval*

Studies, 18 (1956), pp. 46-47; Knut B. Westmann, *Birgitta Studien* (Uppsala: Akademica Boktryckeriet, 1911), p. 267.

[15] Bibliotheca Uppsaliensis MS. 17, fols. 50-51; *ASS* Oct 4; "Vita S. Birgittae," in *Scriptores rerum svecicarum medii aevi* (henceforth *SRSMA*) (Uppsala: Edvardus Berling, 1876) 3:186-206; *Birgerus Gregorii Legenda S. Birgitte*, ed. Isak Collijn (Uppsala: Almquist and Wiksells, 1946).

[16] The canonization materials and this text give her mother's name as Sighrid. It has become customary to say her mother's name was Ingeborg; Magnus O. Celsius, *Monasterium Sko in Uplandia* (Stockholm: Wernerianis, 1728), p. 14; *ASS*, 50, Oct. 4, p.377.

[17] *SRSMA*, 189,190; *ASS* Oct 4:381C; on the island of Öland a stone cross still stands said to have been raised by Bride in memory of this event.

[18] *SRSMA*, 190,227; the Virgin with the Book indicates the sense women had of their loss of learning and their desire for access to the Word. Bishop Hemming of Äbo in Finland was later to be associated with Bride, serving as her envoy to the Pope, but is here mistakenly identified with this priest.

[19] *SRSMA*, 190.

[20] Jacobus de Voragine, *The Golden Legend*, trans. Granger Ryan and Helmut Ripperger (New York: Longmans, Green, 1941) Nov. 22, pp. 689-695; Chaucer, *Canterbury Tales*, Second Nun's Tale. British Library Add MS 37790 combines Bride, Julian, and gives "Saynte Cecylle," at fol. 97^v; commented by James Grenehalgh, Sheen Carthusian associate of Brigittine Abbey of Syon, Michael Sargent, *James Grenehalgh as Textual Critic* (Salzburg: Institute für Anglistik, 1984, 2 vols.)

[21] Jørgensen 1:48-49.

[22] This text, as do others, has Ulf Ulfsson.

[23] *SRSMA*, 192-193: on this pilgrimage the Cistercian monk Svenung had vision of Bride as crowned with seven crowns whose light obscured the sun, the sun representing King Magnus, Bride, the seven gifts of the Spirit: *ASS* Oct 4:398E,514; Plate 21 in Andreas Lindblom; Bride and her husband also went on pilgrimage to the shrine of St. Olav in Trondheim, Norway, *ASS* Oct 4:398A; repeating what had been done by Birger Persson and by his father, grandfather and great-grandfather: Jørgensen 1:99.

[24] Her husband placed his wedding ring on her finger while he lay dying, but she shortly removed it from her finger, saying her love died with him and she wished now to dedicate herself to God: *SRSMA*, 227; Jørgensen 1:129-130.

[25] *SRSMA*, 188; Scandinavians were great pilgrims, Sigurd Jorsalafa, 1108-1130, journeying to Myklegaard, Constantinople, as well as the Holy Land: Paul Riant, *Expeditions et Pelèrinages des Scandinaves en Terre Sainte* (Paris: Lainé et Harvard, 1865).

[26] Victor Turner, *The Ritual Process: Structure and Antistructure* (Chicago: Aldine, 1969); liminality, from *limen*, threshold, means the state in between, where there is freedom from structure.

[27] Jørgensen 1:71; *Libellus de Magno Erici rege et Commentarii historici super nonullis Revelationibus S. Birgittae de Magno Erici rege et successoribus ejus*, pp. 12-20.

[28] Jørgensen 1:158; *ASS* Oct 4:400C,D.

[29] Joinville and Villehardouin, *Chronicles of the Crusades*, trans. M.R.B. Shaw (Harmondsworth: Penguin, 1963), pp. 347-349.

[30] Jørgensen 1:82-83.

[31] *SRSMA*, 204-205; Rudulph Bell, *Holy Anorexia* (Chicago: University of Chicago Press, 1985); Caroline Walker Bynum, *Holy Feast and Holy Fast: The Religious Significance of Food to Medieval Women* (Berkeley: University of California Press, 1988).

[32] *SRSMA*, 204-205; gentian has a blue flower, of medicinal use.

[33] Catherine and Peter Olavi, at Bride's process for sainthood, remembered her work visiting the sick, feeding the poor, washing the feet of travelers, providing dowries for young girls who wished to marry or enter convents, rescuing harlots from their trade, and caring for the dying: *ASS* Oct 4:392F, 393AB; Jørgensen 1:54-55.

[34] Jørgensen 1:170-172. Stephan Grundy tells me of a similar tax paid in pagan times to the priestess at Uppsala. It is quite possible that Bride made use of pagan paradigms in which women had been priests and prophets.

[35] Sheila Delany, "Sexual Economics: Chaucer's Wife of Bath and *The Book of Margery Kempe*," *Minnesota Review*, 5 (1975), 104-115, p. 114, quotes Marx: "Religious distress is at the same time the *expression* of real distress and the *protest* against real distress. Religion is the sigh of the oppressed creature, the heart of a heartless world, just as it is the spirit of a spiritless situation. It is the opium of the people."

[36] Canon of Linköping, *ASS* Oct 4:374F, 405A, 406A; Westmann, *Birgitta-Studien*, pp. 272-276, noting Master Mathias and Nicholas Lyra commentary "super totam Biblia" manuscripts in Prague, Krakow, Genoa, Cologne, Berlin, Florence, Munich, Uppsala; Marguerite Tjader Harris, Albert Ryle Kezel, and Tore Nyberg, *Birgitta of Sweden: Life and Selected Writings* (New York: Paulist Press, 1990), pp. 17-28.

[37] *ASS* Oct 4:374F-375,390C,D,404C,405A,406A; he is mentioned in *Revelationes*, I.3,52, V, VI.75,89, and elsewhere; Thomas Gascoigne makes copious marginal notes on Master Mathias in Digby 172B, noting that he was Bride's sprititual director, leaving in 1346 on crusade, and that he is buried in Stockholm in the Dominican house, "Iste doctor sepultus est in Stockholm in domo fratrum predicorum," fol 48; Jørgensen 1:46-57; Colledge, "Epistola solitarii," p. 22, fn. 17.

[38] Jørgensen 1:285, Lindblom, Plate 10.

[39] *ASS* Oct 4:419E.

[40] See *Letters of Abelara and Heloise*, trans. Betty Radice (Harmondsworth: Penguin, 1974), pp. 109,119,137,159-271.

[41] Sancta Birgitta, *Opera Minora I: Regula Salvatoris*, ed. Sten Eklund (Stockholm: Alquist and Wiksells, 1975), pp. 102-103; Roger Ellis, *Syon Abbey: The Spirituality of the English Brigittines* (Salzburg: Institüt für Anglistik und Amerikanistik, 1984), pp. 19-26.

[42] For controversy in the Church concerning whether women could receive consecrated wine, see Bynum, *Holy Feast*, pp. 48-69.

[43] *Regula Salvatoris*, pp. 132, 171-172; Jørgensen 1:180-181.

[44] Jørgensen 1:174-175; medieval English texts became obsessed with the cult of the Five Wounds, and with Bride and Syon motto "*Amor meus crucifixus est*," "My love is crucified." Connected to this is the outcry against Henry IV's 1405 Whit Monday execution of Archbishop of York Richard le Scrope, who had stated the Five Wounds of Christ were analogous to those which the sword would inflict upon his neck: Bodleian Library MS Lat. lit. f.2=Arch f.F.11, fols. 4, 143^v; Thomas Gascoigne,

MS. Auct. D.4.5; John Fletcher, vol 3 of unpublished notebooks on Syon, University of Exeter.

[45] Jørgensen 1:176, 2:104. Bride spoke of the two kinds of Franciscans, those who lived according to the Rule Christ revealed to Francis, those by that which the devil taught Brother Adversarius (her name for Elias of Cortona), 2:251.

[46] *ASS* Oct 4:419F, observing parallel of Rule to those of Benedict and Francis. See also Roger Ellis, *Syon Abbey: The Spirituality of the English Brigittines*, pp. 19-26.

[47] *ASS* Oct 4:419E.

[48] Jørgensen 1:200-201.

[49] Sancta Birgitta, *Opera Minora II: Sermo Angelicus*, ed. Sten Eklund (Uppsala: Almquist and Wiksells, 1972). The monastic offices were the services carried out by monks and nuns in praise of God, the *Opus dei*, work of God, and were generally chanted, sung. Books of Hours were similarly produced for the laity for their more private reading.

[50] Jørgensen 1:301.

[51] *ASS* Oct 4:426C, 427D, 428A; *SRSMA*, 197. The letter takes the form of Christ telling Bride to write to Pope Clement these words: "*Scribe, ex parte mea Papae Clementi haec verba: Ego exaltavi te, et ascendere te feci super omnes gradus honoris. Surge igitur ad faciendum pacem inter reges Franciae et Angliae, qui sunt periculosae hostiae, animarum proditores*," "I will raise you up and place you in the highest grade of honor. Rise therefore and make peace between the kings of France and England, who have become dangerous enemies, with treacherous hearts."

[52] *ASS* Oct 4:423A; ed. Cummings, p. xxiv: "*Christus loquitur Sponsae existenti in Monasterio Alvastri, dicens: Vade Romam, et manebis ibi, donec videas Papam, et Imperatorem, et illis loqueris ex parte mea verba, quae tibi dicturus sum. . . . ,*" "Christ spoke to his Bride residing in the monastery of Alvastra, saying 'Go to Rome and remain there until you see the Pope and the Emperor, and speak to them of my words which I will say to you.'"

[53] *ASS* Oct 4:428B.

[54] *ASS* Oct 4:420A,B; Jørgensen 1:255, 2:74.

[55] Jørgensen 2:4. Christ appearing to Bride used the image of the Mediterranean vineyard for the Rule, he used that of the northern ploughman for the plague.

[56] Jørgensen 2:5; *ASS* Oct 4:397D; Alphonse de Jaen, *Revelaciones Extravagantes*, ed. Lennart Hollman (Uppsala: Almquist and Wiksells, 1956), "*Arabo terram istam in iudicio et tribulacione, donec inhabitantes addiscant petere misericordiam Dei*," "I will plough this land in judgement and punishment, so that the inhabitants will be brought to seek God's mercy."

[57] Jørgensen 2:6.

[58] Jørgensen 2:311. I visited the Brigittine cloister at Altomünster, which is unchanged from the fifteenth century, its 1773 church carefully built according to Brigittine requirements except that it is not "humble, simple, strong." The Lady Prioress handed me the staff and bowl through the grille, and many manuscripts, then invited me inside.

[59] *ASS* Oct 4:398A.

[60] She was accompanied by the two Peter Olavis, "*ad Romam peregrinando devenit . . . habens semper secum . . . duos seniores antiquos et maturos, virtuosos et expertos patres spirituales qui usque ad mortem ei secuti sunt*," "She came to Rome

on pilgrimage, having always with her two older, mature, virtuous and skilled spiritual fathers who remained with her until her death," Jørgensen, II. 311.

[61] ASS Oct 4:443E, "*praeparabat se quotidie in eadem camera ad scribendum cum pugillari et carta et penna in manibus,*" "every day she was ready in her chamber with malls and paper and pen in hand.":

[62] Jørgensen 1:22. Earlier, Christ had told Bride to go to Rome where the streets are gold and "rubricated" with the blood of the saints, ASS Oct 4:423A.

[63] Jørgensen 2:102: Petrarch, *The Revolution of Cola di Rienzo*, ed. Mario Emilio Cosenza and Ronald G. Musto (New York: Italica, 1986).

[64] Leviticus 25. 8-7.

[65] ASS Oct 4:428B.

[66] ASS Oct 4:435E,F, 437F; SRSMA, 202.

[67] Jørgensen 2:36-37; ASS Oct 4:426A, on Bride's veneration of St. Ambrose's Milan relics.

[68] Jørgensen 2:43; ed. Roger Ellis, pp. 355-356.

[69] ASS Oct 4:427F, citing Matteo Villani, *Cronica*, 3:42-43.

[70] Christ had told her, "*Vade, quia camera prö te parata est,*" "Go, to where there is a chamber prepared for you." ASS Oct 4:432E; SRSMA, 228.

[71] ASS Oct 4:432D,E.

[72] ASS Oct 4:424C; SRSMA, 248.

[73] ASS Mar 3:507D,E.

[74] ASS Mar 3:508C.

[75] ASS Mar 3:509B,C,D; SRSMA, 250-252; Jørgensen 2:70-77. Margaret Clausdotter, later the Abbess of Vadstena, was to say that she never heard Catherine say a cross word: ASS Mar 3:512D.

[76] Voragine, *Golden Legend*, pp. 689-695; *Christine of Markyate*, ed. C.H. Talbot (Oxford: Clarendon, 1959); Chaucer, Second Nun's Tale.

[77] Jørgensen 2:74-75.

[78] Jørgensen 2:85; Liber de Miraculis Beate Brigide de Sueccia, Codex S. Laurentii de Panisperna in Roma, 1374, fols. 20-21, and passim.

[79] ASS Mar 3:512A; ASS Oct 4:437 C,D; SRSMA, 253; Jørgensen 2:103.

[80] Jørgensen 2:210.

[81] Jørgensen 2:104.

[82] Codex Saint Lawrence in Panisperna, fol. 15ᵛ. The Cardinal was Hugues Roger, Pope Clement VI's brother: A.J. Collins, *The Brigittine Breviary of Syon Abbey* (Worcester: Stanbrook Abbey Press, 1969), p. xvii.

[83] Her title, *principessa Nericie*, of Nericia or Närke, came from her husband's as *legifer Nericie*. Her brother Israel was almost King of Sweden.

[84] Jørgensen 2:105.

[85] Jørgensen 2:106.

[86] P. 000.

[87] Jørgensen 2:72-73, 113. Emperor Charles of Bohemia was scholarly and liberal, protecting Jews in his kingdom from the virulent anti-semitism that flourished during the Black Death. His daughter, Anne, Richard II's queen, similarly protected the learned reformist Wyclif and his followers.

[88] Jørgensen 2:119-120; Florence, Biblioteca Nazionale, Magl. II.II.90, fol. 47. Boccaccio had dedicated *De mulieribus claris*, "On Famous Women," to Andrea Acciaiuolo, Isak Collijn, *Birgittinska Gestalta: Forskeninger i italienska arkiv och*

bibliotek (Stockholm: Gillet, 1929), p. 6. Bride healed an Acciaiuolo child named Esau, *ASS* Oct 4:514F-515A.
[89] *ASS* Oct 4:447D. The account notes that the lake beside the convent is so clear that a coin thrown into it can be easily seen.
[90] Jørgensen 2:208; relevant passage from *Rev. Extravag.* 44, giving Christ's words, endorsed by the Virgin, God the Father, and God the Holy Ghost, is chiseled in Swedish upon the wall of Vadstena's Blue Church; Francis, likewise, believed the indulgence was given to him by Christ rather than by the Pope.
[91] *ASS* Oct 4:445E,F, 446A-447A.
[92] *ASS* Oct 4:445B; *SRSMA*, 223; Jørgensen 2:211.
[93] Celsius, pp. 131-132; Jørgensen 2:217.
[94] Jørgensen 2:159.
[95] Jørgensen 2:171,322-323, "*Una corona di spine in testa la teneva, con una mano il libro leggeva . . . prima di morire, Santa Brigida ci viene a visitare,*" "A crown of thorns she wears on her head, in her hand the book she reads . . . before dying, St. Bride will come to visit you."
[96] Colledge, "Epistola Solitarii," pp. 19-49; Arne Jönsson, *Alfonso of Jaén: His Life and Works with Critical Editions of the Epistola Solitarii, the Informaciones and the Epistola Servi Christi* (Lund: Lund University Press, 1989). The Escorial belongs to Hieronomyte Order: Jørgensen 2:218; its court painter was to be Hieronymus (or Jerome) Bosch, King Philip owning his *Garden of Earthly Delights.*
[97] Celsius, pp. 132.
[98] Judith C. Brown, *Immodest Acts: The Life of a Lesbian Nun in Renaissance Italy* (New York: Oxford University Press, 1986), pp. 8, 167; Augustine, Letter 211, *Letters,* trans. Sr. Wilfrid Parsons (New York: Fathers of the Church, 1956), vol. 32. The Dominicans, unlike the Franciscans, not being allowed a Rule of their own, observe the Augustinian one.
[99] Jørgensen 2:221-222.
[100] *ASS* Oct 4:438A.
[101] The *Processus, SRSMA*, 227, describes Joan as weeping copiously, Bride as immobile, a column of patience, at his death. See also *ASS* Oct 4:449F, 454C. On her return Bride gave Joan a little gold cross which Joan later used to heal a child, writing to Catherine of that miracle, II. 234.
[102] Jørgensen 2:270-273.
[103] Aron Andersson, *St. Birgitta and the Holy Land* (Stockholm: Museum of National Antiquities, 1973), trans. Laurie Seterwall, pp. 20-87; Sabinlo de Sandoli, *Viaggio di Santa Brigida de Svezia da Roma a Gerusalemme, 1372* (Jerusalem: Franciscan Printing Press, 1991), p. 29.
[104] *ASS* Oct 4:449C.
[105] Jerome's and Paula's Letters, *Epistolae,* in *Patrologia Latina,* ed. J.P. Migne (Paris, 1854), 22; *The Letter of Paula and Eustochium to Marcella about the Holy Places (365 A.D.),* trans. Aubrey Stewart (London: Palestine Pilgrims' Text Society, 1896); *Select Letters of St. Jerome,* trans. F.A. Wright (Cambridge: Mass.: Harvard University Press, 1963) Loeb Classical Library, 262. Because Alfonso de Jaen was a Hieronomyte (a follower of Jerome), there are strong associations with Paula and Jerome in Brigittine writings, as in Lambeth Palace MS 432. A Spanish nun, Egeria, had likewise journeyed to Jerusalem and written of her experiences.
[106] Jørgensen 2:249-250.

[107] Biblioteca Nazionale, Magl. II.I.249, fols. ccs-ccxi[v], II.X.57, fols, 55-64; Biblioteca Riccardiana 1258, fols, 53[v]-58, 1731, fols. 145v-154[v], etc.
[108] See Middle English *Pearl*.
[109] Jørgensen 2:332; Meiss, *Painting in Florence*, pp. 106, 150.
[110] Portraits of King Canute of Denmark and King Olav of Norway, both pilgrims to the Holy Sepulchre, are painted there on two columns with the attributes, "STS CHNUTUS REX DANORUM; STS OLAVOS REX NORVEGE," Jørgensen 2:258,331; de Sandoli, between pp. 60-65.
[111] Jørgensen 2:278.
[112] *ASS* Oct 4:453B.
[113] He figures in Chaucer's Monk's Tale and in the Spanish Chapel fresco as the dark ruler, second to the left of the Emperor.
[114] *ASS* Oct 4:436B, 452A,B.
[115] Jørgensen 2:284.
[116] Jørgensen 2:287, who says she was Turkish; Albert Ryle Kezel, *Birgitta of Sweden: Life and Selected Writings* (New York: Paulist Press, 1990), p. 246, says she was Black and from India.
[117] As Francesca di Panisperna she would be a witness at the process: Codex Saint Lawrence in Panisperna, fol. 23[v], Vatican MS Ottab. lat 90, fol. 1[v], Jørgensen 2:303. the iron grill of this story can still be seen in the church of Saint Lawrence in Panisperna in Rome: Isak Collijn, Plate V. The healing from a stomach disorder mirror reverses Bride's terminal illness from a stomach disorder.
[118] *The Myroure of oure Ladye*, ed. John Henry Blunt, EETS, ES 19 (Millwood, N.Y.: Kraus Reprint, 1981), pp. lvii-lviii, gives these last three stories from the 1516 Pynson *Life of St. Bridget*; trans. Julia Bolton Holloway, *The Life of Saint Birgitta* (Toronto: Peregrina Publishing Co., 1991), pp. 30-31.
[119] ASF, Carte Strozziane, Serie prima, CCCLII. e. 4, 352; Vatican MS Ottob. lat. 90, fol. 99.
[120] Jean Gerson, *Oeuvres Complètes* (Paris: Desclée, 1973) 9:179, "De Probatione Spiritum."
[121] Bygdén, et al. *Les reliques de Sainte Brigitte de Suéde, passim.*
[122] Giovanni Lami, *Sanctae Ecclesiae Monumenta* (Florence: Angelo Salutati, 1758) 1:204-205. The original letter was found in the late Renaissance and carefully transcribed, then sealed and placed in the library's reliquary, marked with a cross of gold, but is now lost again.
[123] Lami 2:1381; Domenico Moreni, *Notizie Istoriche dei Contorni di Firenze* 5(Florence, 1794):127-168; ASF, Carte Strozziane; *Il Paadiso degli Alberti*, ed. Alessandro Wesselofsky (Bologna: Romagnoli, 1867), Scelta di Curiosità Letterarie Inedite o Rare dal Secolo XIII al XVII, 86, 2:196-6.
[124] ASF Monastero di Santa Brigida detto del Paradiso, 322. One is "Camilla Alberti, figlia illegitt[a]." We see portraits of these nuns in the illuminated leaf now in America and on exhibition at the Pierpont Morgan, 1991. My thanks to Christopher de Hamel for this information.
[125] *ASS* April II, "De Beata Clara Gambacorta ordinis S. Dominicis Pisis in Hetruria," 519, noting that, through the influence of Alfonso of Jaen and the Hermits of St. Jerome in Fiesole, she imitated St. Bride.
[126] *ASS* Mar 3:503-531.
[127] *ASS* Oct 4:430C

[128] Siena, Biblioteca Comunale degli Intronati, MS G. XI. 20, on Bride, written out the year of her death, perhaps under Alfonso of Jaen, could have been known to Catherine of Siena; MS I.V.25/26 is Christopher Di Ganno's rendition of Birgitta's texts.

[129] Tore Nyberg, "Klastor Brygidek w Gdansku i jego najwczesmejsze kontaktu z krajami skandynawskimi na przelomie XIV i XV wieku," *Zapiski Historyczne* 20 (1962), 53-77.

[130] Document in ASF, Archivio diplomatico di S. Bonifazio, May 14, 1425, is request from Catherine, Duchess of Bavaria (sister-in-law of Philippa who aided founding of Syon), that three or two members of Paradiso be sent to instruct youth of new monastery, in Eychelberg, near Nuremburg.

[131] Tore Nyberg, *Birgittinische Klostergründungen des Mittelalters* (Leiden: Gleerup, 1965); *SRSMA*, 297-298; Uppsala University Library, MS C77, fols. 161-199; MS C153, fols. 123ᵛ-125ᵛ. There were about twelve Brigittine convents in Poland.

[132] Syon Abbey MS 7, fol. 52ᵛ, gives "1587 Angelopoli in Provincia Mexicana." My colleague, Professor John Hoag, showed me a slide of a fine portrait of a Mexican Brigittine nun.

[133] *ASS* Oct 4:467D, on Pope Urban VI writing in 1381 to Bishop Nicholas of Linköping, saying canonization of Bride was to counter schismatics and heretics, including Wyclif.

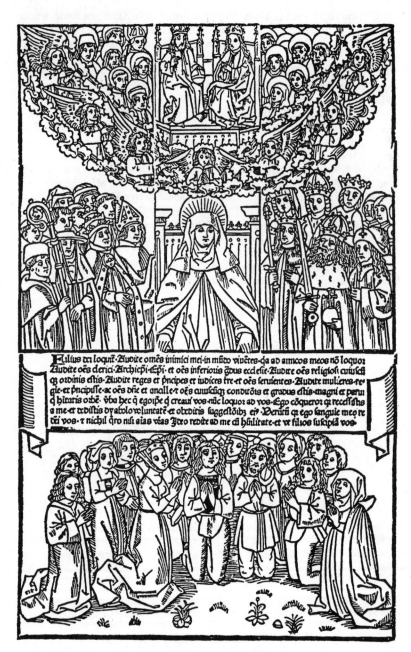

UR BIRGITTA: REVELATIONES.
Lübeck 1492.

The Book of Saint Bride

Our Lord Jesus Christ tells Saint Bride why he choses her to be his spouse, and how as a bride she ought to array herself and be ready for him. [Book I, chapter 2]

 "I am the Creator of Heaven and earth and sea and of all the things that are in them. I am one with the Father and the holy Spirit, not as gods of stone or gold, as was sometimes proclaimed, nor as many gods, as used to be the custom; but one God, Father and Son and holy Spirit, three Persons and one in substance, Creator of all things and made of none, unchangeable and almighty, enduring without beginning and without end.[1] I am he who was born of the Virgin, not leaving the God head but knitting it to the manhood, so that I should be in one person the very Son of God and the Son of the Virgin. I am he who hung upon the cross and died and was buried, the Godhead remaining unhurt. For though the manhood and body which I, the Son, alone took upon myself, was dead, yet in the Godhead, in which I was one God with the Father and the holy Spirit, I lived eternally. I am also the same who rose from death and ascended into heaven who now speaks with you through my Spirit. I have chosen and taken you to myself to be my bride to reveal to you my secret counsels, for this so pleases me. And also you are mine by all manner of right, when in the death of your husband you gave your will into my hands, and also after his death, when you thought and prayed how you might become poor for me and for me abandon all things.[2] And therefore by right you are mine and for so much

[1]See p. 9 on Magister Mathias' translation of Genesis into Swedish.
[2]See Edward Cutts, "Consecrated Widows of the Middle Ages," *Scenes and Characters of the Middle Ages* (London: Vertue, 1902), pp. 152-156; Elizabeth M. Makowski, "Canon Law and Medieval Conjugal Rights," *Journal*

charity it is right for me to prepare for you; therefore I take you as my Bride and for my own proper delight, such as seems good to have with a chaste soul.[3]

"To the Bride therefore it is right to be ready when her husband will make his wedding, that she be beautifully arrayed and clean. Then are you well cleansed, if your thought is always about your sins; how I cleansed you from the sin of Adam in your baptism and how often I have permitted you and supported you when you have fallen into sin. The Bride also ought to have tokens of her husband on her breast; that is, to take heed of the benefits and works which I have done for you; that is to say, how nobly I made you, giving you a body and a soul, and how nobly I have endowed you, giving you health and temporal goods, and how sweetly I redeemed you when I died for you and restored you to your heritage, if you would have it. The Bride ought also to do the will of her husband. What is my will, but that you will love me above all things and to desire no other thing but me? I have made all things for man, and all of them subject to him; but he loves all things except me, and truly hates nothing but me. I redeemed for him his heritage which he had lost. But he is so alienated and turned away from reason that he prefers this transitory praise that is but like sea spume, which suddenly rises up like a mountain and as soon falls down to nothing, than everlasting worship in which there is endless good.

"But you, my Bride, if you desire nothing but me, if you despise all things for me, not only your children and kindred, but also respect and riches, I shall give you the most precious and sweetest reward, not gold and silver, but myself, to be your husband and endless reward, who am the king of bliss. And if you are ashamed of being poor and despised, see that I, your God, go before you, whom servants and friends abandoned on earth; for I looked not for earthly friends, but heavenly ones. And if you fear and dread the burden of labor and sickness, consider how grievous it is to burn in the fire which you

of Medieval History 3 (1977):99-114.

[3]Bridget is influenced by Bernard on the Song of Songs of Solomon from her residence at Cistercian Alvastra. The topos, or convention, had already been used, for instance, in writings to anchoresses; Elizabeth Robertson, "An Anchorhold of Her Own: Female Anchoritic Literature in Thirteenth-Century England," in *Equally in God's Image*, pp. 170-183. Its origins lay in the *Ordo* for the Consecration of Nuns, derived in turn from the Roman marriage rites.

would have deserved, if you had offended a temporal lord as you have offended me. For though I love you with all my heart, yet I shall not go against justice in the least point, but according to how you have transgressed in all your members unless in all that you have performed satisfaction. Nevertheless, if you have a good will and purpose to amend, I change justice into mercy, forgiving grievous torments for a little amending. Therefore, take upon yourself gladly a little labor, so that you may the sooner be made clean and come to a great reward. For it is right for the bride to work with her husband until she is weary, so that she afterwards may more surely and trustingly take her rest with him."

Our Lord Jesus Christ stirs Saint Bride not to be afraid of his speaking with her, teaching her the difference between the good Spirit and the evil one. [I.4]

"I am Creator of all things and Redeemer: why do you dread my words and why did you think of what Spirit they were, whether of the good or the evil? Tell me what you found in my words that your own conscience told you not to do? Or ordered you anything against reason?"

The spouse, Saint Bride, answered: "Nothing, Lord, but all that you said is true and I erred sinfully."

Then said our Lord: "I told you of three things by which you may know a good Spirit. First, I told you to worship your God who made you and gave you all that you have, and this your own reason teaches you, to worship him above all things. Second, I told you to keep and hold the right faith; that is, to believe that nothing is done nor may be done without God. The third, I told you to love all things with reasonable temperance and continence; for the world is made for man and he should use it according to his need.

"So also are there three things contrary to these. You may know the unclean spirit because he stirs you to seek your own worship and praise and to be proud of the gifts that God gave you; and he stirs you to intemperance in all your members and of all other things, and to these he inflames your heart. He deceives also sometimes under the appearance of what is good; and therefore I have asked you to examine your conscience and open it to spiritual wise men. Therefore do not doubt that the good Spirit of God is then with you when you desire nothing but God, and of him you are all inflamed. For that I alone may do and it is impossible for the fiend to come near to you. Nor may he come near to any evil man, unless he is permitted by me, other than because of his sins or for some secret judgment known to me.

For the fiend is my creature[4] as are all other things; and of me he was well made, but by his own malice he is evil, and therefore I am Lord over him. And therefore they who say that they who serve me with great devotion go mad or have a fiend in them, they blame me incorrectly. For they make me as though like a man who had a chaste wife who trusted her busband greatly, and he put her to an adulterer. Such a one should I be, if I suffered a rightful man who had a loving heart towards me to be taken to the fiend. But because I am trusty and true, the fiend shall never have lordship over any soul which devoutly serves me. For though my friends seem sometimes as if mad, yet that is not for passion of the fiend, nor because they serve with fervent devotion, but for default of their brain or for some other privy cause which is to them the cause of more humility. It may also be sometimes that the fiend takes power from me upon the bodies of good men to the increase of their reward, and upon him who darkens his conscience; but in the souls of those who have faith and delight in me he may never have lordship or power."

Here our Lord Jesus Christ informs Saint Bride how the world stands in relation to him in all states and degrees under the likeness of five men, where comfort and help is promised to the good and hard sentence is given against evil. [I.41. The body of the chapter is omitted here. It describes Christ speaking as Judge within a law court, after commencing with the following address:]

"I am Creator of all things. I am born of the Father before Lucifer. And I am inseparable in the Father and the Father in me, and one Spirit in both. Therefore there is one God, Father, Son and holy Spirit, and not three gods. I am he who promised to Abraham an endless inheritance, and who through Moses brought my people out of Egypt. I am also the same who spoke through the Prophets. The Father sent me into the Virgin's womb, not separating himself from me, but abiding inseparably with me, that man who was gone from God should by my charity turn again to God.

"But now before you, my heavenly law court,[5] though you see and know all things in me, yet for knowledge and instruction of this my Bride, who is present and may not perceive spiritual things, I make a complaint against these five men who stand before me, that they offend me in many ways.[6]

---

[4]That is, a thing created by God.

[5]Latin text has *exercitu*, army.

[6]Bridget's "theater of devotion" (Gail McMurray Gibson's term), is also that of the law courts, from her father's profession as *legifer*, Lawman, as

Our Lord Jesus Christ tells saint Bride of the harsh sentence of judgment that he will do against all mankind if they do not amend themselves. [IV.37]

The Son of God asks of Saint Bride and says: "Daughter, how stands the world now?"

She answered: "It stands as an open sack to whom all run, and as a man running who does not heed what will happen."[7]

Then said our Lord: "Therefore it is just that I go with my plough upon all the earth and world, both heathen and Christian.[8] I shall neither spare the old nor the young, neither the poor nor the rich. But each shall be judged according to justice and each shall die in his sin; and their houses shall be left without inhabitants; and yet I shall not make an end of the world."

Saint Bride said: "O Lord, do not be displeased though I speak. Send some of your friends to warn them and admonish them beforehand of their peril."

Our Lord answered: "It is written that the rich man in Hell, despairing of his own health, asked that one might be sent to warn his brothers so that they would not perish in the same way. And it was answered to him, 'That shall not be, for they have Moses and the Prophets, by whom they may be taught.' So I say to you: They have the Gospel and sayings of Prophets; they have parables and the writings of the Church Fathers; they have reason and understanding. If they use these they shall be saved. For if I send you, you may not cry loud enough to be heard; and if I send my friends, they are but few; and if they cry, it is not enough for them to be heard. Nevertheless I

well as being religious and liturgical.

[7]Latin has, punningly, "*sicut homo curens, non curans, quid sequitur,*" Jørgensen 1:369.

[8]Two years following this prophecy made by Saint Bridget to King Magnus, the Black Death hit Sweden. At that date Saint Bridget was already traveling as a pilgrim towards Rome. Magnus ordered his kingdom to carry out penance, giving their wealth to the poor. There may be a connection between this prophecy and the later use of the theme of the Ploughman by William Langland, *Piers Ploughman*, Johannes von Tepl, *Der Ackerman* (in which the Ploughman, Death and God dialogue), ed. Willy Krogmann (Wiesbaden: F.A. Brockhaus, 1964), and Holbein's engraving of *Death and the Ploughman*.

shall send my friends to those as I approve and they shall prepare a way to God."

Our Lord Jesus Christ teaches Saint Bride the difference between good death and evil death, and how God's servants ought not to despair though they are in this life. [IV.40]

The Son of God speaks to Saint Bride thus: "Daughter, do not be afraid; this woman who is sick shall not die, for her work pleases me." And when the woman was dead, the Son of God said again to Saint Bride: "So, daughter, it is true what I said, this woman is not dead, for her bliss is great. For the separation of body and soul of just men is only a sleep, for they awake in endless life. But it is truly to be called death when the soul, separated from the body, lives in death everlasting. There are many who take no heed of things to come, desiring to die in Christian death. But what is Christian death, but to die as I died, innocently, willingly and patiently? Am I therefore to be despised, because my death was despicable and harsh? Or are my chosen therefore fools, because they suffered despicable torments? Or does it come because of Fortune, or was it wrought by the course of planets and of stars? No, but therefore I and my chosen suffered great passion to show in word and by example that the way to Heaven is hard, and that it should be intensely borne in mind how much need the wicked have to be cleansed since the innocent and chosen suffered such poignant things. Therefore you are well aware that he dies despicably and evilly who, living dissolutely, dies in the state of sin, and likewise he who goes out into the world desiring to live longer and not thanking God; but he who loves God with all his heart and is troubled innocently with despicable death or weighed down with longer sickness, he lives and dies blessedly. For a poignant death lessens sin and the punishment for sin, and increases the reward in Heaven.

"So, I bring two men to your mind who after men's judgment died in bitter and contemptible death, who, unless they had obtained such deaths by my great mercy, should never have been saved. But because God does not punish twice those who are contrite in heart, therefore they gained the crown of endless reward. Therefore the friends of God ought not to despair, though they have their temporal tribulation or though they die a bitter death. For it is most blessed to sorrow here for a time and to be troubled in this world, that they do not come to more grievous Purgatory, where there is no fleeing nor time of laboring."

Of the tribulation and sorrow that our Lady suffered and of the fruit of our Lord's words. And of three houses that Christ and man's soul ought

to have together. [II.24]

Our blessed Lady speaks to Saint Bride and says: "It is as if there were a great host of men, and one who had a great and heavy burden on his back and in his arms and his eyes full of tears, went up to them, and looked to see if any of them would have pity on him and help him with his burden; just so was I; for from the birth of my Son to his death I was full of tribulation. I bore a very great burden on my back, for I heeded continually the labor of God's service, and I suffered patiently all that ever came to me. In my arms I bore the most heavy burden, for I suffered tribulation and sorrow of heart more than did any other creature. I had my eyes full of tears when I beheld in the members of my Son the place of the nails, and his Passion that was to come, and when I saw fulfilled in him all that I had heard before prophesied by the Prophets. But now I look to all who are in the world, that I might find any who had pity and compassion on me and would think on my sorrow. And I found only a few who think on my sorrow and tribulation. Therefore, my daughter, if I am forgotten and counted little, yet do not you forget me, but see my sorrow and follow it as much as you may. Behold my sorrow and tears and be sorry; for the friends of God are but few. And now stand firmly, for, see, my Son comes to you."

[The rest of this chapter and some of the next is omitted here. They discuss the relationship of the Christian spouse in terms of allegorical housekeeping, a metaphor appropriate to Bride as the noblewoman in charge of large households.]

Mark how in the first house ought to be bread of goodwill, drink of goodly premeditation, and food of goodly wisdom. [II.25]

"I who speak with you am the Creator of all things and made of none. Before me there was nothing, nor after me may any thing be; for I was and am always. I am also the Lord whose power none may withstand, and from whom comes all power and lordship. I speak to you as a man speaks to his wife. My wife, we must have three houses. In one must be bread and drink and food. But you may ask what this bread signifies, whether I mean the bread that is on the altar. Truly that is bread before the words, '*Hoc est enim corpus meum*,' are said.[9] But the words said by the priest, 'It is not bread but my blessed body that I took of the Virgin and was crucified on the cross,' this

---

[9]See Carolyn Walker Bynum, *Holy Feast and Holy Fast: The Religious Significance of Food to Medieval Women* (Berkeley: University of California Press, 1987), pp. 113-149,

bread I do not mean here; but the bread that we must gather into one house is a good and clean will. Bodily bread, if it be clean and pure, is useful for two things. First, it comforts and gives strength to all the veins and sinews of the body. Second, it gathers to it all inward filth, and with it is purged from men, and so men are cleansed. It is the same with a clean will. First, it comforts; for if a man wills nothing but what God wills, nor works nothing but to God's worship, and desires with all his heart to be out of the world and to be with God, this will comforts a man in God and incresses the worship of God and makes the world vile and foul. It strengthens patience and makes strong the hope of obtaining bliss, so much that he takes and suffers gladly all that falls to him. Second, a good will draws out all filth that harms the soul, such as pride, covetousness, and lechery. But when the filth of pride or of any other sin comes to mind, than it goes away if the man thinks thus: 'Pride is vanity, for it is not correct for him to be praised who takes gifts; but the giver is to be praised. Covetousness is vanity, for all earthly things shall be left, and lechery is but stink. Therefore I do not want these; but I will follow the will of my God, whose reward shall never have end, nor his goods become old.'

Mark how Saint Lawrence followed the patience and Passion of our Lord Jesus Christ in life and death.[10] **And how in the second house must be linen cloth of peace and patience, and woolen cloth of deeds of mercy, and silken, of abstinence from evil.**[11] [II.26. The body of this chapter is omitted here.]

Of the instruments of the third house, that are good thoughts, virtues, manners, and true confession. And of the sparing of all three houses. [II.27. The body of this chapter is omitted here.]

Our Lord Jesus Christ teaches Saint Bride how active life and contemplative ought to be kept through the example of Mary and Martha;

[10]St. Bride in Rome was associated with several churches dedicated to St. Lawrence, Saint Lawrence in Panisperna, Saint Lawrence in Damaso, Saint Lawrence Outside the Walls. See Voragine, *Golden Legend*, August 10, pp. 437-445.

[11]Ancient and medieval thought carefully differentiated between the moral meanings of linen, from vegetable matter, and wool, from animals, pilgrims first wearing wool, then changing to linen upon reaching their shrine, the first signifying mortality, the second, eternity: J. Quasten, "The Garment of Immortality," *Miscellanea liturgica in onore di sua eminenza il cardinale Giacomo Lercaro* (Rome: Desclée, 1966-67), I:391-401.

and first, of contemplative life. [VI.65]

The Son of God says: "Bride, there are two lives which are compared to Mary and Martha; which lives, if a man or a woman would follow he must first make clean confession of all his sins, being himself truly sorry for them, having the desire never to sin again.[12] The first life, as the Lord bears witness, Mary chose; and it leads to the contemplation of heavenly things; and this is the best part and day's journey to everlasting health. Therefore every man and woman who desires to take and hold to the life of Mary, it is enough for him to have two things that are necessary to the body; that is, clothing without vanity or showing of pride, and food and drink in scarceness and not in superfluity. He must also have charity without any evil delight, and reasonable fasting after the rules of holy Church. And in his fasting he must take heed that he not become ill from unreasonable abstinence, unless by such sickness his prayers or preaching or other good deeds thereby are lessened, by which he might profit both his neighbor and himself. He must also carefully examine himself, that by his fasting he is neither made dull nor hasty to the rigor of justice or slow to the works of pity, to punish those who are rebellious, and to make unfaithful men subject to the yoke of faith, It is necessary to have bodily strength as well as spiritual. Therefore anyone who is sick or feeble, who would rather fast to my praise than eat, he shall have as great reward for his good will as does he who fasts reasonably for charity. And in the same way he who eats out of holy obedience, willing rather to fast than to eat, shall have the same reward as he who fasts.

"Second, Mary ought not to delight in the praise of the world nor of its prosperity; nor ought he to sorrow at its adversity, except in that he ought to delight when wicked men are made devout and that lovers of the world are made lovers of God, and when good men profit in goodness and, by laboring in the service of God, are made more devout. Of this also ought he who is Mary to sorrow; that sinners fall into worse sin, and that God is not loved by

[12]The androgynous Middle English grammar of this section is powerful, where the female Mary Magdalen and Martha are to be enacted by the male, as well as female, readers of Saint Bride's text, and referred to as "he" and "him." In Latin this effect does not occur, though it would have in the original Swedish. Bride visited the Sainte Baume, the region legendarily associated with Mary Magdalen, and had named one of her daughters, Martha. Mary Magdalen was considered by the medieval world to be the first monk.

his creature, and that God's commandments are despised and not kept.

"Third, Mary ought not to be idle any more than is Martha; but after he takes his necessary sleep, he ought to rise, and with inward attentiveness of heart thank God who of his charity and love made everything from nothing; and of that same charity, taking the body of man, he made all things again; showing by his Passion and death his love for man, more than you who might not be. Mary must also thank God for all those who are saved; and for all who are in Purgatory, and for them who are in the world, praying God humbly that he suffered them not to be tempted beyond their strength. Mary must also be discreet in prayer, and orderly in the praising of God, for if he has the necessities of life without business, he ought to make longer prayers. And if he grows bored with praying, and temptations grow upon him, then he may labor with his hands at some honest and profitable work, either to his own profit if he have need, or else to the profit of others. And if he is weary and bored both in prayer and in labor, then he may have some honest occupation, or hear words of others' edification with all seriousness, and without dissolution and vanity, until the body and soul be made more able and quick to the service of God. If he who is Mary be such that he has not bodily sustenance but of his own labor, then he must make his prayer shorter for such needful work; and that same labor shall be profiting and increasing of prayer. If Mary can not work, or may not, then be not too ashamed or despairing about begging, but rather joyful; for then he follows me, the Son of God; for I made myself poor that man should become rich.[13] And if he who is Mary be subject to obedience, he should live in obedience to his prelate, and the crown of reward shall be double the more than he was at his own liberty.

"Fourth, Mary ought not to be covetous, no more than was Martha. But he ought to be truly generous; for Martha gives temporal goods for God, so ought Mary to give spiritual goods. And therefore, if Mary has loved God entirely in his heart, he should be careful of that word that many have in their mouths, saying: 'It is nothing to me, if I may help my own soul, What do I care about the works of my neighbors?' Or this: 'I am good: why should I care about how other men live?' O daughter, they who say and think such words, if they see their friend troubled or dishonestly treated, they should risk

---

[13]Saint Bride herself, when in Rome, during which time this portion of the *Revelations* was being written, was forced to beg for her sustenance.

their deaths to deliver their friend from tribulation. So must Mary do; he ought to sorrow that his God is offended, and that his brother, or his neighbor, is hurt; or if any fall into sin, Mary ought to labor as much as he may that he be delivered—nevetheless, with discretion. And if for that Mary is persecuted, he must seek another more secure place. For I myself who am God have said so: '*Si vos persecuti fuerint in una civitate fugite in aliam*'; that is, if they persecute you in one city, flee to another. And so did Paul, for it became necessary at one time; and therefore he was let down over the wall in a basket.

"Therefore, that Mary be generous and merciful, five things are necessary to her: first, a house in which guests can sleep; second, clothes to cloth the naked; third, food to feed the hungry; fourth, fire to make the cold hot and warm; fifth, medicine for the sick.

"The house of Mary is his heart, whose wicked guests are all the things that come to him and trouble his heart, such as anger, despair, sloth, greed, pride, and many others, which enter in by the five senses. Therefore all these vices, when they come, ought to lie as guests who sleep at rest. For as an innkeeper receives guests both good and bad with patience, so ought Mary to suffer all things for God by the virtue of patience, and not consent to sin nor delight in it, but remove it from his heart as much as he may little by little with the help of God's grace; and if he may not remove them and put them away, let him endure them patiently against his will, as guests knowing certainly that they will reap him more rewards, and in no ways to damnation.

"Second, Mary ought to have clothes to clothe his guests, that is, humility, inward and outward, and compassion of heart for the disease of one's fellow Christian.[14] And if Mary is despised by men, then he should think how I, God, was despised, taunted and suffered it patiently: how I was judged and spoke not; how I was scourged and crowned with thorns, and did not complain. Mary must also take heed that he show no tokens of wrath or impatience to them who taunt him or despise him; but he ought to bless them who persecute him, so that they who see it may bless God, whom Mary follows; and God himself shall return blessings for curses. Mary also must beware that he neither backbite nor criticize those who burden him or trouble him. For it is damnable to backbite and to hear a backbiter and to criticize his neighbour impatiently; and therefore, that Mary may have the gift

[14]The Middle English, in this text and in others, is one's "*eyn cristen*," one's "even Christian," one's "equal Christian," which has no equivalent democratic term in modern English usage.

of meekness perfectly, he must study to admonish and to warn them of the perils for backbiting others, exhorting them with charity by speech and example to true humility. Also the cloth of Mary ought to be compassion; for if he sees his fellow Christian sin, he ought to have compassion on him, and to pray to God to have mercy on him. And if he sees his neighbor suffer wrong or harm or be taunted, he ought to be sorry for that, and to help him with his prayers and other help and actions. Yes, against the great men of the word; for true compassion seeks not what he wants for himself, but for his fellow Christian. But if Mary is such who is not heard amongst princes and great men and at leaving his cell gains nothing, then he should pray to God carefully for those who are in pain; and God, beholder of the heart, shall for the charity of him who prays turn the hearts of men to peace which are diseased. And either he shall be delivered of his tribulation, or else God shall give him patience, so that his reward in heaven shall be doubled. Therefore such a cloth of humility or of compassion ought to be in Mary's heart. For there is nothing which draws God so into a soul as humility and compassion for his fellow Christian.

"Third, Mary must have food and drink for guests. For grievous guests are lodged in Mary's heart, when the heart is ravished out of itself and desires to see delectable things in this world and to have temporal possessions; when his ear desires to hear his own praises; when the flesh seeks to delight in fleshly things; when the spirit pretends to be frail and excuses sin; when there is tardiness to do good and forgetfulness of things that are to come; when good deeds are considered to be many and the evil thought to be few and forgotten. Against such guests Mary has need of counsel, that he dissemble not nor fall asleep. Therefore Mary, heartened with faith, must rise firmly and answer thus to these guests: 'I will not have any temporal things, except those which are necessary to sustain the body. I will not spend the best hour or time, except to praise God. Nor will I take heed of fair or foul, nor what is profitable or unprofitable to the flesh, nor what is savory or unsavory to the taste, except only the pleasure of God and profitable to the soul; for I do not wish to live hour by hour, except to praise God.' Such a will is food to guests who may come, and such an answer quenches inordinate delights.

"Fourth, Mary must have a fire to make her guests warm, and to give them light. This fire is the heat of the holy Spirit; for it is impossible for any man to forsake his own will or the carnal affection of his friends or the love of riches, but by the working inspiration and heat of the holy Spirit. Neither may Mary himself, be he never so perfect, begin nor continue any good life without sweetness and information of the same holy Spirit. Therefore, that Mary illumines and lights the guests that come first, he must think thus: 'God made me for that skill that I should praise him, love him and dread him above all things; and he was born of a Virgin to teach the way to heaven, which I should follow with humility. And after, with his death, he opened heaven, that by desiring and advancing I should haste there.' Mary must also examine all his works and thoughts and desires, and how he has offended God, and how patiently God suffered man, and how in many ways God calls man to him. For such thoughts and others like them are the guests of Mary, which are all in darkness; but if they are lightened with the fire of the holy Spirit, which fire comes to the heart when Mary thinks it is reasonable to serve God, and when he would rather suffer all pain than wittingly provoke God to anger, by whose goodness his soul is made and bought again with his blessed blood. The heart also is lit by this good fire, when reason thinks and discerns by what intent each guest, that is, each thought, comes, when the heart examines if the thought goes to everlasting joy or to transitory joy; if it leave no thought undiscussed, none unpunished, none without dread. Therefore, that this fire may be got, and kept when it is obtained, it is necessary for Mary to gather together dry wood, by which this fire is fed; that is, that he be concerned about the stirrings of the flesh, that the flesh begin not to be wanton; and that he put to all diligence, that the works of pity and devout prayer be enlarged and increased, in which the holy Spirit delights. But above all it is to know and see that where fire is kindled in a close vessel and has no ash, the fire is soon quenched and the container becomes cold. And so is it with Mary; for if Mary desires to live only to praise God, then it is necessary for him that his mouth be opened and the fame of his charity to go out. Then is the mouth opened, when by speaking in fervent charity he gets spiritual sons for God.

"But Mary must be very careful that he open the mouth of his preaching when they who are good may be made more fervent, and they who are wicked may be amended, where righteousness may be increased and evil habits removed. For my Apostle Paul would sometimes have spoken; but he was forbidden by my Spirit, and therefore at the right time he was still, and at the convenient time he spoke; and sometimes he used soft words, and sometimes sharp; and all his words and deeds were to the praise of God and to strengthen faith. But if Mary may not preach,[15] and has the desire and the knowledge how to preach, he must do so as a fox that goes about seeking many places with his feet; and when he finds the best and most suitable places, there he makes a den to rest in. So Mary must with words, examples, and prayers try the hearts of many; and when he finds hearts more able to receive the word of God, there must he stay and rest, admonishing and stirring whom he may. Mary must also work that a fitting show be given to his flame of fire: for the greater the flame is, the more people are illumined and enflamed by it. The flame has then a fitting show, where Mary neither dreads criticism nor shame, nor seeks his own praise, when he dreads neither contrarious things, nor delights in wealth and prosperity. And then it is more acceptable to God that Mary do his good deeds in the open rather than in private, to that extent that they who see them may praise and worship God.

"Also, Mary ought to give out two flames, one in private, another openly: that is, to have double humility; the first in the heart, inwardly, the other outwardly. The first is that Mary thinks himself unworthy and unprofitable in all goodness, and that he prefers not nor exhalts himself in his own conceit above any person; and that he does not desire to be seen and praised, but that he flees from all pride and haughtiness, desiring God above all things and following his words. If Mary send out such a flame in his deeds, then shall his heart be lit with charity, and all contrary things that come to him shall be overcome and easily endured. The second flame must be in the open; for if true humility is in the heart, it ought to appear in clothing and to be heard in the mouth and to be fulfilled in deeds. True humility is in the clothing when Mary chooses cloth of less price, from which he may gain warmth and profit, rather than cloth of more value, of which he might be proud and show off. For cloth which is cheap and is called by men vile and

[15]Bride is remembering that Paul forbade women to preach, I Corinthians 7.3-6. Mary Magdalen preached, according to the *Golden Legend*, "And when Mary Magdalen saw the pagans going into their temple to offer sacrifice to their gods, she arose with calm mien and prudent tongue, and began to draw them away from the worship of the idols and to preach Christ to them. And all wondered at her, not only for her beauty but for her eloquence, which eloquence was not indeed a matter of surpise on lips that had touched the Lord's feet," p. 357. Bride is also playing positively with the negative *topos* of the "preaching fox."Chaucer's Nuns' Priest's Tale uses that topos. Is Bride talking about herself?

abject is truly fair to God because it provokes humility.[16] But that cloth which is bought with great price and is called fair is foul to God; for it takes away the fairness of angels, which is humility. Nevertheless, if Mary is compelled by any reasonable cause to have better clothing than he would want, be not troubled therefore; for by that shall his reward be greater.

"Also Mary ought to be meek in mouth, speaking humble words; fleeing from vain words and such as cause laughter; being careful of much speech; not using subtle nor pretty words; nor professing his own will or words before the comprehension and feeling of those who are better. And if Mary is praised for any good deed, he should not be exalted thereby with pride, but should answer thus: '*Laus sit deo qui dedit omnia,*' that is, praising God who gave all goodness. For what am I but dust before the face of the wind; or what good comes of me, earth without water? And if he is criticized, he should not be downcast but answer thus: 'It is appropriate; for I have so often offended in the sight of God and not done penance for which I should earn greater torment. Therefore pray for me that by enduring temporal reprimands, I may escape everlasting ones.' If Mary is provoked by wrath to any misjudgment of his fellow Christian, he must be prudently careful of any indiscreet answer; for pride is often associated with wrath, and therefore it is wholesome advice that when wrath and pride come about, that he hold his lips tightly together until he can ask for help from God for endurance and patience; and until he may be advised what and how to answer; or until he may overcome himself. For then wrath is quenched in the heart and men may answer wisely to those who are unwise.

"You know also that the devil is greatly envious of Mary; and therefore if he may not stop him by breaking God's commandments, then he stirs him to be easily moved with great wrath, or else to the dissoluteness of vain mirth, or else to dissolute and playful words. Therefore Mary must ask for help from God that all his words and deeds may be governed by God and addressed to God. Also Mary must have meekness in his actions, that he does the right not because of earthly praise; that he attempt nothing new, that he be not ashamed of being humble; that he flee singularity in his works, that he respect all; and that in all things he consider himself unworthy. Also Mary ought rather to sit with the poor than with the rich; rather he should obey than be obeyed; rather to be silent than to speak; rather to be alone solitary

---

[16]We recall Bride's shabby, patched mantle in which she begged at Saint Lawrence in Panisperna.

than be constantly amongst the great of the world and among his worldly friends. Mary must hate his own will and think always on his death. Mary ought not to be idle, nor complain, nor be forgetful of the justice of God and of his own affections. Mary must be fervent in confession, careful concerning temptations, desiring to live for the right and for nothing else but the praise of God and that the health of souls be increased and enlarged.

"Therefore, if Mary, who is thus disposed as I have now said, be chosen by Martha, and obeying, for the love of God takes the rule of many souls, there shall be given to him a double crown of reward, as I show you in a parable. There was a certain lord of great power who had a ship filled with precious merchandise, and said to his servants: 'Go to such a harbor, and you shall gain much for me, and glorious fruit. If the wind rises against you, work hard and do not become weary; for your reward shall be great.' Then the servants sailed away. And the wind became strong, and tempests arose, and the ship was grievously battered. Because of this the ship's captain was exhausted and all despaired of their lives. And then they agreed to come to any harbor that the wind could blow them to, and not to the haven that the lord had assigned to them. When one of the servants who was more loyal than the others heard this, he wailed and out of fervent love and zeal that he had for his lord, he violently seized hold of the steering board of the ship and with great strength he brought the ship to the harbor the lord desired. Therefore this man who thus manfully brought the ship to the harbor is to be rewarded with more singular rewards than any other.

"It is the same with a good priest who for love of God and salvation of souls takes charge of the steering, not paying heed to fame, for he shall be doubly rewarded: first, because he shall be partner of all the good deeds of those whom he has brought to the haven; second, because his joy and bliss shall be increased without end. And so shall it be against those who desire fame and responsibility; for they shall be partner to all the pains and sins of those that they have chosen to govern. Second, for their confusion shall be without end. For the priests who desire fame are more like whores than priests. For they deceive souls with their evil words and examples; and they are unworthy to be called either Mary or Martha, unless they make amends with penance. Fifth, Mary ought to give his guests medicine; that is, delight and comfort them with God's words. For to all things that ever happen to him, whether they be joyful or burdensome, he ought to say: 'I will this; whatever God wills, I will do; and to his will I am readily obedient; though I should go to Hell." For such a will is medicine against evil things that occur to the heart, and this will is delight in tribulation and a good restraint in prosperity. But because Mary has many enemies he must therefore make his confession frequently. For as long as he remains in a state of sin and could have confessed and is negligent and takes no heed, then is he rather to be called an apostate before God than Mary."

Of the deeds of the active life which are understood by Martha. Chapter 11. [VI.65 continued]

"You must know also that though the part of Mary is best, yet the part of Martha is not evil, but praiseworthy and very pleasing to God. Therefore I shall tell you how Martha ought to be governed. For he ought to have five good things as well as Mary. First, the right faith regarding God's Church. Second, to know the commandments of the Godhead and the counsels of the truth of the Gospel; and these he ought perfectly to keep in thought and deed. Third, he ought to keep his tongue from evil words that are against God and his neighbor, and his hand from all dishonest and unlawful actions, and his heart from too much greed and pleasure. He ought also to be content with the goods God has given him, and not to desire superfluous things. Fourth, he ought to fulfill the deeds of mercy reasonably and modestly, that in doing those deeds he offends in no way. Fifth, he ought to love God above all things and more than himself. So did Martha, for he gave joyfully of himself, following my words and deeds; and after she gave all her goods for my love. And therefore she loathed temporal things, and sought heavenly things, and suffered heavenly things patiently, and took heed and care of others as of herself. And therefore she thought always on my charity and Passion; and she was glad in tribulation and loved all as a mother. The same Martha also followed me every day, desiring nothing but to hear words of life. She had compassion on those who were grieving; she comforted the sick; she neither cursed nor said evil to any. But she did not imitate the pushiness of her neighbor and prayed for all. Therefore every man who desires charity actively ought to follow Martha in loving his neighbor, to bring him to heaven, but not in favoring and nourishing his vices and sins. He ought also to flee his own vanity, pride and doubleness. Also he ought not to use wrath or envy.

But mark well that Martha, praying for her brother Lazarus when he was dead, came first to me. But her brother was not yet raised until Mary came after, when she was called. And then for both sisters their brother was raised from the dead to life.[17] So in spiritual life he who perfectly desires to be Mary must first be Martha, laboring physically to my praise. And he ought first to learn how to withstand the desires of the flesh and the temptation of the fiend and afterwards he may with deliberation ascend up the height of Mary. For he who is unproved and tempted, and he who has not overcome the lusts of his flesh, how may he continually heed and choose heavenly things? Who is the dead brother of Mary and Martha, but an unperfect work? For often a good work is done with an indiscreet intent and with an ill advised heart, and therefore it is done dully and slowly. But for the working of good deeds to be acceptable to me, it must be raised and quickened by Martha and Mary; that is, when the neighbor is clearly loved for God and to God, and God alone is desired above all things. And then every good work of man is pleasing to God. Therefore I said in the Gospel that Mary chose the better part; for then the part of Martha is also good, when he grieves for the sins of his fellow Christians; and then is the part of Martha better, when he labors that men may continue in the good life wisely and honestly, and that only for the love of God.

"But the part of Mary is best when he beholds only heavenly things and the profit of souls. And the Lord enters into the house of Martha and Mary when the heart is fulfilled with good affections; and at peace away from the noise of worldly things; and thinking of God as always present; and not only contemplating and meditating on his love, but laboring in that day and night.

Our Lord Jesus Christ tells Saint Bride of his blessed Incarnation; and how man offends God and breaks his baptismal promise; and of the mercy that is for them who make amends; and of the harsh judgment to them who do not repent; and how sweetly he calls stalwart souls to his bliss. [I.1. The body of this chapter is omitted here.]

Our Lord Jesus Christ tells Saint Bride of the sin and of the uncleanness of Christian people; and how they may have mercy if they will repent; and otherwise how hard they shall be punished. Chapter 13. [I.57. the body of this chapter is omitted here.]

Our Lord[18] tells Saint Bride by example that nothing pleases God so

---

[17]John 11.1-24; see, for instance, the liturgical drama, the *Resuscitatio Lazari*, the Raising of Lazarus, from Orléans MS 201, published in Fletcher Collins, Jr., *Medieval Church Music Dramas: A Repertory of Complete Plays* (Charlottesville: University of Virginia Press, 1976), pp. 189-239.

[18]Error for "Our Lady."

much as that he be loved above all things. [VI.50]

The Mother of God speaks to the spouse of Christ, Saint Bride, and says: "Nothing pleases God so much as that man love him above all things. See, I shall tell you by the example of a heathen woman who knew nothing of the Christian faith; but she thought thus to herself: 'I know,' she says, 'of what matter I am, and how I came to be in my mother's womb. I believe also that it is impossible for me to have a body, joints, bowels, and senses, unless someone had given these to me. And therefore there is some creator and maker who made me so fair a person of mankind, and would not make me as foul as worms and serpents. Therefore it seems to me that though I had many husbands, if they all called me, I should rather go at one call from my maker than at the calling of them all. I have also many sons and daughters, yet if I see them with food in their hands and I know that my maker was hungry, truly I would take away the food from my children's hands and gladly give it to my maker. I have also many possessions which I dispose of at my own will. Yet if I knew the will of my maker, I would most desire to leave my own will and dispose of them according to his praise.'

"But see, daughter, what God did with this heathen woman. Truly, he sent his friend to her, who informed her in the holy faith. And God himself visited her heart, and you may well understand by the woman's words, for when that man of God preached to her that there was one God without beginning and end who is the Creator of all things, she answered: 'It is well to be believed, that he who made me and all things has no maker above him. And it is likely true that his life is everlasting who could give me life.'

"When this woman heard that the same Creator took mankind of a Virgin and preached with his own mouth, she answered: 'It is well to believe all virtuous works are of God. But, friend of God, tell me what are the words that come from my Creator? For I will leave my own will and obey his according to all his words.'

"Then, the friend of God preaching to her of his Passion, Crucifixion and Resurrection, she answered with weeping eyes and said: 'Blessed is that God who so patiently showed his charity on earth that he had for us in heaven. Therefore if I have loved him first, for he made me, now I am much more bound to love him, for he showed me the right way and bought me with his holy blood. I am also bound to serve him with all my might and all my limbs, for he bought me with all his limbs. And furthermore, I am bound to put away from me all my own will and desire that I previously had for my goods, possessions, children, family relations and friends, and only to desire my Creator in his bliss and in that life that never ends.'"

Then said the Mother of God: "See, daughter, this woman obtained a many fold reward for her love, and so is each day reward given to each one after that time that God had lived in this world."

How our Lady and Saint Peter kept a woman from falling into sin, by whose counsel she changed her life, and of special grace she fell ill, and so was purged and went to Heaven. Chapter 25. [VI.93]

The spouse of Christ, Saint Bride, saw spiritually a woman sitting in a rope whose one end a fair man held up, and a virgin of great beauty held up the other end.[19]

Then our Lady appeared and said: "This lady whom you know is wound up in much business of the flesh and the world, and it is miraculous that she has balanced herself so well that she has not fallen. For she has often desired to sin, but never had the place nor the time to do so. And that caused the prayer of the Apostle Peter to be made by my Son, whom this woman loved. Sometimes she had time and space, but not the will; and that was made by the love of me who am the Mother of God. And therefore now because her time draws near, Saint Peter counseled her to take upon her some harshness in clothing and wearing, putting away soft garments. For he was the chief Apostle; and yet he endured nakedness, prison and hunger, although he was mighty in heaven and on earth. I also, Mother of God, who never passed an hour on earth without tribulation and discomfort of heart, counsel her that she not be ashamed to be meek and to obey the friends of God."

After this soon Saint Peter the Apostle appeared and said to Saint Bride: "You now, spouse of our lord God, go and ask of this woman whom I have loved and preserved, if she will wholly be my daughter."

When Saint Bride had asked, and she consenting, said, "I will, with all my heart," Saint Peter answered: "I shall arrange for her as for my daughter, Peronell, and take her into my charge."[20]

[19]This vision is not unlike that which Monica reported to Augustine that she had had, *Confessions* 3:11, of seeing herself standing on a wooden rule, someone asking her joyously why she wept and her answer that it was for her son, his reply being that her son would come to stand there with her.

[20]"Saint Petronilla," May 31, *Golden Legend*, pp. 300-301. In the Legend Saint Peter arranged for his daughter to become ill with fever in order not to be attractive to men, and to die when her hand was demanded in

Then, as soon as this lady heard this, she changed her life. And not long after, she fell ill, which continued for the rest of her life, until she was purged and with very great devotion gave up her spirit. For, when she came to the end of her life, she saw Saint Peter arrayed like a bishop, and Saint Peter Martyr in the habit of the Friars Preachers, for he was of that Order, both of whom she had loved entirely during her life.

And then she said openly: "Who are these lords?" When the ladies and women who stood about her asked her what she saw, she answered: "I see," she said, "marvelous things. For I see my lords, Peter the Apostle dressed pontifically and Peter the Martyr in the habit of the Preachers, whom I have always loved and always hoped for their help." And then, crying: "Blessed be God. See, I come," she passed to our Lord.

Our Lord Jesus Christ stirs up his Bride to love him, and tells her how little love many have toward him, and how much to the world. Chapter 16. [I.3]

"I am your Lord God, whom you worshipped. I am he who by my power bears up heaven and earth; and it is born up with no other arches or pillars. I am he who each day is offered on the altar as very God and man. I am the same who has chosen you. Worship my father. Love me. Obey my spirit. Do reverence to my Mother, as to your Lady. Praise all my saints. Keep the right faith, which he shall teach you who has felt in himself the strife of the two spirits of falsehood and truth; and by my help he shall overcome. Stay truly humble; that is, a man to show himself such as he is, and to give praise to God for his life.

"But now there are many who hate me. My words and deeds they hold in contempt and as vanity; and the adulterer, the fiend, they kneel to and love. Whatever they do for me, it is with complaining and bitterness. Nor would they acknowledge my name if they would not be damned by me. The world they love so clearly that they are not weary to work concerning it night and day; and always they are fervent in their love for it, their service is as pleasing to me as if a man gave his enemy money to slay his own son. So do they who give me a little charity. And they worship me with their lips to the intent that they may increase in worldly prosperity, and remain in power and in sin; therefore their good will is slain from profiting in God.

"But if you will love me with all your heart and desire nothing but me,

marriage.

I shall draw you to me by charity, as the magnet draws to itself the iron. And I shall take you on my arm, that is so strong that no one may draw it out, and so mighty that when it is stretched out, none may bend it. It is also so sweet that it surpasses all sweetness; and it is beyond comparison with worldly delight."

How Saint Bride sees in her spiritual sight the judgment of a soul whom the fiend accused, and at the last was helped by our Lady; and how she saw all Hell and Purgatory and many other marvels; and how needful it is to help them who are in Purgatory. Chapter 17. [IV.7]

It seemed to a person who was awake in prayer and not sleeping as though she had seen in her spiritual sight a palace of incredible greatness, in which were countless people, clad in white and shining clothes. And each of them seemed to have a proper seat to himself. In this palace stood principally a judgment seat, in which it was as if there were a sun; and the brightness that went from that sun was more than may otherwise be told or understood, in length, depth and breadth. There stood also a Virgin close to that seat, having a precious crown on her head. And all who were there served the Son sitting on the throne, praising him with hymns and songs.

Then appeared there an Ethiopian, fearful in sight and bearing, as though he had been full of envy and greatly enraged. He cried and said: "O you rightful Judge, grant me this soul, and hear his works; for now his life is near the end. Allow me therefore to punish the body with the soul, until they are separated."

When this was said, it seemed to me that one stood before the throne, like a knight armed excellently, and wise in words, and sober in hearing, who said: "You, Judge, see, here are his good works that he has done up to this hour."

And then there was heard a voice out of the sun sitting on the seat: "Here are vices," he said, "more than virtues. And it is not justice that vice be joined to him who is supreme virtue."

Then answered the Ethiopian: "Therefore it is rightful that this soul be joined to me; because if it has any vice in it, in me is all wickedness."

The knight answered: "The mercy of God follows every person until the last moment of his life, and then comes the Judgment. And in this man that we speak of are yet both soul and body joined together, and discretion remains in him."

The Ethiopian answered: "The Scriptures say, that may not be: you shall love God above all things, and your neighbor as yourself. See you therefore, that all the works of this man are done out of dread, and not out of love and charity as they ought to be. And all the sins that he is cleansed of, you will find him cleansed with little contrition. And therefore he has deserved Hell; because he has forfeited the kingdom of Heaven. And therefore his sins are here opened before the Judgment of God. For he never yet was contrite in goodly charity for the sins that he has done."

The knight answered: "Truly, he hoped and believed he would become contrite before his death."

"You," he said, "have gathered all the deeds that he had ever done well, and you know all his words and his thoughts for the salvation of his soul. And all these, whatever they may be, may not be likened to that grace gained by contrition for the love of God with holy faith and hope, and much less they may not cancel out all his sins. For justice is in God who is without beginning, that no sinner shall enter Heaven who is not perfectly contrite. And therefore it is impossible that God should judge against the disposition ordained from before time. Therefore the soul is to be judged to Hell and to be joined with me in everlasting pain."

When this was said, the knight held his peace and answered nothing to these words. After this appeared innumerable fiends, like sparks out a hot fire. And they all cried out with one voice saying to him who sat in the seat as a sun: "We," they say, "know that you are God in two Persons, without beginning and end, and there is no other God but you. You are that charity to which is joined mercy and righteousness. You were in yourself from before the beginning, having not lessened nor in any little way changed, as it seemed God without you is not, and nothing has joy without you. Therefore your charity made angels of no other matter but the power of your Godhead. And you did as mercy stirred you. But after that we were burned within with pride, envy and greed; your charity, loving righteousness, cast us out of heaven with the fire of our malice into dark and unseeable deepness that is now called Hell. So did your charity, then, which shall not yet be separated from the Judgment of your justice, whether it be after mercy or after equity. And yet we say more, if the thing which you love before all things, the Virgin who bore you, who never sinned, had sinned mortally and died without goodly contrition, you love justice so that her soul should never have got to Heaven, but it should have been with us in Hell. Therefore, Judge, why do you not condemn this soul to us, that we may punish it after his works."

After this was heard as it were the sound of a trumpet, and all who heard it were still. And then was heard a voice saying: "Be still and listen, all angels, souls and fiends, to what the Mother of God speaks."

And then, the same Virgin appearing before the seat of Judgment and having under her mantle as it had been some great private things, said: "O, you enemies, you persecute mercy and without charity you love justice, though here appears a lack of good works for which this soul ought not to get Heaven, yet see what I have under my mantle."

And when the Virgin had opened both the fronts of her mantle, under the one appeared as like a little church, in which seemed to be some men of religion; and under the other appeared women and men, friends of God, religious and other.[21] And they all cried with one voice saying, "Have mercy, merciful Lord."

Then after there was silence and the Virgin spoke and said: "The Scripture said, he who has perfect faith may thereby move mountains in the world. What then may and ought the voices of these do, who had faith and also served God with charity? And what shall those friends of God do, whom this man asked that they pray for him, that he might be separated from Hell and obtain Heaven? And he sought no other reward for his good works but heavenly things, where all their tears and prayers may not or are not of power to take him and lift him up so that he get goodly contrition with charity before his death, and furthermore I shall add to my prayers the prayer of all the saints that are in Heaven, whom this man specially worshipped." Yet then further said the Virgin: "O, you fiends, I command you by the power of the Judge to take heed of these things that you see now in justice."

Then they all answered as if it had been with one mouth: "We see," they said, "that in the world a little water and great air balance out the anger of God. And so by your prayer is God weighed to mercy with charity."

After this was heard a voice from the Son, saying: "For the prayers of my friends shall this man now get goodly contrition before his death, in so much that he shall not come into Hell; but he shall be purged with them who

[21]See the medieval paintings of Mary in this attitude with people gathered within her cloak; also the Giotto Arena Chapel Last Judgment fresco with Ernesto Scrovegni donating that chapel shown self-referentially within it, Sarel Eimerl, *The World of Giotto: c. 1267-1377* (New York: Time Incorporated, 1967), p. 129. Here Birgitta is speaking of Nicholas Acciaiuoli and of his founding Certosa from similar motives as had Scrovegni the Arena Chapel.

suffer most grievous pain in Purgatory. And when the soul is purged, he shall have reward in Heaven with them who had faith and hope on earth with right little charity."

When this was said, the fiends fled away. Then after that it seemed to the Bride as if there had opened a fearful and dark place wherein there appeared a furnace all burning within; and that fire had nothing else to burn but fiends and living souls. And above that furnace appeared that soul whose judgment was just completed. The feet of the soul were fastened to the furnace, and the soul stood up like a person. It did not stand in the highest place nor in the lowest, but as if on the side of the furnace. The shape of the soul was fearful and marvelous. The fire of the furnace seemed to come up between the feet of the soul, as when water ascends up by pipes. And that fire ascended upon his head, and violently thrust him together; so much that the pores stood as veins running with burning fire. His ears seemed like smiths' bellows which moved all his brain with continual blowing. His eyes seemed turned upside down and sunk in as if they were fastened to the back part of his head. His mouth was open and his tongue drawn out by his nostrils and hung down to his lips. His teeth were as iron nails fastened to his palate. His arms were so long that they stretched down to his feet. Both his hands seemed to have and to press together a kind of fat with burning pitch. The skin which seemed to be upon the soul seemed like the skin upon a body, and it was as a linen cloth all fouled with filth; which cloth was so cold that each one could see it tremble and shiver. And there came from it pus from a sore with corrupt blood, and so wicked a stench that it could not be compared to the worst stench in the world. When his tribulations were seen, there was heard a voice of the soul that said five times, "Woe, woe, alas, alas," crying with tears and all his might.

First he said: "Alas and woe to me, that I loved God so little for his truly great virtues and grace given to me." The second: "Alas and woe to me, that I did not fear the Judgment of God as I ought." The third, "Alas and woe to me, that I loved the body and the lust of my sinful flesh." The fourth, "Alas and woe to me, for my worldly riches and pride." The fifth, "Alas and woe to me, that ever I saw you, Lewes and Joan."[22]

[22]Latin text gives "*Ludovicum et Ioannam.*" This is the vision Bride relayed to Nicholas Acciaiuoli, Grand Seneschal of Naples, who had been Queen Joan's lover and tutor to Prince Lewes of Taranto and whose marriage he arranged in 1347, following her murder of her previous husband and King of Naples, Andrew of Hungary, 1345. Acciaiuoli had founded

Then the angel said to me: "I will explain this vision to you. This palace you have seen is the likeness of heaven. The multitude of those who were on the thrones, clad in white and shining clothes, are angels and the souls of saints. The sun means Christ in his Godhead. The woman means the Virgin who bore God. The Ethiopian means the fiend who accuses the soul. The knight means the angel who tells of the good works of the soul. The furnace means Hell, which is so burning within, that if all the world burnt with all things that are within, it would not be like the greatness of that furnace. In this furnace are heard diverse voices, all speaking against God, and all beginning their utterances with "Woe and alas," and ending in the same way. The souls appeared as people whose members are stretched out without comfort and who never can rest. Know also the fire that seemed to you in the furnace, burns in everlasting darkness, and the souls that burn within it do not all have the same pain. The darkness that appeared about the furnace is called 'limbus,'[23] and it comes from the darkness that is in the furnace and yet they are both the same place and one Hell. Whoever comes there shall never dwell with God. Above this darkness is the greatest pain of Purgatory that souls may suffer. And beyond this place is another place where there is less pain, that is none other but the lack of firmness in strength, beauty and such other: as I tell you by a parable, as if there were a sick man; and when the sickness and the pain had ended, he was left so feeble that he had no strength, until he recovered little by little. The third place is above, where there is no other pain but the desire of coming to God. And that you should understand this better in your conscience, I tell you by a parable, as if other metals were meddled with gold and burnt in a most hot fire and should so long be purged, that the other metals were refined away; and the gold stayed pure and clean though the other metal was strong and thick, so that it should need the hotter fire, and the gold was like running water, and all burning. Then the master of the work puts the gold in another place, where it shall take its true form and shape by sight and by touch. And after that, he puts it in the third place, where it is kept until it is presented to

Carthusian Certosa in Florence, 1342: ASF Monastero de Santa Brigida detto del Paradiso 61, fols. 21^v-24^v; Vatican MS Ottob. lat, fol. 120; Jørgensen 2:121-122.

[23]To be in 'limbo' is to be betwixt and between, neither in Heaven nor in Hell. See Dante, *Inferno* 4.

the owner.

"It is the same spiritually. In the first place above the darkness is the greatest pain of Purgatory, where you see the said soul being purged. There is tormenting by fiends. There appear the likeness of venomous worms and the likeness of savage beasts. There is heat and cold. There is darkness and confusion that comes from the pain that is in Hell. Some souls there have less pain and some more, according to whether their sins were amended or not, during the time that the soul dwelled in the body. Then the master, that is, the justice of God, puts the gold, that is the souls, in other places, where there is less strength, in which the souls abide until they have refreshing of their friends or of the continual prayers of holy Church. For a soul, the more help it has from its friends, the rather will it become strong and be delivered from that place. After this, the soul is born to the third place, where there is no pain except the desire to come into the presence of God and to his blessed sight. In this place dwelled many and for a very long time, without, those who had perfect desire while they lived in the world to come to the presence and sight of God. Know also that many die in the world so virtuously and innocently, that soon they come to the sight and presence of God. And some have so amended their sins with good works, that their souls shall feel no pain. But there are few who come not to the place where there is desire to come to God. Therefore all souls abiding in these three places have a part in the prayers and good works of holy Church that are done in the world; namely of those that they did while they lived, and of those which are done by their friends after their death. Know also that as sins are many and diverse, so are the pains many and diverse. Therefore as the hungry one delights in food when it comes to his mouth, and the thirsty in drink, and as he who is downcast, is gladdened with joy, and the naked with clothing, and the sick with going to his bed, so the souls joy in and are partners of the good deeds that are done for them in the world."

Then said the angel furthermore: "Blessed is he who has in the world helped souls with prayers, good works and the labor of his body. For the Justice of God may not lie which says that souls either must be purged after their death with the pain of Purgatory, or else they must be loosed by the good works of their friends."

After this were heard many voices out of Purgatory, saying: "O Lord Jesus Christ, just Judge, send your charity to them who have spiritual power in the world; for then shall we have more part than we have now, of their song, readings and offerings."

Above this space from where this cry was heard, it seemed as if it were a house in which were heard many voices, saying "let those be rewarded of God who send us help from our errors."

In the same house the sun seemed to go forth as if it had been the spring of a day. And under that dawn appeared a cloud that had not the light of the morning time. Out of which came a great voice, saying: "O Lord God, give of your unspeakable power to each of them in the world a hundredfold reward, that with their good deeds lift us up into the light of your Godhead and into the sight of your face."

Then after that the angel tells of the pains of the said soul and says: [IV.8-9]

"That soul whose disposition you have seen, and heard his judgment, is in the most grievous pains of Purgatory. And that is because it does not understand whether it shall come to rest after purgation, or else be damned; and this is the Justice of God, for this one had conscience and great discretion, which he used bodily to the world and not spiritually to his soul. For he was too negligent and forgot God too much, while he lived. Therefore his soul suffers now from burning in flames, and it trembles for cold. It is also blind from the darkness and fearful with the horrible sight of the fiends. It is deafened from the fiend's cry, hungry and thirsty within, and all wrapped in confusion without. Nevertheless, God gave it one grace after death; that is, that it should not be subjected to torment by the fiends. For he spared and forgave grievous faults to his chief enemies, only for the praise of God; and he made friendship and accord with his chief enemy. Know also that whatever he did of good and whatever he promised and gave of justly obtained riches, and most of all the prayers of the friends of God, these lessen and refresh his pain, after it is determined in God's Justice. But other goods that he gave, that were not justly obtained, profit those who had them rightfully in their possession spiritually or physically, if they are worthy after the disposition of God."

After this the angel called, furthermore, for the Judgment of the afore-mentioned soul, and said: "You have heard already that for the prayers of the friends of God, this man obtained goodly contrition through charity for his sins, a little before his death; which contrition separates him from Hell. Therefore after his death, the Justice of God judges that he should burn in Purgatory for six times the age that he has, from that hour that he did first knowingly deadly sin, until the time when he repented fruitfully of goodly charity, but he obtained help from God, of the world, and from the friends of God. The first was that he loved not God for the death of his noble body, and for his manifold tribulations, that he suffered for no other cause but for the salvation of souls. The second age was that he loved not his own soul as a Christian man ought; nor did he thank God for his baptism, for being neither Jew nor heathen. The third age was that he knew well the things that God commanded, and he had very little desire to fulfill them. The fourth age was that he knew well the things that God forbade to them who desire to go to Heaven; and he acted bodily against these, not following the prickings of his conscience, but his own carnal desire. The fifth age was that he did not use grace and confession as was appropriate, while he had the time to do so. The sixth age was that he cared little for the body of Christ, not willing to receive it often, for he would not keep himself from sin; neither had he charity to receive the body of Christ until the end of his life."

After this there appeared one like a man of great solemnity, whose clothes were white and shining like a priest's alb[24]; he was girt with a linen girdle and a red stole about his neck and under his arms; and he began his words in this way. [IV.9]

"You who see these things, take heed, mark and commend to your mind the things that you see and that are said to you. For you who are living in the world may not understand the power of God and the everlasting stability of it, in the same way as we who are with him. For the things that are with God, done in a moment of time, may not be understood amongst you, but with words and likeness after the disposition of the world. I am one of them whom this man, who is condemned to purgatory worshiped with his gifts in his life. Therefore God has granted me of his grace that if any man would do these things that I tell you, then his soul might be translated to a higher place, where it should get his true shape, and feel no other pain than as if he had a great sore, and all the sorrows would be gone, and he would lie like a man without strength, and yet he should rejoice, as much as he should know certainly that he should come to live.

"Therefore, as you heard the soul of this man had cried five times, 'Woe and alas,' so I say now to him five things of comfort. The first woe was that he loved God too little. Therefore, that he may be delivered from this, there needs to be given for his soul thirty chalices, in which the blood of God

---

[24]*Alba*, white, dawn. An alb is a white gown worn by clergy during church services.

can be offered, and God himself be more praised. The second woe was that he did not fear God. Therefore, to cancel out this, let there be chosen thirty priests devoted to the man's judgment, and each of them to say thirty masses, when they may: twelve of the Martyrs, twelve of the Confessors, twelve of All Saints, twenty-eight Masses of the Angels, twenty-nine of our Lady, and thirty of the holy Trinity. And all of them must pray intensely for his soul, that the anger of God be assuaged, and his justice bowed down to mercy. The third woe was for his pride and greed. Therefore, to do away with these, let there be received thirty poor men, whose feet are to be washed with humility, and food and drink and money and clothes to be given to them, with which they can be comforted; and each of them, both he who washes, and they who are washed, should pray to God meekly, that for his meekness and bitter Passion he forgive this soul the greed and pride that he has enacted. The fourth woe, for the lechery of his flesh. Therefore, whoever gives a maiden into a monastery and also a widow, and a maid into true wedlock, giving with them as much goods as they might be sufficiently endowed in food, drink and clothing; then should God forgive the sin of this soul which he had done in the flesh. For these are three lives that God commanded and chose to stand in this world.[25] The fifth woe was that he had done many sins to others' tribulation. That is to say, he did all in his power that the two named before should come together in wedlock, which were no less of kin together than if they had both been next of kindred; and this marriage he procured more for himself than for the realm, and without permission from the Pope, against the praiseworthy disposition of holy Church. And for his deed, many were made martyrs, that such things should not be endured against God and holy Church and Christian custom.[26]

"If any man who would repent of his sin went to the Pope and said: 'A certain man did such a sin' (not expressing the person), 'nevertheless at the end he repented and obtained absolution, though the sin was not amended. Tell me therefore what penance you would give, that I may bear; for I am ready to amend that sin for him.' Truly, if he were to say for him no more than one *Pater noster*, it should be worthwhile to that soul to the lessening of his pain in Purgatory."

Words of praise between our Lady and her Son and what grace our Lady obtains for those who are in Purgatory and in the world. Chapter 18.

[25]The three states: Virginity, Marriage, Widowhood.
[26]Queen Joan of Naples' marriage to Prince Lewes of Taranto.

[I.50. The body of this chapter is omitted here.]

How our Lord likens our Lady to a flower that sprang up in a valley and grew above taller than mountains. Chapter 19. [I.51. The body of this chapter is omitted here.]

Our Lady prays that these revelations might be rooted in men's hearts and spread abroad in the world: and how our Lord praises our Lady and grants her request, and bids that these be taken to the Pope and other prelates.[27] **Chapter 20.** [I.52. A part of this chapter is omitted.]

Then said our Lord to his spouse, Saint Bride: "Say to my friend, your father, whose heart is after my heart, that he expound diligently these words that are written;[28] and that he take them to the archbishop and afterward to another bishop, and when they are wisely informed, then that he send them to the third bishop. Say also to him on my behalf: 'I am your Creator and the Redeemer of souls. I am he whom you love before all other things. Behold and see that the souls which I bought with my blood are as it were the souls of them that knew not God. And they are taken prisoner by the fiend so horribly that he punishes them in all their members, as it were in a narrow press. Therefore if my wounds are savored in your heart, if you care anything about my scourging and my sorrows, show in your works how much you love me; and make my words that I have spoken with my own mouth to be published, and bear them yourself to the head of the Church. For I shall give you my Spirit that wherever there is any debate between two, you shall make them more accord in my name by your virtue that is given you, if they give faith and credence to my words. And for the greater obedience to my words, you shall bear to the bishops the witness of them to whom my words savour and delight. For my words are as it were made of grease or tallow that melt so much the sooner as a man has within him more kindly heat; for where there is no kindly heat a man casts out such fatness and receives it not into his stomach. So are my words. For the more fervent a man in his charity who eats and chews them, the more fat he grows in sweetness of heavenly joy and inward love, and the more he burns in my love. But they to whom my words please not, have as it were fatness in their mouth which they taste, and soon they cast it out and tread it under their feet. So my words are despised by some, for the sweetness of spiritual things pleases them not. The prince of the land whom I have chosen into membership and made truly mine shall

[27]*Prelates*, ecclesiasts, churchmen, priests.
[28]Master Mathias of Linköping.

help you greatly; and he shall give you your necessities for the way of well obtained goodness."[30]

An angel tells Saint Birgitta of the difference between the good spirit and the evil; and how a man should behave who is encumbered by the evil spirit. Chapter 21. [I.54]

An angel spoke to the spouse of Christ, Saint Birgitta, and said: "There are two spirits, one uncreated and another created. The uncreated Spirit has three attributes: first, he is hot; second, he is sweet, third, he is clean. He is hot, for he kindles not with anything that is made, but of himself, for he is, with the Father and the Son, Creator of all things and almighty; and then he kindles the soul which is all inflamed for the love of God.[33] He is sweet, when nothing is sweet nor pleasing to the soul but God alone and the mind contemplating on his works. He is clean, so that no sin may be found in him nor nothing foul, corrupt or changeable. He kindles, not with material fire, nor as the visible sun, that melts things; but his heat is the inward burning love of the soul and a desire fulfilling and swelling the soul to God. He is also sweet to the soul, not as desirable wealth, lust or any such worldly thing; but that sweetness of the Spirit is unlike any temporal sweetness and unthinkable to all those who have never savored it. Third, that Spirit is as clean as are the beams of the sun, where there is found no spot.

"The second spirit, that is, a created spirit, also has three things: he is burning, he is bitter, and he is unclean. First, he is burning and wasting as fire. For the soul that he has in possession, he burns all with the fire of lechery and of wicked desire; so that the soul may not think nor desire anything but the fulfilling of these things; so much, that sometimes temporal life and all worship and comfort are thereby lost. Second, he is as bitter as gall; for he inflames the soul with his delight, that the joys that are to come seem to him as if nothing, and endless good seems to him folly; and all things that are of God and that he owes to God are bitter to him and abhorred, as if they were vomit or gall. Third, he is unclean; for he makes the soul so vile and ready to sin that he is not ashamed of any sin, nor should he leave off sinning, unless he dreaded more the shame of man than of God. And this spirit is as burning as fire; for he is burning in himself to wickedness and so

[30]King Magnus "Smek" Eriksson of Sweden.

[33]Luke 24: The pilgrim disciples on the road to Emmaus noted later that their hearts were "*ardens*," "burning," as the disguised unrecognized Christ had spoken with them. This particular passage gave rise to sublimated erotic imagery in Christian writings.

burns others with him. And he is bitter; for all good is bitter to him, and he makes others bitter with him. And he is unclean; for he delights in uncleanness himself and he seeks to have others be like him.

"But now you might ask and say to me: 'Are you not a created spirit like him? Why are you therefore not such a one as he is?' I answer: 'Truly, I am made by the same God as he is; for there is but one God, Father and Son and holy Spirit, and they are not three Gods but one God. And we both were well made and to a good end, for God never made anything but good. But I am as a star, for I stood in the goodness and charity of God, in which I was made; and he is as a dead coal, because he departed from God's charity. Therefore as a star is not without brightness and shining, and a coal is not without blackness; so a good angel, that is, a star, is never without lightness, that is to say, the holy Spirit. For all that he has he has of God, that is, Father and Son and holy Spirit, by whose love he is hot and by whose shining he is bright. And to him he cleaves intensely and conforms himself to his will, and because he never wills anything but as God wills; and therefore he is hot and clean. But the devil is such a foul black coal and more foul than all creatures. Because he was more fair than any other, so must he be fouler than any other; for he was contrary to his Creator. And as the angel of God shines without ceasing by the light of God and burns in the light of his charity, so does the fiend burn and is anguished in his malice. And as his malice may never be satiated, so the goodness of the Spirit of God and the grace of God are unspeakable; for there is none so rooted with the fiend but that the good Spirit sometimes visits and stirs his heart. So is there also none so good on earth but that the fiend is busy gladly to touch him with temptation. For there are many who are good and just who are tempted by the fiend with God's permission. But that is not for their harm, but for their greater glory. For the Son of God, that is one in Godhead with the Father and the holy Spirit, was tempted in his manhood. How much rather his chosen ones must be tempted to their greater reward. There are also many good people who sometimes fall into sin; and their conscience is darkened by falsehood of the fiend; but by virtue of the holy Spirit, they rise more mightily and stand more strongly. Nevertheless, there is no one but he understands in his conscience whether the suggestions of the fiend lead to the filth of sin or to good, if he will carefully think and examine it. Therefore, you Bride of my Lord, hasten not to doubt the spirit of your thoughts, whether they be good or evil; for your conscience tells you which things are to be left and which are to be done. But what shall he do with those of whom the fiend is full? For the good Spirit may not enter into him, for he is full of the evil spirit. Three things ought he to do. First, he must make a pure and complete confession of his sins which, though it may not be yet with a contrite heart for hardness of his heart, yet because of that confession the fiend will give way to the good Spirit and a manner of ceasing and skipping away. Second, he must have humility, that he intends to amend the sins which he has done. Third, to the intent that he obtains again the good Spirit, he ought to pray to God with humble prayer and to be contrite for his sins that he has done with true charity, For charity to God makes the devil flee; for he would rather die a hundred times than that a man should give the least good of charity to his God, so envious and malicious is he."

After this the blessed Virgin our Lady spoke to the spouse of Christ, Saint Birgitta, and said: "You new Bride to my Son, clothe yourself in his clothes and set your brooch on your breast; that is the Passion of my Son."

Saint Birgitta answered: "My Lady, could you set that brooch on my breast?"

Our Lady said: "I will. Truly, I will tell you how my Son was disposed and why he was so fervently desired by his holy Father. For he stood as a man between two cities; that is, Heaven and Hell. Out of the first city cried a voice to him and said: 'You who stand in my way between the cities, you are a wise man and can beware of the perils that will occur. You are strong to endure difficult things that happen to you; and you are strong-hearted, for you did nothing. We have wanted you and wait for you. Therefore, open our gate, for our enemies beseige it that it may not be opened.' Out of the second city was heard a voice, saying, 'You man, most manly and strong, hear our quarrel and wailing. We sit in the darkness and we suffer insufferable hunger and thirst. Therefore, behold our wretchedness and our wretched poverty. For we are smitten as grass is smitten with a scythe; and we are dried from all goodness, and all our strength fails. Come to us and save us; for you only we wait, and we hope that you will be our deliverer. Come and loose our poverty and turn our wailing into joy. Be you our help and our health. O most worthy and blessed body that was born of a pure Virgin, come.' These two voices my Son heard out of the two cities, Heaven and Hell; and therefore he was moved to mercy; and by his most bitter Passion and giving of his blood, he opened the gate of Hell. Think about these things, my daughter, and have them always before your eyes."

After our Lady had sent many revelations to a king,[34] at last she sent him one and said that it should be the last letter that should be sent to him. But in this revelation following, our Lady spoke again to the same king and declared her first statement and informed Saint Birgitta why the words of God are spoken so darkly that they may have diverse ways of being understood. Here is also shown the blessed Trinity under the likeness of a pulpit; and of three beams of three diverse colors; and of the judgement of three kings, of which one was alive, another was in Hell, and the third in Purgatory. Chapter 22.

The Mother of God speaks to the Bride and says: "Daughter, I told you before that that should be my last letter that should be sent to the king, my friend; that is to be understood of those things which touch his singular person and mine. For if a man heard a useful thing sung about his friend, and he sat and heard it in order to tell it to him, whether it were a song of mirth or a letter of wholesome criticism, both he who wrote it and he who sung it would be worthily rewarded. Right so the Justice of God, judging in justice and justifying in mercy, will sing of justice and mercy.[35] And therefore whoever will hear, let him hear. For it is no letter of criticism, but a song of justice and charity. Sometimes when a letter was sent to someone, it contained warnings and criticism; for it blamed unkindness of benefits and warned and stirred to conversion and the amending of manners. But now the justice of God sings a fair song, that belongs to those whoever hear it, believe it, and receive it indeed, that he shall find fruit of health and fruit of endless life.

"But you might ask why the words of God are said so darkly that they may be diversely understood and sometimes they are otherwise understood of God and other times of men. I answer: God is like to a man who makes burning wine. For this man has many pipes, some going up and some down, by which the wine runs now up and now down through the working of the

[34]King Magnus "Smek" Eriksson of Sweden.

[35]This passage plays with the Four Daughters of God *topos*, here reduced to two, taken from Psalm 85.10, "Mercy and truth are met together; righteousness and peace have kissed each other," and used again in Langland, *Piers Ploughman*, B, Passus 18, where Truth, Mercy, Justice and Peace embrace. See Ernst Robert Curtius, *European Literature and the Latin Middle Ages* (New York: Harper, 1963), p. 131; Shakespeare, *The Merchant of Venice* 4.1.184-205.

heat of the fire until it is made perfectly. Right so does God in his words, for sometimes he goes up by justice, and sometimes he comes down by mercy; as it is shown in King Isaac, to whom, I say, the prophet said out of justice that he should die, and yet afterwards mercy gave him many years of life. Sometimes also God comes down by simple showing of words bodily expressed, but he goes up again by spiritual understanding; as it was in David, to whom many things were said under the name of Solomon which were understood and fulfilled in the Son of God. Sometimes also God speaks of things to come as if they were things past, and touches both things present and things to come; for all things, both present, past, and to come, are in God as one point.[36] And you ought not to marvel though God speaks in diverse ways, for it is done for four reasons. First, that God should show his great mercy, that no man hearing the justice of God should despair of his mercy. For when a man changes the will of sin, then God changes the strictness of his sentence. The second cause is that they who give faith to the justice and to the promises of God should be crowned and rewarded the more largely for faith and constancy. The third cause is that if the counsel of God were known in a certain time, some should be greatly troubled by that, knowing of contrary cases, and others for weariness should cease in their fervor and desire. And therefore when I write any words to anyone, it is not expressed to you in the conclusion whether the words shall be received and be believed with the effect of them or not. Nor is it declared to you whether he shall believe and fulfill the words in deed or not, for it is not lawful to you to know it. The third cause is that no one should presume bodily to discuss the words of God, because he makes him low who is high, and of one he makes a second. The fourth cause is that he who seeks occasion to depart from God may find it, and those who are foul will be more foul, and the good be made more knowledgeable."

After this, the Son of God spoke to Saint Birgitta and said: "If a man spoke by a pipe that had three holes and said to the hearer, you shall never

[36]For this argument concerning God's eternity versus man's temporality, see Augustine, *Confessions* 11, Boethius, *Consolation of Philosophy*, 4. 6, 5. 6. Dante voices the concept, *Paradiso* 33.94-96: *"Un punto solo m'é maggior letargo/che venticinque secoli a la 'mpresa/che fé Nettuno ammirar l'ombra d'Argo,"* "A single point makes a larger lethargy than do the twenty-five centuries since the enterprise that amazed Neptune by the shadow of the Argo."

hear my voice by this hole, he would not be blamed though he spoke afterwards by the other two holes. So it is now in our speech; for though the Virgin my Mother said that should be the last letter to be sent to the king, that is to be understood of his person. But now I, God, who am in the Mother and the Mother in me, send my messenger to the king, as well as for them who are now at present alive as for them who are not yet born. For justice and mercy are endless in God, for eternally this justice was in God, that while God was, before Lucifer, full of wisdom of goodness and of power. He would that many should be partners in his goodness. And therefore he made angels; of which some, beholding their fairness, desired to be above God. And therefore they fell and are made under the feet of God wicked fiends. And yet in them God in a manner has mercy; for when the fiend by the justice and permission of God fulfilled the evil that he wanted, he is as it were in a manner comforted by the prosperity of his malice. Not that the pain of the fiend is lessened thereby; but as a sick man who has a most strong enemy is comforted by hearing of his death, though the pain of his sickness is not lessened by that hearing, so the fiend of envy, wherein he is hotly burning, rejoices and is glad when God does justice against men; for the thrust of his malice is in a manner refreshed and eased. But after the fall of the fiends, God, seeing the lack in his army, made man, that he should obey his precepts and bring forth fruit, until as many men and women were ascended into heaven as angels fell out of heaven. Therefore man was made perfect; who, when he had taken the commandment of life, paid no heed to God nor to his power. But consenting to the suggestion of the fiend, he trespassed, saying, "Let us eat of the Tree of Life, and we shall know all things, good and evil." Thus Adam and Eve would not harm God, as would the fiend; neither would they be above God, but they would be as wise as God. And they fell, but not as did the fiend; for the fiend had envy of God, and his wretchedness shall never end. But man would other than God would that he should will, and therefore he deserved and suffered justice with mercy. Then felt they justice when they had nakedness for clothing of glory, and hunger for plenty, stirring of the flesh for virginity, dread for security, and labor for rest. But soon they obtained mercy; that is to say, clothing against nakedness, food against hunger, security through coming together for the increasing of mankind.[37] Truly, Adam was of most honest life, in that he had no wife but Eve, nor other woman but her alone. Also, God has showed justice and mercy to the beasts, for God has made three worthy things: first, angels who have spirit

[37]Genesis 3.8-21.

but no body, second, man who has a soul and a body; third, beasts which have bodies but no souls as man has. Therefore an angel, because he is spirit, cleaves continually to God and needs no man's help. But man, because he is flesh, may not cleave continually to God, until the mortal body be separated from the soul. And therefore, that man may live, God has made to his help unreasonable beasts to obey and serve him better. And upon these unreasonable beasts God has great mercy, for they have no shame of their members nor sorrow of death until it comes. And they are content with simple living. Also after the Flood of Noah was passed, God did justice with mercy. For God might well have brought well the people of Israel into the Land of Promise in a short while. But it was right that the vessels that might hold the best drink should first be proved and purged and afterwards sanctified. To whom also God did great mercy, for by the prayers of one man, who was Moses, their sin was taken away and the grace of God given to them. In the same way, after my Incarnation, justice is never used without mercy nor mercy without justice."

Then there followed a voice on high, saying; "O Mother of mercy, Mother of the eternal king, purchase you mercy; for to you are come the prayers and tears of your servant, the king.[38] We know very well that it is rightful that his sins are punished, but be merciful so that he may be converted and do penance and reverence to God."

Then answered our Lord Jesus Christ and said: "There is fourfold justice in God. The first is that he who is made and is without end shall be worshipped above all things; for of him and in him all things live and have their being. The second justice is that to him who always was and is and was born in time, in time before prophesied, to do service to all; and for that he is loved in all cleanness. The third justice is that he who of himself may not suffer but of his manhood was made able to suffer; and in the mortality that he took upon himself has earned for man immortality, to be desired by man above all things that may be desired or are to be desired. The fourth justice is that they who are unstable should seek true stability, and they who are in darkness desire light, that is, the holy Spirit, asking his help with contrition and true meekness. But of this king, the servant of my Mother, for whom mercy is now asked, justice says that his time is not sufficient to purge worthily, as justice demands, the sins that he has done against God's mercy, so that his body might not suffer the pain that he has deserved for his sins.

[38]Magnus.

Nevertheless the mercy of the Mother of God has deserved and obtained mercy for the same, her servant, that he shall hear what he has done and how he may make amends, if he will in time be concerned and converted."

"Then after that," said Saint Bride, "I see in Heaven a house of marvelous fairness and greatness. And in that house was a pulpit and in the pulpit a Book. And I see two standing before the pulpit; that is to say, an angel and the fiend.

"Of which the one, that is, the fiend, spoke and said: 'My name,' he said, 'is Wailaway. For this angel and I follow one thing that is desirable to us; for we see the Lord's most mighty plans to build a great thing. And therefore we labor; the angel for the perfection of the thing, and I to the destruction of the same. But it happens that when that desirable thing comes sometimes into my hands, it is so fervent and hot that I may not hold it; and when it comes into the hands of the angel, it is so cold and slippery that soon it slides out of his hands.'

"And when I," said Saint Birgitta, "behold carefully with all consideration of my mind the same pulpit, my understanding is not allowed to conceive it as it was, that my soul might not comprehend the fairness of it, nor my tongue express it. For the appearance of the pulpit was as if it had been the sunbeam, having a red color and a white color and a shining color of gold. The golden color was as the bright sun. The white color was as snow, most white. And the red color was as a rose. And each color was seen in the other. For when I beheld the gold color, I see within it the white and red color. And when I see the white color, I see in it the other two colors. And when I behold the red color, I see in it the white and golden color. So that each color was seen in the other, and yet each was distinct from the others and by itself; and no color was before the other, nor after the other, nor less than the other, nor more than the other; but over all and in all things they seemed even.[39] And when I looked upwards, I might not comprehend the length and the breadth of the pulpit; and looking downward, I might not see nor comprehend the greatness nor the deepness of it, for all was incomprehensible to the consideration. After this I see a Book in the same pulpit, shining like most bright gold, that had the shape of a book.[40] Which

[39]See Brunetto Latino on rainbows, *Li Livres dou Tresor*, ed. P. Chabaille (Paris: Imprimerie Impériale, 1863), 3:107, p. 118, which Bride appears to know; likewise Dante Alighieri, *Paradiso*, 33.115-141, who derives the rainbow, as does Bride, from Ezekiel 1.28.

[40]Bride constantly returns to self-referential imagery concerning the

Book, and the Scripture of it, was not written with ink, but each word in the book was alive and spoke itself, as if a man should say, do this or that, and soon it was done with speaking of the Word. No man read the Scripture of that Book, but whatever that Scripture contained, all was seen in the pulpit and in the three colors. Before this pulpit I see a king who was alive in the world; and on the left side of the pulpit I see another king who was dead and in Hell; and on the right side I see the third king who was in Purgatory. The said king who was alive sat crowned as if it had been a vessel of glass closed about.[41] Above that glass hung a horrible sword with three edges, continually drawing nearer to that glass as does a gnomen in a sun dial draw near to its mark. On the right side of the same king stood an angel who had a vessel of gold and his lap open. And on his left side stood a fiend who had a pair of tongs and a hammer. And both the angel and the fiend strove which of their hands should be nearer the vessel of glass when the three-edged sword should touch and break it.

"Then I heard the horrible voice of the fiend, saying: 'How long shall this be? For we both follow one prayer, and do not know who shall overcome.'

"Then soon the Justice of God spoke to me and said: 'These things that are shown to you are not physical but spiritual. For neither angel nor fiend have bodies; but they are shown to you in such a manner, because you may not understand spiritual things but through a physical likeness. This living king appears to you as if in as it were a vessel of glass, for his life is but as it were frail glass and suddenly to be ended; the three-edged sword is death, for when it comes it does three things. It enfeebles the body, it changes the conscience, and it departs it from all strength, separating as by a sword the soul from the body. That the angel and the fiend seem to strive about the glass means that either of them desires to have the king's soul, which shall be accorded to him to whose counsel he is most obedient. That the angel has a vessel and a lap means that just as a child rests in his mother's lap, so does the angel labor that the soul be presented to God as if it were in a vessel and rest in the lap of endless comfort. That the fiend has tongs and a hammer means that the fiend draws the soul to him with the tongs of wicked delight

book, including the Bible, and her own Book of Revelations, the *Revelations*.

[41]Jørgensen suggested that Bride here is remembering King Magnus' royal seal, 2:134.

and breaks it asunder with the hammer; that is, with the consent and commission of sin. That the vessel of glass is sometimes very hot and sometimes very cold and slippery means the inconstancy and instability of the king; for when he is tempted he thinks thus: 'Though I know well that I offend God, if I fulfill now the conceit of my heart, yet at this time I shall fulfill my conceit in deed.' And so knowingly he sins against his God, for as he sins so knowingly he comes into the hands of the fiend. Afterwards the king makes his confession contritely, and so he escapes the hands of the fiend and comes into the power of the good angel. And therefore, unless the king leave his inconstancy, he stands in great peril, for he has a feeble foundation.

"After this I saw on the left side of the pulpit the dead king who was damned to Hell clad in kingly array and sitting as if on a throne. But he was dead and pale and very fearful to look upon. Before his face was as if it were a wheel that had four lines to the outermost part; and this wheel turned about at the breathing and blowing of the king. And each of the four lines went upward and downward as the king would, for the moving of the wheel was in the king's power. The three lines had writing but in the fourth line was written nothing.[42] On the right side of this king I saw an angel as if like a most beautiful man, whose hands were empty; but he served the pulpit. On the left side of the king appeared a fiend whose head was like a dog's; his womb might not be filled, his navel was open and boiled out venom, colored with all manner of venomous colors. And on each foot he had three claws, great, strong and sharp.

"Then there was one who shone more brightly than the sun, that for brightness was marvelous to see. And he said to me: 'This king whom you see is full of wretchedness, whose conscience is now shown to you as he was in his kingdom, and what state he was in when he died. What his conscience was or how he came to his kingdom you do not need to know. Nevertheless, know that his soul is not before your eyes, but his conscience. And for the soul and the fiend are not physical but spiritual, therefore the fiend's temptations and torments are shown you through physical aspects.'

"Then soon that dead king began to speak, not of his mouth, but as if it had been from his brain, and said: 'O you, my counsellors, this is my will, that

---

[42]See Michael Camille, "Seeing and Reading: Some Visual Implications of Medieval Literacy and Illiteracy," *Art History* 8 (1985):26-49, concerning the medieval use of writings within illustrated material; also death dream sequence in Ingmar Bergman, *Wild Strawberries*.

whatever is subject to the crown of my realm, I will hold it and keep it. I will also labor that the things that I have be increased and not lessened. But in what wise those things were obtained, that I hold, what is it to me to inquire? It is enough to me if I may defend and increase the things that I have.'

"Then cried the fiend and said: 'See, it is throughout. What shall my hook do?'

"Justice answered out of the Book that was in the pulpit, saying to the fiend: 'Put your hook into the hole and draw it towards yourself.'

"And as soon as the Word of Justice was spoken, the hook was put in. But with it at the same moment a hammer of mercy came before the king with which the king could have smitten away the hook, if he would have inquired into the truth of all things and fruitfully have changed his will.

"Then spoke the same king again and said: 'O, my counselors and my men, you have me as your lord, and I have taken you as my counselors. Therefore I tell you that there is a man in my realm who is a traitor to my worship and of my life, who lies in wait to hinder my realm and to disturb the peace and the common people of the realm. In this,' said the king, 'there has been given proof from both learned and unlearned, both lords and common people, believing the words that I said to them, in so much that that man whom I defamed of treason took great harm and shame, and sentence of exile was passed against him. Nevertheless, my conscience knows well what the truth was in all this deed, and I know well that I said many things against that man out of ambitiousness for the kingdom and for dread of losing it, and that my fame should be spread abroad, and that the realm should cleave more surely to me and to my successors. I thought also myself that though I knew the truth as to how the kingdom was obtained, and what wrong was done to him, yet if I receive him again into favor and tell the truth, then all reproach and harm shall fall upon myself. And therefore I firmly set my heart that I would rather die than tell the truth or revoke my wrong words and deeds.'

"Then said the fiend: 'O Judge, see how the king gives me his tongue.'

"The Justice of God answered: 'Put down your snare.' And when the fiend had done so, soon there hung before the king's mouth a most sharp blade, with which he might if he would have cut away the snare and entirely broken it.

"Then spoke the same king and said: 'O my counselors, I have counseled with clerks and learned men of the state of the realm, and they say to me that if I should resign the realm into other men's hands I should do harm to many, and be a traitor to their lives and goods and a breaker of the law of justice; and therefore that I might keep the kingdom and defend it from enemies, we must think of and imagine some new things, for the old rents of the exchequer are not sufficient to govern and to defend this realm. And thus I thought of new impositions of taxes and of guileful exactions to be imposed upon the realm, both to the harm of them dwelling in it and of innocent people traveling through it and merchants.[43] And in these devices I planned to continue until my death, although my conscience told me that they were against God, against all justice, and against common honesty.'

"Then cried the fiend and said: 'O Judge, see how this king has bowed both his hands under my vessel of water. What shall I do?'

"Justice answered out of the Book: 'Put your venom on it.' And soon as the venom of the fiend was put on his hands, there came before the king a vessel of ointment with which the king might well have halted that venom.

"Then the fiend cried out loudly and said: 'I see a marvelous thing that passes my ability to understand. For my hook is put to the heart of the king, and then there is given a hammer to his bosom. My snare is put into his mouth, and there is offered to him a most sharp blade. My venom is poured on his hands, and there is given to him a vessel of ointment.'

"Justice answered out of the Book of the pulpit and said: 'All things have their time; and Mercy and Justice shall meet together.'[44]

"After this the Mother of God spoke to me and said: 'Come, daughter, and hear and see what the good Spirit does, and what the evil; for every man has infusions and visitations some time of the good Spirit and sometimes of the evil. For there is not one but that he is visited by God as long as he lives.'

"And soon there appeared again the same dead king, whose soul the holy Spirit inspired while he lived, in this wise: 'O friend, you ought to serve God with all your strength, for he gave life, conscience and understanding, health and power; and yet he suffers you in your sins.'

"The king's conscience answered, speaking by a resemblance: 'It is

[43]See John Gower against Richard II's tax-farming, *The Major Latin Works of John Gower: The Voice of One Crying and The Tripartite Chronicle*, trans. Eric W. Stockton (Seattle: University of Washington Press, 1962).

[44]Again, reminiscent of the Four Daughters of God in *Piers Ploughman*, which is based upon Psalm 85.10. This concept was to be echoed by Shakespeare in the *Merchant of Venice* with Shylock and Portia as Justice and Mercy.

true,' he said, 'that I am required to serve God, by whose power I am made and bought, and through whose mercy I live and have my being.'

"But here the wicked spirit stirred against the king and said: 'Brother, I give you good counsel. Do as he does who pares an apple, for the parings and the core he throws away, and the inside and the best he keeps to himself. So do you. God is meek and merciful and patient and needs nothing. Therefore give him of your goods such as you may easily part with, and other goods that are more profitable and desirable keep to yourself. Do also what you desire according to your flesh, for that may lightly be amended. And what you do not desire to do, though you are bound to do it, leave it; and instead with it give alms. For by this many may be helped.'

"The king's conscience answered: 'This,' he said, 'is a profitable counsel. For I may give some things that I have without any great harm to me, and yet God sets much store with that. And other things I shall keep to my own use and to obtain friendship with many others.'

"After this the good angel who was given to guard the king spoke to him through inspiration, saying: 'O friend, think that you, a mortal, shall die. Think also that this life is short and that God is a rightful and patient Judge who examines all your thoughts, words and deeds from the beginning of your age of understanding unto the end, who also judges all your desires and intentions and leaves none undiscussed. Therefore, use your time and your strength reasonably and govern your members to the profit of your soul. Live soberly, not fulfilling the lust of your flesh in desires, for those who live according to the flesh and after their own will shall not come to the kingdom of God.'

"But here again the fiend with his suggestions stirred the king and said: 'O brother, if you will give a reckoning to God of all your times and moments, when shall you then have pleasure? But hear my counsel. God is merciful and may easily be pleased, for he would not have redeemed you if he would have lost you. Therefore the Scripture of God says that all sins are forgiven by contrition. Do you therefore as did he who owed another twenty pounds of gold. And when he lacked the amount of the payment, he went to his friend and asked his counsel. And he advised him to take twenty pounds of copper and gild it with one pound of gold, and with that false money pay his creditor. And he did after the counsel given him and paid his creditor twenty pounds of copper gilded over; and nineteen pounds of pure gold he kept to himself. Do so likewise. Spend nineteen hours to your delight, lust and joy; and one hour is sufficient for you to be sorry and repent of your sins. Therefore do what delights you both before and after confession; for as copper that is gilded seems gold, so the works of sins that are meant by the copper, when they are gilded over with contrition, shall be removed, and all your works shall shine like gold.'

"Then the king's conscience answered: 'This counsel seems to me delightful and reasonable. For if I do this I shall have more time for my own delight.'

"The good angel spoke again to the king through his inspiration, saying: 'O friend, think first with what skill God brought you out of the narrow womb of your mother. Second, think with what great patience God suffered you to live. Third, think with what great bitterness God has redeemed you from endless death.'

"But again the fiend stirred the king, saying: 'O brother, if God has brought you out of the narrow womb of your mother into the breadth of the world, think also how he shall lead you again out of the world through bitter death. And if God lets you live long, think also that you have had in your life many diseases and sorrows against your will. If God has bought you with his harsh death, who compelled him? Did you pray to him?'

"Then the king answered as if through speaking within his conscience: 'It is true,' he said, 'what you say. For I grieve more that I shall die than that I was born from my mother's womb. It is also more grievous to me to bear the adversities of the world and the things that are contary to my will than any other thing. For I would, if I could choose, rather live in the world without tribulation and to stay in comfort there, than to depart from the world. And I would rather desire to have endless life in the world with wordly happiness than that Christ had bought me with his blood. And I care not if I never get to Heaven, if I might have the world at my will on earth.'[45]

"Then I heard a Word from the pulpit, saying this: 'Now take away from the king the vessel of ointment, because he has sinned against God the Father. For God the Father who is endless in the Son and in the holy Spirit gave a true and right law by Moses. But this king has made an evil and a contrary law. Nevertheless, because this king has done some good deeds, although he did not do them with good intent, therefore he shall be allowed to have possession of the kingdom while he lives, and so be rewarded in this

---

[45]Chaucer's Wife of Bath: "That I have had my world as in my tyme," *Canterbury Tales* 3:473.

world.' A second time the Word spoke out of the pulpit and said this: 'Take away the most sharp blade from this king's eyes. For he has sinned against the Son. For he said in his new law that judgement shall be done without mercy to them who do no mercy. But this king would not do mercy to him who was unrighteously vexed nor amend his error nor change his evil will. Nevertheless, for some good deeds that he has done, be it given to him as a reward that he have words of wisdom in his mouth and that he be held to be wise by many people.' The third time the Word of Justice spoke from the pulpit and said: 'Let the hammer be taken away from the king, because he has sinned against the holy Spirit. For the holy Spirit forgives sins to all those who repent, but this king intends to persevere in his sin to the end. Nevertheless, because he has done some good deeds, therefore let that thing be given to him that he desires most to the delight of his body, that is, that woman whom he desires to be his wife, the delight of his eye, and that he have a fair and desirable end after that world.'

"After this, when the end of his life drew near, the fiend cried and said: 'See, the vessel of ointment is borne away. Therefore shall I now make his hands heave, that he shall do no fruitful goods.' And as soon as the word of the fiend was said, the king was deprived of his strength and health. And then soon the fiend cried and said: 'See, the sharp blade is taken away; therefore I shall increase my snare upon him.'

"And then the king was deprived of his speech. And in the moment of his privation, Justice spoke to the good angel who was given to the king to be his keeper, and said: 'Seek in the wheel and see what line of it goes up, and read the writing on it.'

"The angel looked and the fourth line went up, in which that nothing was written, for all of it had been erased. Then said Justice: 'Because this soul has loved what is void, therefore he now goes to the delight of his reward.' And soon the soul of the king was separated from the body.

"And as soon as the soul was gone out, the fiend cried and said: 'Now I shall break and tear apart the heart of this king, because I possess his soul.'

"And then I see how the king was all changed from the top of his head to the soul of the foot, and he seemed as horrible as a flayed beast. His eyes were removed and his flesh all clumped together. Then his voice was heard, saying: 'Woe to me, for I am made as blind as a whelp that is born blind, seeking the hind parts of the mother. For, through my unkindness, I cannot see the mother's teats. Woe to me, for I see in my blindness that I shall never see God, for my conscience understands now from where I fell, and what I ought to have done and did not do. Woe to me, for by the providence of God I was born into the world and born again by baptism. And yet I was negligent and forgot God. And because I would not drink the milk of the sweetness of God, therefore am I now more like a blind dog than to a living and a seeing child. But now against my will, though I were a king, I am compelled to say the truth. For I was bound as if it had been with three ropes to serve God: that is to say, through baptism; through wedlock; and through the crown of the kingdom. But the first I despised when I turned my affection and will to the vanity of the world. Of the second I took no heed when I desired another man's wife. The third I despised when I was proud of earthly power and thought not of the power of heaven. Therefore, though I am now blind, I see in my conscience that for the contempt of my baptism I ought to be bound to the hatefulness of the fiend. And for the inordinate stirring of the flesh I ought to suffer the fiend's lust. And for my pride I ought to be bound to the fiend's feet.'

"Then the fiend answered: 'O brother, now it is time that I speak and with my speaking I shall work. Therefore come to me, not with charity but with hate; for I was the fairest of the angels, and you were a mortal man. And God most mighty gave me free choice of will. But because I used it inordinately and would rather hate God and surpass him in praise than love him, therefore I fell as he who has his head downward and his feet upward. But you, as each other man, were made after my fall and given a special privilege above me, in as much as you were bought with the blood of the Son of God. Therefore, because you have despised the charity of God, turn your head to my feet and I shall take your feet into my mouth; and so we can be joined together as they are where the one has a sword in the other's heart, and the other has a knife in his innards. And because I had a head, that is to say, understanding, to worship God if I would, and you had feet, that is to say, strength to go to God and would not, therefore my fiery head shall consume your cold feet, and you shall be devoured without ceasing, but not consumed, for you shall be revived again to the same punishment. We shall also be joined together with three ropes, of which the first shall be in the middle, with which your navel and mine shall be bound together; so that when I breathe, you shall draw my venom into yourself, and when you breathe, I shall draw your entrails into myself. And worthily, for you love yourself more than your redeemer, as I loved myself more than my maker. Your head shall be bound to my feet with the second rope, and with the third rope my head shall be bound to your feet.'

"After this, I see the same fiend having three sharp claws in each foot, saying to the king: 'Because you, brother, had eyes to see the way of life and conscience to discern between good and evil, therefore my two claws shall enter and claw your eyes; and the third claw shall enter your brain, with which you shall be so strangled that you shall be all under my feet. For you were made to have been my lord, and I the sole of your foot. You also had ears to hear the way of life, and a mouth to speak to the profit of your soul. But because you despised to hear and speak to the health of your soul, therefore two claws of my other foot shall enter into your ears, and the third into your mouth, where you shall be so tormented that all things shall be to you the most bitter that seemed to you before most sweet, when you offend God.'

"When these things were said, soon the head and the feet and the navel of the king were joined in this manner with the head and feet and navel of the fiend, and so both bound together fell down into Hell.

"And then I heard a voice crying, saying: 'O, O what has the king got now of all his wealth? Certainly nothing but harm. And what has he now of all his power? Certainly, nothing but shame. And what has he now of his avarice, through which he desired so much from his kingdom? Truly, nothing but pain. Because he was anointed with holy and sacred oil and consecrated with holy words and crowned with a king's crown, that he should worship the words and deeds of God, and defend and govern the people of God, knowing himself under the feet of God, and God his rewarder. But he despised being under the feet of God; therefore he is now under the feet of the fiend. And because he would not redeem his time with fruitful works when he could, therefore from henceforth he shall have no fruitful time.'

"After this spoke Justice out of the Book that was in the pulpit, saying to me: 'All the things that are thus seriously shown are done against God in a moment. But because you are bodily, therefore it is necessary that spiritual things be shown to you through a bodily likeness. Because the king and the angel and the fiend seemed to speak together is nothing else but the inspirations of the good and evil spirits made by them to the soul of the king, or by his counselors or friends. That the fiend cried and said: "It is truth," it is to mean that when the king said that he would hold and keep all that belonged to the crown, however it was obtained, and not to heed justice, then the king's conscience was bored through with the iron of the fiend, that is to say, with the hardness of sin, when he would not speak and discuss which were the things that belonged rightfully to the realm, and which not, and when he cared not to examine what right he had to the crown.

"'And then was the hook put to the king's soul, when the fiend's temptation prevailed so much in his soul that he would abide in his injustice until death. But because there came a hammer to the king's bosom after the hook, means the time of contrition given to the king; because if the king had had such a thought, saying, "I have sinned; I will no longer knowingly own ill-gotten goods, but I will amend me from henceforth," then the hook of righteousness would be broken with the hammer of contrition, and the king would have come to the good life and the good way. That the fiend cried, "See, the king gives me his tongue," and then the snare was put on it, which was when the king would not do grace to the man whom he had defrauded. This is to understand, that who ever wittingly blames and defames his neighbor to increase his own fame, is governed with the spirit of the fiend, and snared with the snare of a thief.

"'But because there came a sharp iron before the king after the snare means the time of changing and of correction of his will and work. Because when a man corrects his trespass with amendment and with good will, such a will is a most sharp blade, with which the snare of the fiend is cut asunder and remission of sins is obtained. Therefore if this king had changed his will and done grace to the man who had been wronged and slandered, then the snare of the fiend would have been cut away. But because he formed his will for an evil purpose, therefore the justice of God was that he should be more hardened in sin. And that when the king thought to put new exactions of taxes upon his realm, you saw the venom poured upon his hands, meaning that his works were governed by the spirit of the fiend and by evil suggestions. For as venom makes the body cold and sick, so was the king troubled and restless with wicked suggestions and thoughts, seeking means how he might obtain goods and possession of other men and gold from them who went by the way. For then wayfaring men slept and trusted that their gold would be in their purse, but when they awoke, they found that it was in the king's power.

"'But because the vessel of ointment came after the venom means the blood of Jesus Christ, by which the sick soul is raised to life. For if the king had weighed his works in consideration of the blood of Christ and prayed God to be his help and said: "O Lord God, who has made and bought me; I know that by your permission I can come to the kingdom and crown, therefore beware the enemies who war against me, and pay you my debts; for the goods of the realm are not sufficient." I truly should have made his works and his burden easier to bear. But because he desired other men's goods and would be seen as just when he knew very well that he was wrong, therefore the fiend governed his heart and stirred him against the ordinance of the Church, and to wage war and defraud innocents, until Justice out of the pulpit of God's majesty cried for judgement and justice.

"'The wheel which was moved at the king's breathing means his conscience, which was stirred in the manner of a wheel, now to mirth, now to sadness. The four lines that were in the wheel mean the fourfold will that each man ought to have; that is to say, a perfect will, a strong will, a right will and a reasonable will. The perfect will is to love God and have him above all things; and this will ought to be in the first line above. The second line is to desire and to do good to his neighbor and to himself for God. This will must be so strong that it be neither broken with hate nor with greed. The third will is to abstain from fleshly desires and to desire eternal things. And this will must be right that it not be done to the pleasure of man, but of God. The fourth will is not to will to have the world, but reasonably and only to your need.

"'Therefore when the wheel was turned, there appeared in the last line going upward that the king loved the delights of the world, and set at nought the love of God. In the second line was written that he loved the men of the world. In the third line was written the love that he had inordinately for worldly riches and possessions. In the fourth line was written nothing, but all was void in which ought to have been written the love of God. Above all things, therefore, the blankness of the fourth line means the absence of love and fear of God; for by fear God is drawn into the soul, and by love God is fastened in a good soul. Because if a man had never loved God in all his lifetime, and at his last end might say or think in his heart, "O God, I think with all my heart that I have sinned against you; give me your love and I shall repent me from this time," a man of such love may not nor shall go to Hell. But because the king loved him not whom he ought to have loved, therefore he has now the reward of his love.'

"After this, I see the other king on the right side of Justice, who was in Purgatory, who was like a newborn child that might not move himself about, but only open his eyes. And I see that the fiend stood on the king's left side, whose head was like a pair of bellows with a long pipe, his arms were like two serpents, and his knees like a press, and his feet like a long hook. On the right side of the king stood a most fair angel, ready to help him.

"And then I heard a voice saying: 'This king appears now such as his soul was disposed when it departed from the body.'

"And then the fiend cried to the Book in the pulpit, saying: 'Here is seen a marvelous thing. This angel and I have waited for the birth of this child, he with his cleanliness, and I with my filth. But now the child is born, not in the body, but from the body, uncleanness in him appears which the angel, loathing, might not touch the child. But I torment him, for he is fallen into my hands. But I do not know where to lead him; for my dark eyes do not see him, for the light of a clearness that comes out of his breast. The angel sees him and knows where to lead him, but he may not touch him. Therefore you, who are the rightful Judge, separate us from our strife.'

"The Word answered out of the Book which was in the pulpit and said: 'Tell, you who speak, from what cause this soul comes into your hands.'

"The fiend answered: 'You are righteous, and you said that no one shall enter Heaven who does not first make restitution of things which are unrightfully obtained. But this soul is all befouled with ill-gotten goods. Second, you said that treasures should not be hoarded which rust and moths destroy, but those which last without end.[46] But in this soul that place was empty where heavenly treasure should have been gathered and that place was full where worms and frogs were nourished. Third, you say that a man's neighbor should be loved like God. But this soul loved his body more than God, and of the love of his neighbor he cared not at all; for he, while in the body, rejoiced when his neighbor's goods were taken away. He wounded the hearts of his subjects, not taking heed of the harm to others, as long as he himself had plenty, and he did whatever he desired, and commanded whatever he would, and took little heed of justice. These are the principal causes, after which follow others without number.'

"Then answered the Word out of the Book of Justice, saying to the angel: 'O you angel, keeper of the soul, who are in light and see light, what right or power have you to help this soul?'

"The angel answered: 'This soul,' he said, 'had holy faith, and believed and hoped that all of which he had sinned should be done away by contrition and confession. And he feared you, his God, though less than he ought to have.'

"Then Justice spoke again and said: 'O you, my angel, now it is granted to you to touch the soul and to you, you fiend, to see the light of the soul.

[46]See Chaucer's Wife of Bath, *Canterbury Tales* 3:555-562, "Thise wormes, ne thise motthes, ne thise mytes, Upon my peril, frete hem never a deel; And wostow why? for they were used weel," who quotes, as does Birgitta, from Matthew 6. 19-2l, "Lay not up for yourselves treasures upon earth, where moth and rust doth corrupt, and where thieves break through and steal: But lay up for yourselves treasures in heaven, where neither moth and rust doth corrupt, and where thieves do not break through nor steal."

Inquire therefore both what this soul loved when it lived in the body and had all his members intact.' The angel and the fiend both answered: 'He loved men and wealth.'

"Then said Justice again out of the Book: 'What did he love when he was in agony with the pain of death?'

"Then both answered: 'He loved himself, for he was more agonized with the sickness of his body and of the tribulation of his heart, than he was of the Passion of his Redeemer.'

"Then spoke Justice again and said: 'Still seek and look for what he loved and thought in the last moment of his life, while he still had a whole consience and understanding.'

"Only the good angel answered: 'The soul thought thus. "Woe," he said, "to me, for I have been overbold against my Redeemer. Would God I now had time in which I might thank God for his benefits. Because it grieves me more that I have sinned against God than the pain of my body; and though I should never attain heaven, yet would I serve my God."'

"Justice answered out of the Book: 'For as much as you, fiend, may not see the soul for the brightness of his light, and you, my angel, may not touch the soul for his uncleanness, therefore this is the judgement; that you, fiend, purge it; and you, angel, comfort it until it be brought into the brightness of bliss. And to you, you soul, it is granted to look to the good angel and to have comfort from him; and you shall obtain the blood of Christ and the prayers of his Mother and of his Church.'

"Then said the fiend to the soul: 'Because you have come to my hands filled with food and ill-gotten goods, I shall now therefore empty you with my press.'

"And then the fiend put the brains of the king between his knees, like a press, and strained it strongly in length and breadth, till all the marrow was as thin as the leaf of a tree.

"Second, the fiend said to the soul: 'Because the place is empty where virtues should be, I shall therefore fill it.'

"And then he put the pipe of his bellows in the king's mouth, and blew strongly, and filled him very full of horrible wind; so much so that all the king's being and sinews were wretchedly broken and burst asunder.

"The third time, the fiend said again to the king's soul: 'Because you were cruel and without mercy towards your subjects, who ought to have been to you as if your sons, my arms therefore shall bitingly grip you together; that as much as you grieved your subjects, so shall my arms, as if serpents, rend you with the most grievous horror and sorrow.'

"After these three pains, that is to say, of the press, of the bellows, and of the serpents, when the fiend would have accumulated these same pains again, beginning at the first, then I saw the angel of God put out his hands upon the fiend's hands, that he should not make the pains so great as they were the first time. And so each time, the angel of God eased the pains; and after each pain, the soul lifted up his eyes to the angel, saying nothing but showing in his bearing that he was comforted by him; and that he should quickly be saved.

"Then said the Word out of the pulpit to me: 'All these things which are thus seriously shown to you are done with God in a moment; but because you are bodily, they are shown to you in bodily likeness. But this king, though he were greedy to have the world's praise and to obtain goods that were not his, yet, because he fears God and left for that dread some things that were pleasurable to him, therefore that dread drew him to the love and charity of God. For you know well that many who are involved with many heavy sins become very contrite before their death, whose contrition may be so perfect that not only their sin is forgiven them, but also the pain of Purgatory, if they die in the same contrition. But the king obtained no charity until the last moment of his life; for then his strength and his conscience were failing, yet he obtained of my grace godly inspiration, by which he sorrowed more of not worshipping God than of his own sorrow and harm. And this sorrow means that light by which the fiend was blinded and knew not where to lead the soul. Yet he said not that he was so blinded for lack of spiritual understanding, but because he marveled how that in that soul should be such clearness of light and so much uncleanness. The angel knew well enough whether to lead the soul, but he could not touch it until it was purged. As it is written, "No man shall see the face of God but he be first made clean."'

"Then the Word out of the pulpit spoke again to me and said: 'That you see the angel put out his hands upon the soul and of the fiend that he should not increase the pains means the power of the angel above the power of the fiend by which he restrains the fiend's malice. For the fiend should have no measure nor order in punishing unless he were restrained by the virtue of God. And therefore God does mercy in Hell; for though there be no redemption, remission nor comfort to them who are damned, yet in as much as they are not punished but after their deserts and after justice, therefore in that is shown God's great mercy. Otherwise the fiend should have no temperance nor measure in his malice. That the king was seen as a child just born means that those who will be born out of the vanity of the world to the life of heaven, must be innocent and by the grace of God grow in virtues to perfection. That the king lifted up his eyes to the angel means that by the angel, his guardian, he had his comfort; and of hope he had joy, in as much as he hoped to come to endless life. And these are spiritual things understood by bodily likeness; for neither fiends nor angels have such members nor such speaking together, for they are spirits. But by such likeness their goodness or wickedness are shown to bodily eyes.'

"Also the Word spoke out of the pulpit, saying to me: 'The pulpit which you see means the Godhead's self; that is to say, Father and Son and holy Spirit. That you might not understand the length, breadth, depth, and height of the pulpit means that in God is not found either beginning or end. For God is and was without beginning, and shall be without end. And that each color of the three said colors was seen in the others, and yet each color was discerned from the others, means that God the Father is endless in the Son and in the holy Spirit, and the Son in the Father and in the holy Spirit, and the holy Spirit in them both, which are truly one in nature and distinct in property of persons.

"'That one of the colors seemed to be sanguine and red means the Son, who without hurt of his Godhead took man's nature into her person. The white color means the holy Spirit, by whom is washing away of sins. The golden color means the Father, who is the beginning and the perfection of all things. Not that any perfection is more in the Father than in the Son, nor that the Father is before the Son; but that you understand that the Father is not the same in person, that is the Son. For the Father is other in person, and other is the Son in person, and other is the holy Spirit in person; but one in nature. Therefore three colors are shown to you both separated and joined together; separated for distinction of persons, and joined together for union of nature.

"'And as in each color you see the other colors, and you might not see one without another, and there was nothing in the colors before nor after, more nor less, right so in the Trinity is nothing before nor after, more nor less, separated nor joined; but one will, one eternity, one power and one glory. And though the Son is of the Father, and the holy Spirit of both, yet the Father was never without the Son and the holy Spirit, nor the Son and the holy Spirit without the Father.'

"Also the Word spoke to me and said: 'The Book that you see in the pulpit means that in the Godhead is endless justice and wisdom, to which nothing may be added or lessened. And this is the Book of Life, that is not written as the scripture, that is and was not; but the scripture of this Book is forever. For in the Godhead is endless being and understanding of all things present, past and to come, without any variation or changing. And nothing is invisible to it, for it sees all things.' That the Word spoke itself means that God is the endless Word, from whom are all words, and in whom things have life and being. And this same Word spoke then visibly when the Word was made man and was conversant among men. So, this goodly vision has the Mother of God made to be shown to you; and this is the mercy called to the kingdom of Sweden, that men dwelling there should hear the words that proceed out of the mouth of God. But because few receive and believe these heavenly words given you from God, that is not God's fault, but men's. For they will not leave the cold of their own souls. Nevertheless, the words of the Gospel were not fulfilled with the first kings of our time; but the times shall yet come when they shall be fulfilled."

How the Father of Heaven showed to Saint Birgitta a severe judgement upon a king who was unkind and disobedient to the counsels of God. And how they who are in Heaven, on earth, in Purgatory, and in Hell ask wrath upon kings and princes and how our Lady prayed for them. Chapter 23.

God the Father spoke to the spouse, Saint Birgitta, and said: "Listen to the things that I say, and speak of the things that I order you; not for your power, nor for your reproach. But singly and evenly hold in your heart the praiser and the reprover, so that you may never be moved to ire for reproof, nor raised to pride for praising. For he is worthy of praise who is and was endless in himself, who has made angels and men only to that end, that many should be partners in his glory. I am now he, and the same in power and in will that I was when the Son took man's nature; in which Son I am and was, and he in me, and the holy Spirit in both. And though it were secret to the world that he was the Son of God, yet it was known to some, though it were few. And know that the Justice of God which had no beginning nor end, no more than God himself, was first shown to angels as light before they see God; for they fell not from ignorance of the law of the Justice of God, but because they would not hold it or keep it. For they understand that all who love God should see him and abide with him for ever, and they who hated God should be punished endlessly and never see him in his glory. And yet in their ambition and desire for praise they chose rather to hate God and to have the place where they shall be punished, than to love him that they might rejoice endlessly. And of like justice is that of a man as of angels. For man ought first to love God and afterward see him, that he should more be seen in manhood; for he might not be seen in his Godhead. And free choice is given also to man as to angels, that they should desire heavenly things and despise earthly. Therefore I, God, visit many in many ways, although my Godhead is not seen. And in many parts of the world I have shown to many persons how the sin of each land might have been amended, and how mercy might have been obtained, before ever I did justice and my righteousness in those places. But men take no heed of these things, nor consider them. This justice is also in God, that all who are upon earth first hope surely for those things that they do not see, and which they believe in relation to the Church of God and to the holy Gospel. And furthermore that they love God above all things, who has given them all things; and he has given himself to death for them, that all should endlessly rejoice with him. Therefore I, myself, God, speak to such as desire me, that it be known how sin ought to be amended, and how pain may be lessened and bliss increased."

"After this I see," said Saint Birgitta, "as if all the heavens had been one house, in which sat a Judge on a throne. And the house was full of servants and praisers of the Judge, each of them in his voice. And under this Heaven was seen a kingdom. And soon there was heard a voice that all might hear it, which said: 'Come, both angels and fiends, to the Judgement; that is to say, you angel who are guardian of the king, and you fiend who are governor of the king.'

"And as soon as the word was spoken, an angel and a fiend stood before the Judge. The angel seemed like a man troubled, and the fiend like a joyous man. Then said the Judge: 'O you angel, I put you as the king's guardian, when he made the covenant of peace with me and made confession of all his sins that he had done from his childhood, that you should be nearer to him than the fiend. How is he now therefore so far from you?'

"The angel answered, 'O Judge, I am burning in the fire of your charity, with which the king was warmed for a time. But when the king loathed and despised those things that your friends said to him, and it was tedious to him to do the things that you counseled to him, then the king went according as his own lust drew him, away from me, and nearer each hour to the enemy.'

"The fiend answered, 'I am the self which is cold, and you are the self which is hot with godly fire. Therefore such as who comes closer to you is more fervent to good works, so likewise the king, drawing near to me, is made more cold towards your charity and hot towards my works.'

"Then answered the Judge: 'The king was stirred to love God above all things, and his neighbor as himself. Why, therefore, have you taken from me the man whom I bought with my own blood, and made him to deny to his neighbor, not only his temporal goods but even his life?'

"The fiend answered: 'O Judge, now it is for me to speak and the angel to keep silence. For when the king went from you and from your counsels and came to me, then I counseled him to love himself more than his neighbor; and that he should not care for the health of souls, if he had the power of the world; and that he should not take heed of those who were needy or defrauded, if his friends had plenty.'

"Then said the Judge to the fiend: 'Who so will go from you, they may; for you may hold none with violence. Therefore I shall yet send some of my friends to the king, who will warn him of his peril.'

"The fiend answered: 'Justice is that who ever will obey me, he ought to be governed by me; and therefore I shall send my counselors also to the king, and it shall be seen to whose counsel he would rather give audience.'

"Then said the Judge: 'Go, for my justice is to judge to the tormenter what is his, as well as to him who has action of what is due to him in his cause.'

"After this," said Saint Birgitta, "when certain years were past, I see again the same Judge with his heavenly host, more moved than he was wont to be, and as though he were angry. And then he said to the angel and to the fiend: 'Tell,' he said, 'which of you has overcome.'

"The angel answered: 'When I came to the king with godly inspiration, and your friends with spiritual words, soon the messengers of the fiend whispered in his ears and said: "Will you spare temporal goods or your praise or souls or bodies, that your friends whom you love more than yourself may have praise and prosperity?" To this stirring the king assented and to the stirring of the friends he, saying, answered: "I am sufficient enough and wise enough from counsel without you. Go your way from me with shame." And so the king turned his back to them, and his face to the enemy, and put from him friends with dishonest reproof and the scorn of the friends of the world.'

"Then cried the fiend and said: 'Judge, see, now it is for me to govern the king and to give him counsel by my friends.'

"The Judge answered: 'Go, and as much as you are allowed, punish the king. Because he has provoked me to indignation against him.'

"Two years after this, the Judge appeared again, and the angel and the fiend before him. Then said the fiend: 'O Judge, decide now whether I shall pronounce judgement. You are truly the essence of charity, and therefore it is not fitting to you to be in the heart of him where envy and anger are rooted. You are also true wisdom and therefore you ought not to be in the heart of him who desires to deny the life of his neighbors, their goods, and their praise. You are also the true truth, and therefore it is not proper to dwell with that man who has bound himself with oaths to do treason and deceit. Therefore because this king has spit you out from him as that thing is spit out that is abominable, therefore allow me to stir him and oppress him, that he be all out of his mind and actions. For my counsels he holds as wisdom, and your counsel he takes for scorn. And with such reward I desire to reward him, for he has done my will. Nevertheless I may not harm him without your permission.'

"And when this was heard, the Judge seemed to have a marvelous changing; for then he appeared as bright as the sun, and in the sun were seen three words: that is, Virtue, Truth and Justice. Virtue spoke and said: 'I have made all things without merit beforehand. And therefore I am worthy to be praised by my creature and not to be despised. I am also worthy of being praised by my friends for my charity. I ought also to be praised and feared by my enemies, for I support them patiently without their merits, where they have worthily deserved damnation. And therefore, you fiend, it is fitting to me to decide all after my justice and not after your malice.'

"Then soon Truth spoke also and said: 'I in my Godhead took manhood of a Virgin, in which manhood I spoke and preached to people. I sent also the holy Spirit to the Apostles, and I spoke by their tongues. As I spoke each day by spiritual infusion to such as I chose, therefore my friends must know that I myself who am Truth have sent my words to a king, which he has despised.[47] Therefore, you fiend, hear now; for I will speak that it be known whether the king has obeyed my counsel or my stirrings. For I will tell all the counsel I gave to the king, rehearsing now in a few words what I expressed earlier at greater length. For the king was stirred and counseled to

[47]See *Piers Ploughman*, B. Passus 7.

beware of all sins forbidden by holy Church and to have moderate fastings, so that he might hear and answer his subjects' complaints, and be ready to do right to rich and poor who asked it; so that for much abstinence the good of the community of the people of the realm and the governance of the common profit not be lessened, nor that he should not be the more slothful from overmuch excess to give audience to all. Also the king was counseled and stirred how he should serve God and pray, and which days and times he should leave other occupations and purposes for the common profit of his realm. Also the king was counseled which days he should treat all his counsels with men who loved Truth and with the friends of God; and that he should never knowingly pass over truth nor law; and that he should not put any unwanted grievance to the common people of his realm but for the defence of the same, and for war against the pagans. Also the king was counseled to have a number of servants in his household, according to the faculty of livelihood and rents of the exchequer of his realm. And all that was left over, he should share with his knights and friends. Also the king was counseled wisely to admonish them who were insolent and lewd with charitable words, and manfully to correct them; and that he love in goodly charity those who were prudent and sober; and that he should defend the people dwelling in his realm and give his gifts with discretion; and all those things that belong to the crown he should not diminish nor alienate; and he should judge rightfully both men of the land and strangers; that he should love the clergy, and charitably gather to him his chivalry, and nourish in peace the common people of his realm.'

"When these things were heard, the fiend answered to the Judge and said: 'And I counseled the king to do some sins privately which he dared not do in the open. I counseled him also to say long and many prayers and psalms without attention and devotion of heart, so that he should prolong and occupy the time in vain, and not hear any who would complain, nor do any right to such as had suffered wrong. Also I stirred the king to leave and despise other good men of the realm; and to lift up and prefer one man above all others; and to love him with all his heart, more than himself; and to hate his own son; and to grieve the common people of the realm with his exactions; and to slay men and spoil churches. I stirred the king also to simulate justice; and to permit each man to deny others, that he should alienate and give lands belonging to his crown to a great prince of another realm, my sworn brother; and this I counseled to that end that treason and war should come about; that good men and rightful should be cast down; wicked people should be drowned the deeper in Hell; and they who shall be purged in Purgatory should be the more grievously tormented; women should be defiled; ships in the sea should be robbed; sacraments of the Church should be despised; lecherous lives should the more boldly be continued; and all my will more freely fulfilled. And thus, Judge, by these sins, and many others, which I do and and which are fulfilled by the king, it may be proved and known whether the king has obeyed your counsel or mine.'

"At this spoke Justice, answering, and said: 'Because the king has hated Virtue and despised Truth, therefore it is now proper for you to increase some of your counsel given to the king. And I ought according to justice to lessen and withdraw from him some of my graces I gave to him.'

"The fiend answered: 'O Judge, I shall multiply and increase my gifts to the king. And first, I shall send him negligence, that he take no heed of the works of God in his heart, and that he think not on the works and examples of your friends.'

"Justice answered: 'And I shall diminish for him the inspirations of the holy Spirit, and I shall withdraw from him the good thoughts and comfort that he had before.'

"Then said the fiend: 'I shall send him boldness to think and to do deadly sins and venial without embarrassment or shame.'

"Justice answered: 'I shall lessen his reason and discretion that he discern not nor discuss the rewards and judgements of deadly and venial sins.'

"The fiend said: 'I shall given him dread that he dare not speak nor do right against the enemies of God.'

"Justice answered: 'I shall lessen his prudence and knowledge of things to be done so lewdly, that he shall seem more like a fool and clown in words and deeds than a wise man.'

"Then said the fiend: 'I shall bring him anguish and tribulations of heart, because he has not prosperity after his will.'

"Justice answered: 'I shall lessen for him ghostly comforts, which he had sometimes in prayers and in his actions.'

"The fiend said: 'I shall put to him evil to think subtle inventions, by which he may beguile and deceive those whom he wishes to destroy.'

"Justice answered: 'I shall lessen his understanding so much that he shall take no heed of his own praise nor of his own profit.'

"The fiend said: 'I shall put to him such joy of heart that he shall not heed his own shame, nor of the harm and peril of his soul, while he may have temporal prosperity after his will.'

"Justice answered: 'I shall lessen his thinking beforehand and that consideration that wise men have in their words and deeds.'

"Then said the fiend: 'I shall give him a woman's boldness, and an unseemly fear, and such a bearing that he shall seem more like a ribald or a harlot than a crowned king.'

"Justice answered: 'Of such a judgement is he worthy, that separates him from God. For he ought to be despised by his friends, and to be hated by the community of his people, and to be cast down of God's enemies; for he has misused the gifts of God's charity, both spiritual and physical.'

"Then spoke Truth again and said: 'These things that are shown to you are not for the merits of the king, whose soul is not yet judged; but it shall be judged in the last moment of his life.'

"After these things were said, I saw that the three, that is to say, Virtue, Truth and Justice, were like the Judge who spoke before.

"And then I heard the voice, as if of a beadle saying, 'O you, all heavens with all planets, be silent; and all you fiends who are in darkness, listen; and all you others that are in darkness, hear; for the sovereign emperor proposes to hear judgement upon the princes of the earth.'

"And then the kings whom I saw were not bodily but spiritual. And my ghostly ears and eyes were opened to hear and to see. And then I saw Abraham come with all the saints who were born of his generation. Then came all Patriarchs and Prophets. And afterwards I saw the four Evangelists, whose shape was like to four beasts, as they are painted upon walls in the world, except that they appeared to be living and not dead.[48] After this, I saw twelve seats, and in them the twelve Apostles, waiting for the coming of the power. Then came Adam and Eve with Martyrs and Confessors and all other saints that came from them. But the manhood of Christ was not yet seen, nor the body of his blessed Mother; but all waited for her arrival. The earth and the water seemed to be lifted up to Heaven, and all things that were in them humbled themselves, and with reverence bowed themselves to the power.

[48]See Dante's similar description of the sculpture in *Purgatorio* 10.94-96, which seems to move, to breathe, and to speak. Bride is probably recalling Swedish church painting. Ingmar Bergman's film, *Seventh Seal*, has a powerful, self-referential scene of a painter depicting Doomsday and speaking of the Black Death.

"Then after this, I saw an altar that was in the seat of the majesty, and a chalice with wine and water and bread in the likeness of a host offered up upon the altar; and then I saw how in a church of the world a priest began mass, arrayed in a priest's vestments.[49] And when he had done all that belonged to the Mass, and came to the words with which he should bless the host, I saw as if the sun and the moon and the stars with all the other planets, and all the heavens with their courses and moving spheres, sounded with the sweetest note and with sundry voices. And all the song and melody was heard, and seemed as if it had been innumerable manners of music, whose most sweet sound was impossible to comprehend by man's wit or to be spoken about. They who were in the light beheld the priest and bowed themselves to the power with reverence and worship, and they who were in darkness shuddered and were afraid.

"But when the words of God were said by the priest upon the host, it seemed to me that the same sacred host was in the seat of the majesty in three figures, staying nevertheless in the hand of the priest. And the same holy host was made a living Lamb, and in the Lamb appeared the face of a man. And a burning flame was seen within and without the Lamb and the face. And when I fastened my eyes intently to behold the face, I saw the same face in the Lamb. And the Virgin sat crowned by the Lamb, and all angels served them, who were of so great a multitude as the beams of the sun. And a marvelous shining proceeded from the Lamb. There was also so great a multitude of holy souls, that my sight could not behold them in length, breadth, height and deepness. I see also some places being empty, that are yet to be fulfilled to the worship of God.[50]

"Then I heard a voice out of the earth, of innumerable thousands, crying and saying: 'O Lord God, rightful Judge, give your judgement upon our kings and princes, and take heed to the shedding of our blood, and behold the sorrows and weeping of our wife and children. Behold our hunger and shame, our wounds and our imprisonments, the burning of our houses, and the violation of the chaste maidens and women. Behold the wrong done to churches and all the clergy. And see the false promises and deceits of kings

[49]Bynum, *Holy Feast and Holy Fast*, pp. 113-149, notes how often women had visions of the Eucharist, because they were being denied the elements of bread and wine.

[50]For similar iconography as in this scene see Jan and Hubert Van Eyck's Ghent Altarpiece.

and of princes, and the pillage that they wreak to them with violence and anger. For they heed not how many thousands die, so that they may spread abroad their pride.

"Then cried there out of Hell as it had been innumerable thousands, saying: 'O Judge, we know that you are maker of all things. Give judgement therefore upon the lords whom we served on earth. For they have drowned us in Hell deeper than we should have been, and though we will you harm, yet justice compels us to complain and say the truth. For our earthly lords loved us without charity; for they cared no more about our souls than about those of dogs. And it was alone to them whether we loved you, our Creator, or no, desiring ever to be beloved and served by us. Therefore they are unworthy of Heaven; for they care not for you. And they are worthy of Hell, unless your grace help them. For they have deserved us; and therefore we would suffer more grievous pains than suffer that their pain should never have end.

"Afterward, they who were in Purgatory, speaking by likenesses, cried and said: 'O Judge, we are condemned to Purgatory for contrition and good will that we had at the end of our life. And therefore we complain upon the lords who yet live on the earth. For they ought to have governed us, and to have warned us with words and criticism, and to have taught us with wholesome counsels and examples. But they comforted us rather, and provoked us rather to evil deeds and sins. And therefore our pain is now the more grievous for them; and the time of pain is the larger; and our shame and tribulation is greater.

"Then spoke Abraham with all the Patriarchs, and said: 'O Lord, among all things desirable, we desire that your Son should be born of our lineage, which is now despised by the princes of the earth. Therefore we ask judgement upon them, for they take no heed of your mercy, nor do they dread your judgement.

"Then spoke the Prophets and said: 'We prophesied the coming of the Son of God; and we said that for the deliverance of the people it was necessary that he should be born of a Virgin and endure treason and be taken and be scourged and be crowned with thorns and at last die on the cross, that Heaven should be opened and sin taken away. Wherefore those things are now fulfilled of which we said; therefore we ask judgement upon the princes of the earth who despise your Son who of your charity died for them.

"Then spoke the Evangelists and said: 'We are witnesses that your Son has fulfilled in himself all things which were prophesied of him.'

"Also the Apostles spoke and said: 'We are Judges, therefore it belongs to us to judge according to the truth. Wherefore he who despises the body of God and his precepts, we judge to perdition.'[51]

"After all this, the Virgin who sat by the Lamb said: 'O most sweet Lord, have mercy upon them.'

"To her the Judge answered: 'It is not right,' he said, 'to deny you any thing. Therefore they who cease from sin and do worthy penance shall find mercy; and judgement shall be turned away from them.'

"After this I saw that the face that was seen in the Lamb spoke to the king and said: 'I have done grace with you, for I have shown you my will: how you should bear and demean yourself in your governing, and how you should govern yourself honestly and worthily. I cherished you also with sweet words of charity like a mother, and I frightened you with warnings like a piteous father. But you, obeying the fiend, have cast me from yourself, as a mother casts away a stillborn child whom she does not touch nor put her teats to his mouth.[52] And therefore all the good that is promised you shall be taken from you and given to one who shall come after you.'

"After this the Virgin who sat with the Lamb spoke to me and said: 'I will tell you how understanding of spiritual visions is given to you; for the saints of God receive the holy Spirit in different ways. For some of them know before the time when those things should happen which were shown to them, such as holy Prophets. Others knew before what end any battle should have, before they who should fight entered battle. Others knew in spirit what they should answer to persons who came to them when any thing was asked of them. Others knew whether they were dead or alive who were far from them. But it is not lawful to you to know other things, but to hear and see ghostly things, and to write the things which you see, and to tell and say them to such people as you are ordered. And it is not lawful to you to know whether they be alive or dead, to whom you are asked to write; or whether they will obey or not the counsels of your writing given to you from God in

[51]*Perdition*, loss, the loss of salvation, damnation.

[52]Birgitta here uses a powerful image drawn from obstetrical practices, at a time when women, midwives, not men, obstetricians, delivered babies, and therefore unlikely to be used by a male medieval writer. Compare this image with the miracle of Elsebi Snara, given p. 20.

spiritual visions from him. But though this king has despised my words; yet shall there come another who shall receive them with reverence and praise and use them to his health. Amen.'",

Our Lord Jesus Christ blames and gives a harsh sentence to all manner of people, of whatever state or class they be, for their sins and unkindness, promising mercy if they will amend. And this revelation our Lord told Saint Birgitta to write last of her revelations, affirming that his judgement shall be fulfilled to all people who turn not to him with true meekness, as it is shown in the same revelation.[53] **Chapter 24. [VII.30]**

"I see a great palace like a bright heaven, where there was a host of heavenly chivalry, innumerable as the rays of the sun, shining bright as the sun beams. In this palace there sat in a marvelous throne, as it were a person of a man of incomprehensible fairness, and as a Lord of great power, whose clothes were marvelous and of unspeakable clearness. And a Virgin stood before him who sat in the throne that was brighter than the sun, whom all of them who were there of the heavenly chivalry praised reverently as the Queen of the Heavens.

"Then he who sat in the throne opened his mouth and said: 'Hear you, all my enemies living in the world: for I do not speak now to my friends who follow my will. Hear you, all you clergy, archbishops, bishops, and you who are of lower ranks in the Church. Hear, also, all you monastics, of whatever Order you may be. Hear you, you kings, princes, and judges of the earth, and all sovereigns and servants. Hear also, you women, princesses, ladies, wives, maidens, and all people of whatever condition or rank you are, great or small, who dwell in the world.[54] Hear these words which I myself who made you speak now to you. I complain, for you are gone away from me, and you have given faith to the fiend, my enemy. You have forsaken my commandments, and you follow the will of the fiend and of his suggestions. You take no heed that I, unchangeable and eternal God, your maker, came down from Heaven into a Virgin, taking of her a body, and was conversant with you. And I by myself opened you the way and showed you counsels by which you should go to Heaven. I was naked, scourged, and crowned with thorns, and so strongly stretched sideways and lengthwise on the cross that all the sinews and joints

---

[53]Actually Birgitta asked that her *Revelations* be ended with her vision in the Church of the Holy Sepulchre concerning the judgement of her son Charles, as indeed the second part of the manuscript gives.

[54]See Lübeck 1492 engraving, given p. 31, visualizing these words.

of my body were as if they had been loosed asunder. I heard all reproaches and suffered most despicable death and bitter sorrow of heart for your salvation. O you, my enemies, of all these things take you no heed, for you are deceived. And therefore you bear the yoke and the burden of the fiend with deceptive sweetness and you know not nor feel not those things, till endless sorrow approaches you; and yet these things suffice not for you. But thus your pride is so much that if you might ascend above me, you would gladly do it; and the lust of your flesh is so much that you would rather be without me than leave your inordinate delights. And also your greed may not be satiated, like a sack which is open at both ends; for there is nothing that may fill your avarice. Therefore I swear by my Godhead that if you die in the state that you are in now, you shall never see my face, but for your pride you shall be drowned so deep in hell that all fiends shall be above you and torment you without comfort. For your lechery you shall be filled with the horrible venom of the fiend, and for your greed you shall be filled with sorrow and anguish and be partners of all the evils which are in hell. O you, my enemies, abhominable, uncourteous and unkind, I seem to you as a dead worm in winter; and therefore you do what you will, and prosper. But I shall arise in Summer, and then you shall be still, and you shall not flee my hand. Nevertheless, O you enemies, because I have bought you with my blood, and I seek nothing but your souls, therefore turn yet again to me with meekness, and I shall receive you gladly, as my children. Shake from you the grievous yoke of the fiend and think of my charity, and you shall see in your conscience that I am easy and mild. Amen.'"[55]

Assint laudes deo [Let there be praises to God][56]

How our blessed Lady is ready to help all, both the wives, widows and maidens.

"Hear," said the Mother of God to Saint Birgitta, "that with all your heart you pray to God that your children may please God. Truly, such prayer

---

[55]The 1628 edition notes that the next Revelation was given to Bride in Rome, Jørgensen 2: 253.

[56]The rest of folio 63 and 63 verso are blank; another scribe begins at folio 64. The selections in this second part of the manuscript are written more emphatically from the stance of women and are likely by a nun of Syon. The first part had more likely been inscribed by a Syon brother or, perhaps, by a Carthusian at Sheen, writing what he knows would affect women.

is pleasing to God. For there is no mother who loves my Son above all things and asks the same of her children, but that I am immediately ready to help her to effect what she asks. There is also no widow who firmly prays for the help of God to remain in her widowhood consecrated to God until her death, but that I am immediately ready to fulfill her will with her. For I was as a widow, in that I had a Son on earth who had no bodily Father. There is also no virgin who desires to keep her maidenhead to God to her death, but that I am ready to defend her and to comfort her. For I myself am truly a Virgin. Nor ought you to marvel why I say these things. It is written that David desired King Saul's daughter, when she was a maiden. He received her also, when she was a widow. He had also the wife of Uriah, while her husband lived. Nevertheless, the desire and lust of David was not without sin. But that spiritual delight of my Son, who is Lord of David, is without all sin. Therefore, as these three lives, that is, maidenhood, widowhood, and wedlock, pleased David bodily, so it pleases my Son to have them in his most chaste delight spiritually. Therefore it is no marvel though I help them and draw their ghostly delight into the delight of my Son, for his delight is in them."

The mantle of meekness. [II.23]

Our Lady Saint Mary speaks to the spouse of Christ, Saint Birgitta and says: "Many marvel why I speak to you. It is certain therefore that my humility is shown, for as the heart delights not in a member of the body which is diseased before it receives back its health again, and when it is whole, the heart rejoices, so do I; sins a man never so much, but if he turn again to me with all his heart, and with true repentence soon, I am ready to receive him. And I take no heed how much he has sinned, but with what intent and will he turns back. I am called the Mother of all mercy. Truly, daughter, the mercy of my Son made me merciful, and his Passion made me have compassion. And therefore he shall be wretched who comes not to mercy when he could. Therefore, you, my daughter, come and hide yourself under my mantle, which is despicable without, but inward it is profitable for three things. First, it shelters from tempestuous winds. Second, it protects from biting cold. Third, it keeps away rain. This mantle is my humility.[57] This

----

[57]Lancia Chadwick suggests that this image is reminiscent of "hiding in the shadows of God's wings" (Psalm 36.7, 91.4, 57.1). It is as well the medieval painterly convention of the Madonna della Misericordia. We also recall Bride's literal hand-me-down cloak of poverty and humility in which she begged for her household outside St. Lawrence in Panisperna and which

seems to lovers of the world to be most despicable and foolish to follow. What is more despicable than to be called a fool, and not be angry nor cry out? What is more despicable than to leave and forsake all things, and to be needy in all things? What is more sorrowful among worldly people than for a man to suffer while pretending no wrong is done to him, and to believe and hold himself lower and more unworthy than all others? Such, daughter, was my humility. This was my love, this was all my will, that I would please no one but my Son.

"And this, my humility, is valuable against three things. First against tempestuous wind and weather; that is, against criticism and contempt from men, for as wind and weather that is full and great with storm troubles a man on all sides and makes him cold, so reproaches bear down quickly a man who is impatient, and who does not think on the time and things that are to come and they make his heart cold from charity. But whoever takes heed intently of my humility, he must think what I, Lady of all, heard, and seek my praise and not his, and consider that words are but wind; and soon he shall be refreshed and find ease. For why are worldly people so impatient in suffering words and reproaches, but because they seek their own praise more than the praise of God? And there is no meekness in them, for they have their eyes closed from seeing their sins. Therefore, though the justice that is written says that a man is not bound to suffer or to hear reproaching words without cause, it is a virtue and a worthy reward to hear and suffer patiently contrarious things that are said or done to them.

"Second, my humility protects from biting cold, that is to say, from carnal friendship and fleshly love. There is a kind of friendship and love by which a man is loved only for those things that are present, as with those who say: 'Feed me and I will feed you while you live. For I do not care who will feed you after you are dead. Praise me and I shall praise you, but I care little what praise might follow hereafter.' This friendship is cold and without the warmth of God's love. And it is like snow before the love and compassion of his neighbor who is in need. And it does not reward fruitfully, for when the friendship is ended and the table taken down, soon all the profit of their friendship and love is dissolved, and the fruit of it gone. But whoever follows my humility, he does well to all of God, both to enemies and to friends. To friends because they remain steadily in the praise of God; and to enemies,

is still preserved as a relic, Aron Andersson and Anne Marie Franzén, *Birgittareliker*, pp. 18-29,33-44.

because they are the creatures of God, and in the hopes they should become good.

"Third, is the sight of my meekness protecting from rain and from the uncleanness of water that comes from the clouds. From where come clouds or skies, but of humors and moisture going up from the earth which are lifted up into the firmament; and which thicken? And so come three things from them, rain, hail and snow.[58] This cloud means man's body, which comes from uncleanness. This body has three things with it, as does the cloud: for the body has hearing, seeing and touch. In that the body has sight, it desires those thing which it sees; it desires good things and fair faces, and it desires many possessions. And what are all these things but as if rain coming out of clouds befouling the heart in its desire and love to gather goods together, making the heart restless with much business, distracting the heart with many, sterile thoughts, and troubling it with leaving those things it has gathered together. In that the body has hearing, it listens gladly to its own praise and the love and friendship of the world. It hears also all that is delightful to the body and harmful to the soul. And what are all these things, but as snow which is soon melted and makes the soul cold to God and hardened to meekness? In that the body has touch, it feels with delight its own lust and comfort of the flesh. And what is this but hail drawn together from the waters of uncleanness, making the soul unfruitful to spiritual things, strongly attached to worldly things, and compliant to the desire of the body? Therefore whoever desires to be defended from this cloud, he should flee to my humility and follow it; for with that he shall be protected from the greed of sight, so that he not desire unlawful things; and from the pleasure of hearing, that he hear not things that are against truth; and from the lust of the flesh, that he not be overcome by unlawful impulses.

"Truly, I say to you that the sight of my humility is like a good mantle, warming those who wear it. That is to say, not those who wear it only in thought, but also in deed; for a bodily mantle does not warm a body if it is worn and threadbare, nor my humility help those who merely think about it, but only if each of them strives to follow it in act according to their power. Therefore, my daughter, put on yourself this humility to your power; for women of the world wear mantles which have much pride outside and in, but to little profit. Such clothing you should avoid in every way; for only if the

[58]Brunetto Latino, *Li Livres dou Tresor* 3:107, pp. 117-120, appears to be the source.

love of the world be first foul and loathsome to you; and only if you think continually upon the mercy of our Lord God shown to you, and your unkindness again towards him; and only if you think always to do those things that you have done and which you ought to do, and what sentence of judgement you deserve for these acts, you may not obtain the mantle of my meekness. Because I humbled myself so much; so much therefore do I deserve grace, unless I thought and knew well that I was worth nothing and had no rights for myself. Therefore I would not praise myself, but praise and worship him only who was giver and maker of all. Therefore, daughter, run to the mantle of my humility, and think and consider yourself as a sinner above all others. For though you see any wicked one, you do not know what shall happen to them tomorrow. Also you do not know with what intent nor with what knowledge they do it, whether out of weakness or conscious will. Therefore do not prefer yourself above others; and you ought not to judge anyone in your heart."

Our Lord Jesus Christ teaches us to humble ourselves in four ways. [IV.91]

The Son of God speaks to Saint Birgitta and says: "You ought to humble yourself in four ways. First, against them who have power by rank or by office in the world. For since man has come to despise and leave off obeying God, it is worthy that he at least obey man. And because people must not be without rulers, therefore reverence and praise must be given to their power. Second, you must humble yourself towards those who are spiritually poor, that is to say, towards sinners, praying for them and thanking God for the ways you are not nor have been any such. Third, towards them who are spiritually rich, that is to say, towards the friends of God, thinking yourself unworthy to serve them or to be conversant amongst them. Fourth, towards the poor of the world, by helping them and clothing and washing their feet."

This is a revelation sent to the holy spouse of Christ, Saint Birgitta, in which our Lady Saint Mary reproached the pride of women in their stance, bearing, speech, dress, and other behavior, with the example of three wretched women: of which one was in Hell, another in Purgatory, and the third, alive. [VII.52]

The holy spouse of Christ, Saint Birgitta, spoke to our Lord Jesus Christ words of love and praise for the great grace that he shaped with her, and said: "Praise to you, almighty God, for all the things that have been made, and praise for all your virtues. Service be rendered to you by all creatures for your great love and charity. I, therefore, always unworthy and sinful from my childhood, thank you, my God, that you do not deny grace to any sinner who asks for it. But you spare and have mercy for all. O my sweetest God, it is truly marvelous that you work with me; for when it pleases you, you bring my body into a spiritual sleep, and then you excite and raise up my soul to see and hear and feel spiritual things. O my most sweet God, how sweet have been your words to my soul, which swallows them as the most sweet food. And then enter with joy into my heart, for when I hear your words, I am both full and hungry; full, because nothing delights me except your words; hungry, because the more I hear them the more fervently I want them. Therefore, blissful God, give me help always to do your will."

Our Lord Jesus Christ answered and said: "I am without beginning and without end. And all things which are are made by my power; all things are disposed by my wisdom and all things are governed by my judgement and will; and all my works are ordered by charity. Therefore for me there is nothing that is impossible. But that heart is over-hard which neither loves me nor fears me, since I am ruler of all things and Judge. And yet man fulfills the will rather of the devil, who is my tormentor and a deceiver, who gives out venom largely through the world, for which souls may not live, but they are drowned down into the death of Hell. This venomous sin, which, though it is bitter to the soul, yet to many tastes sweet, and each day it is drawn out of the devil's hand upon many people. But who ever heard any such things, that life is offered to all, and they choose death rather than life. Nevertheless I, God of all, am patient and have compassion on their wretchedness. For I do as a king who sends wine to his servants and says: 'Pour it forth to many, for it is wholesome. It gives health to the sick, mirth to them who are depressed, and a courageous heart to those who are whole.' But yet the wine is not sent but by an appropriate vessel. So I have sent my words, which are like wine, to my servants by you, who are my vessel, which I will fill and draw out after my own will. My holy Spirit shall teach you where you will go and what you shall say. Therefore speak joyfully and without fear the things that I order; for there is no one who shall prevail against me."

Then answered the spouse, Saint Birgitta: "O king of all glory and bliss, giver of all wisdom and granter of all virtues, why do you choose me for such work, who has wasted my body in sins? I am like a donkey, unlearned and unwise and defective in virtues; and I have trespassed in all things and amended nothing."[59]

Our Lord Jesus Christ answered: "If money or other metal were presented to a lord, who should marvel, though he made of it for himself crowns or rings or coins to his own profit. So it is no marvel though I receive the hearts of my friends presented to me and do my will in them. And just as much as one has less understanding and another more, so do I use the conscience of each as is expedient to my praise. For the heart of a rightful man is my money; therefore be firm and ready to do my will."

Then spoke the Mother of God to Saint Birgitta, saying: "What do the proud women say in your kingdom?

Saint Birgitta answered: "O Lady, I am one of them, and therefore I am ashamed to speak in your presence.

"Though I know it better than you, yet I would hear it from you."

Saint Birgitta answered: "When," she said, "true humility was preached to us, we said that our ancestors willed to us and gave us in heritage great possessions and a good education as to behavior and class. Why therefore should I not follow them? My mother sat with the first and the highest and was clad and arrayed nobly, having many servants and educating them with praise. Why should I not also pass on such things to my daughter, who has learned to bear herself nobly and to live with bodily joy and to die with great praise from the world?"[60]

The Mother of God answered: "Each woman who has these words and follows them in deed goes by the true way to Hell. And therefore such an answer is very difficult. What does it profit to have such words, when the Creator of all things suffered his body to live and dwell on earth in all humility from the time of his birth until his death, and never wore upon himself the clothing of pride. Truly, such women do not consider his face, how he stood living and dead upon the cross, bloody and pale from pain; nor those who reckon nothing of the criticism which he heard, nor of his despicable death which he chose; neither have they in mind the place where

[59]For medieval donkey lore see Julia Bolton Holloway, "The Asse to the Harpe: Boethian Music in Chaucer," in *Boethius and the Liberal Arts*, ed. Michael Masi (Berne: Peter Lang, 1981), pp. 175-186, and *Apuleius through Time*, ed. Constance Wright and Julia Bolton Holloway, forthcoming.

[60]Here Bride speaks of her mother and her daughter Ingeborg, the dialogue echoing that between Boethius and Lady Philosophia, to be repeated in Chaucer's Wife of Bath's Tale, concerning social rank as conferring no value in itself.

he gave up the spirit, for where thieves and robbers had received many wounds, there was my Son wounded. And I, who before all creatures, am most dear to him, and in me is all humility, was present there. And therefore they who did such proud and pompous things, and given other occasion to follow them, are like a sprinkler, which, when it is put to a burning liquid, it burns and befouls all of them whom it sprinkles. Right so do the proud give examples of pride and very grievously they burn souls by evil examples.

"And therefore I will now do like a good mother, who, fearing for her children, makes them see the rod, which the servants also see. But the children, seeing the rod, fear to offend their mother, thanking her for threatening them but not beating them. The servants fear to be beaten if they trespass. And so of the dread of the mother the children do more good deeds than they did before, and the servants do less evil. So truly, because I am the mother of mercy, therefore I will show you the reward of sin, that the friends of God may be more fervent in the charity of God. And sinners, knowing their peril, flee from sin, at least, from fear. And in this way I have mercy on both good and evil; on the good people, that they may obtain and get more crowns and rewards in heaven, on the wicked, that they suffer less pain. And there is none who is so great a sinner, but I am ready to help him; and my Son to give him grace, if he ask mercy with charity."

After this, there appeared three women: that is to say, the mother, and the daughter, and the niece, that is, that daughter's daughter.[61] But the mother and the granddaughter appeared dead, and the daughter appeared to be alive. The said dead mother seem to come creeping out of a foul and dark clay ditch; her heart was drawn out of her body, her lips cut off, and her chin trembled; her teeth, shining, white and long, ground and chattered together; her nostrils were all gnawn; her eyes were put out, hanging down on her cheeks between sinews; her forehead was hollow; and instead of her forehead there was a great and dark depth. In her head the head pan failed and had fallen away, and the brain boiled up as if it had been lead, and flowed out like black pitch. Her neck turned about like wood that is turned in the instrument of a joiner, against which was set a blade of the sharpest iron, cutting and shaving away without any comfort. Her breast was open and full of worms long and short; and each of them wallowed hither and thither upon each other. Her arms were like the hafts or handles of a grinding stone. Her hands

---

[61]In Latin and Italian, there is one word for the two relationships, nephew, niece, grandson, granddaughter, from which comes "nepotism."

were like keys full of knots and long. The chines or vertebrae of her back were all dissolved, each from the other; and one going up, another going down, they never ceased moving. A long and large serpent came forth from the nether part of her stomach to the other parts; and joining the head and tail together as a round bow, went round about her bowels continually, like a wheel. Her hips and her legs seemed like two rough staves of thorns full of most sharp prickles. Her feet were like toads.[62]

Then this dead mother spoke to her daughter who was alive saying: "Hear you, altogether my torn and venomous daughter. Woe is me that I was ever your mother. I am she who set you in the nest of pride, in which you, made hot, grew until you came of age. And then it was pleasing to you that you had spent your time in that nest. Therefore I say to you that as often as you turn your eyes to look at, or see pride, which I taught you, so often cast you boiling venom in my eyes with insufferable burning heat. As often as you speak words of pride which you learned from me, so often swallow I most bitter drink. As often as your ears are filled with the wind of pride which the waves of arrogance and pride excite and stir up in you, that is to say, to hear praise of your own body and to desire praise from the world, which you learned from me, so often comes to my ears a fearful and dreadful sound, with blowing and burning wind. Woe, therefore, to me, who am poor and wretched; poor because I have nor feel anything of good, and wretched because I have abundance and plenty of evil. But you, daughter, are like the tail of a cow which, going in foul clay, as often as she moves her tail, as often does she befoul and sprinkles those near her. So you, daughter, are like a cow; for you have no goodly wisdom, and you go after the works and impulses of your body. Therefore as often as you follow the works of my custom, that is to say, those sins which I taught you, so often is my pain renewed, and the more grievously it burns upon me. Therefore, my daughter, why are you proud of your generation and parentage? For it would be honor and respect to you that the uncleanliness of my bowels was your pillow, my shameful member was your birthing, and the uncleanness of my blood was your clothing when you were born? Therefore, now, my womb, in which you lay, is altogether eaten by worms. But why, daughter, do I complain to you, when I ought more to complain about myself? Because there are three things which torment me most grievously in my heart. The first is that I, made by

[62]Bride here seems to be speaking of her fears concerning her own mother, Ingeborg, or Sighurd, who had died when Bride was a small child.

God for heavenly joy, misused my conscience and have disposed myself to the sorrows of Hell. The second is that while God made me fair as an angel, I deformed and mishaped myself so that I am more like the devil than an angel of God. The third is that in the time given to me, I made a very evil change. For I received a little thing, short and transitory, that is to say, delight in sin, for which now I feel endless evil, that is, the pain of Hell."

Then said this dead mother to the spouse of Christ, Saint Birgitta: "You," she said, "who see me, see me not but by bodily likeness. For if you should see me in that form in which I am, you would die from fear; and all my members are devils. And therefore the Scripture is true which says that as rightful men are members of God, so sinners are members of the devil. Right so I now experience the devil's arms fastened into my soul; for the will of my heart has disposed me to so much filth, deformity and misshapenness. But hear now more. It seems to you that my feet are toads. That is because I stood firmly in sin; therefore now fiends stand firmly in me. And always biting and gnawing at me, they are never full. My legs and my thighs are as staves full of prickly thorns, for I had a will after fleshly delight and my own lust. That each chine of my back is loose, and each of them moves against the other; that is therefore because the joy of my lust sometimes went too much upward for worldly solace and comfort, and sometimes too much downward because of too much depression, grouching, and wrath because of the adversity and disease of the world. And there as the back is moved and stirred after the motions of the head, so ought I to have been stable and moveable according to God's will, who is the head of all good. But because I did not do so, therefore I justly suffer these pains which you now see. That a serpent creeps forth from the lower parts of my stomach to the higher parts, and standing like a bow turned about as a wheel, is because my lust and delight were inordinate; and my will would have had all the world's goods in its possession; and in many ways to have spent them, and indiscreetly. Therefore the serpent now searches about in my entrails without comfort, gnawing and biting without mercy. That my breast is open and altogether gnawn with worms, shows the true justice of God, for I loved foul and rotten things more than God; and the love of my heart was all given to transitory and passing things of the flesh and of the world. And therefore as from small worms are brought longer worms, right so is my soul; for the foul stinking things which I loved are filled with devils. My arms seem as if they are beams; that is because I had my desire like two arms; that is to say, because I desired a long life, that I might have lived longer in sin. I would also and desired that the Judgement of God had been easier than the Scripture said. Nevertheless, my conscience told me very well that my time was short and the Judgement of God insufferable. But again my desire and delight that I had in sinning stirred me to think that my life should be long and the Judgement of God bearable. And of such suggestions my conscience was subverted and turned upside down, and my will and reason followed lust and delectation. And therefore the devil is now lodged in my soul against my will, and my conscience understands and feels that the Judgement of God is right. My hands are like long keys. And that is because the precepts and commandments were not pleasing to me; and therefore my hands are now to me a great burden, and lack any use. My neck is turned like wood which is placed against a sharp blade; that is because the words of God were not sweet to me to swallow and taste them in the charity and love of my heart; but they were too bitter, for they argued and criticized the delight and will of my heart; and therefore now a sharp blade stands at my throat. My lips are cut off, for they were ready with vain, joking, and dishonest words of pride; but they failed and found it irksome to speak the words of God. My chin appears to be trembling, and my teeth grind and beat together; that is because I was wilfull in giving food to my body, so that I might seem fair and desirable, whole and strong to all the delights and pleasures of the body. And therefore now my chin trembles and quakes without comfort, and my teeth beat together; for all that they wasted was but unprofitable work as far as being fruit for the soul. My nose is cut off; because amongst you it is done to them who trespass in such a case to their greater shaming, right so is the mark of my shame set upon me for ever. That my eyes hang down by sinews upon my cheeks is correct for, just as the eyes joyed in the fairness of my cheeks for ostentation and showing-off from pride, so now from much weeping they are put out and hang down to my cheeks with shame and confusion. And right so is my forehead hollow, and instead of it there is a great darkness. For about my forehead was set the veil and array of pride; and I would appear glorious, and be seen of fairness, and seem fair. And therefore is my forehead now dark and foul, deformed and misshapen. That my brain boils up and flows out like lead and pitch, is well deserved. For as lead is soft and may be bent according to the will of him who uses it, so was my conscience, which lay in my brain, bowed to the will of my heart, although I understood well the things that I should have done. And the Passion also of the Son of God was in no way fastened in my heart, but it flowed out like a thing that I knew well and took no heed of. And furthermore, of that holy blood which flowed out of the members of the Son of God, I took no more heed than of pitch, and fled, as if they were pitch, from the words of charity and of the love of God, lest they should convert me or trouble me from the delights of the body. Nevertheless, sometimes I heard the words of God to the shame of man; but as quickly as they entered, so quickly went they out of my heart again. And therefore now my brain flows out like burning pitch, with extremely hot boiling. My ears are stopped with hard stones, for words of pride entered in them joyfully, and softly and sweetly they went down into the heart, for the charity of God was closed out of my heart. And because I did all that I could for pride and for the world, therefore now joyful words have been shut out from my ears.

"But you may ask if I did any meritorious or good deeds. And I answer you I did as does a money changer, who clips and cuts the money; and then reassigns or takes it again to the lord to whom it belongs. So I fasted and made alms and such other good works; but I did them for fear of Hell, and to escape the adversities and disease of the body. But because the charity and the love of God was cut off from my deeds, therefore such deeds were not valuable to me for obtaining Heaven, although they were not without reward. You might also ask how I am within in my will, when so much foulness and distortion is without. I answer: My will is as the will of a manslayer or of him who would gladly slay his own mother. So I covet and desire the worst evil to God, my Creator, who has been to me the best and most sweet."

Then the dead granddaughter, that is, the daughter's daughter of the same dead Beldame,[63] spoke to her own mother who was still alive, saying: "Hear, you scorpion, my mother, woe is me, because you have evilly deceived me. For you showed me your merry face, but you pricked me very grievously in my heart. Three counsels you gave me of your mouth, three things I learned of your works. And three ways you showed me in your process and going out. The first counsel was to love bodily in order to get carnal love and fleshly friendship. The second was to spend temporal goods over abundantly for praise from the world. The third was to have rest for the delectation and

[63]*Beldame*, Belle Dame, "beautiful lady," French term of respect which became denigrated with time to meaning "witch," as in Keats' "La Belle Dame Sans Merci." One suspects this is Ingeborg, Bride's daughter, who had died young and who had perhaps had the same name as her grandmother. See pp. 10-11.

delight of the body.

"These counsels were very harmful to me and a great hindrance. For I loved carnally, therefore I now have shame and spiritual envy. And because I spent wastefully temporal goods, therefore was I deprived of grace and the gifts of God in my life, and after my death I have obtained great confusion and shame. For I delighted in the quest and rest of the flesh in my life, therefore in the hour of my death began the unrest of my soul without comfort.

"Three things also I learned of your works. The first was to do some good deeds, and nevertheless use them and not to leave that sin which delighted me: as a man should do who mixed honey with venom, and offered it to a Judge; and he, moved by that to anger, dropped it on him who offered it. So am I now expert in many fold anguish and tribulation.

"The second is that I learned from you a marvelous manner of clothing myself; that was to conceal my eyes with a kerchief, to have sandals on my feet, gloves on my hands and the neck all naked in front. This kerchief concealing my eyes means the fairness of my body, who so obscured my spiritual eyes that I took no heed nor saw not the fairness of my soul. The sandals, which protect the feet underneath and not above, mean the holy faith of the Church, which I held faithfully, but there followed no fruitful works. For as sandals furthered my feet, right so my conscience, standing in the faith, promoted my soul. But because good works did not follow, therefore my soul was naked. The gloves on the hands mean a vain hope I had; for I extended my works which are meant by the hands, into so great and large mercy of God, which is signified in the gloves, that, when I groped for the justice of God, I felt it not nor took any heed of it. Therefore I was overbold in sinning. But when death came, then the kerchief fell down from my eyes upon the earth, that is to say, upon my body. And then the soul saw and knew itself as naked, for few of my deeds were good, and my sins were many. And for shame I might not stand in the palace of the eternal king of bliss, because I was shamefully clothed. But then devils drove me into hard punishment, where I was scorned with shame and confusion.

"The third thing, mother, that I learned of was to clothe the servant in the lord's clothes,[64] and to set him in the lord's seat, and to praise him as a lord, and to minister to the lord the reliefs of the servant and all things that

[64]Medieval laws were strict about the appropriate quality of garb to be worn by men and women of differing ranks.

were despicable. This lord is charity and the love of God. The servant is a will to sin. Truly in my heart where ought to have reigned godly charity was set the servant, that is, delight and lust of sin, whom I clothed then when I turned my will to all temporal things that are made. And the reliefs and parings and the most abject things I gave to God, not out of charity, but out of fear. So therefore was my heart glad of fulfilling and delight of my own will, for the charity and love of God was excluded from me, and the good Lord cast out and the evil servant closed within. See, mother, these three things I learned from your doings.

"Three ways you showed me also in your going out. The first was bright. But when I entered in it, I was blinded by its brightness. The second was compendious and slippery as ice, in which, when I went one step forward, I slid again backward a whole step. The third was was very long, in which, when I went forth, there came after me a sudden rushing flood and bore me over a hill into a deep ditch.

"In the first way is noted the going forth of my pride, which was too much; for the ostentation and showing which proceeded from my pride shone so much in my eyes that I did not think about the consequences of it, and therefore I was blind.

"In the second way is noted that disobedience in this life is not long; for after death a man is compelled to obey. Nevertheless, to me it was long, for when I went one step forward in meekness of confession, I slid backward a step. Because I would that the sin confessed have been forgiven, but after making confession, I would not flee from the sin. And therefore I did not stand firmly in the step of obedience, but I slid again into sin, as does he who slides upon ice; because my will was cold and would not get up and flee from the things which delighted me. So therefore when I went a step forward, confessing my sins, I slid a step backward; because I would fall again to those sins and delectations that delighted me, of which I had made confession.

"The third way was that I hoped for a thing which was impossible; that is to do more sin and not have lengthy pain; also to live longer, and the hour of death not be near. And when I went forth by this way, there came after me a hasty rushing flood; that is to say, death, which from one year to another caught me and turned my feet upside down with pain of illness. What were these feet, but when sickness comes about, I might take little heed of the profit of the body and less to the health of the soul? Therefore I fell into a deep ditch, when my heart that was high in pride and hard in sin burst, and the soul fell down low into the ditch of pain for sin. And therefore this way was long; for after the life of the body was ended, soon there began a great pain. Woe, therefore, to me, my mother; for all those things that I learned from you with joy, now I wail about them with weeping and sorrow."

Then spoke this same dead daughter to the spouse of Christ, Saint Birgitta, who saw all these things, saying: "Hear, you who see me. To you it seems that my head and my face as like thunder, thundering and lightning within and without; and my neck and my breast as it were put into a hard press, with long sharp pricks; my arms and my feet are as it were long serpents; and my womb is smitten with hard hammers; my thighs and my legs are as it were flowing water out of the gutters of a roof,[65] and my feet are frozen together. But yet there is one pain within that is more bitter to me than all these. Right as if there were any person of whom all the breaths of his living spirits were stopped and all the veins, filled with wind, pressed up to the heart, which for violence and strength of those winds should begin to burst; so am I disposed within very wretchedly for the wind of my pride, which was to me much cherished. Nevertheless, yet I am in the way of mercy, for in my most grievous sickness I was confessed in the best manner I could, for fear of pain. But when death came near, than came to my mind the consideration and vision of the Passion of my God, how that was much more grievous and more bitter than all that I was worthy to suffer for my sins and demerits. And with such consideration, I became tearful and wept and wailed that the charity and the love of God was so much to me and mine so little to him. Then I beheld him with the eyes of my conscience and said: 'O Lord, I believe you, my God. O you Son of the Virgin, have mercy upon me for your bitter Passion; for now from henceforth would I amend my life, if I had time, very willingly.' And in that point of time was there lit and kindled in my heart a spark of charity, by which the Passion of Christ seemed more bitter to me than my own death. And so then burst my heart, and my soul come into the hands and power of devils to be presented to the Judgement of God. Therefore it came into the hands of devils, because it was not worthy that the angels of fairness should come near the soul of so much foulness. But in the Judgement of God, when the devils cried and asked that my soul should be judged and damned to Hell, the Judge answered: 'I see,' he said, 'a spark of

[65]Julian of Norwich makes uses of this metaphor as well, *The Revelations of Divine Love*, trans. James Walsh (St. Meinrad: Abbey Press, 1975), p. 57.

charity in the heart which ought not to be quenched, but it must be in my sight. Therefore I judge the soul to Purgatory, until the time that it be so worthily purged and made clean that it deserve and have forgivenss.'

"But now you might ask if I shall have part of all the goods and good deeds that were done for me. I answer you with a parable. Just as if you saw two balances hanging, and in that one were naturally bearing downward and in the other were some light thing going upward, the greater things and fair that were put in the empty balance, so much the rather should they lift up the other balance that is heavy and of great weight. It is so with me; for the deeper that I was in sin, the more grievously am I gone down into pain. And therefore what ever is done to the praise of God for me, it lifts me up from pain; and specially that prayer and good that is done by rightful men and the friends of God, and benefits that are done by well-gotten goods and deeds of charity. Such things, truly, they were that make me each day become closer to God."

After this spoke the holy Mother of God to the spouse of Christ, Saint Birgitta, and said: "You marvel how I, who am Queen of Heaven, and you who live in the world, and that soul which is in Purgatory, and that other which is in Hell, speak together. This I shall tell you. I, truly, never go from Heaven, for I shall never be departed from the sight of God. Nor that soul which is in Hell shall not be separated from pain. Nor that soul which is in Purgatory, neither, until it is purged clean. Nor shall you come to us before the departure of your bodily life. But your soul with your understanding, by virtue of the spirit of God, is lifted up to hear the words of God in Heaven: and you are allowed to know some pains in Hell and in Purgatory, for warning and amendment of evil livers and to the comfort and profit of them who are good. Nevertheless, know that your body and your soul are joined together on earth, but the holy Spirit who is in Heaven gives you understanding to understand his will."

After this, the third woman who was alive left all the world and entered into the religious life, and lived all her life after in great perfection and holiness.

How our Lady tells Saint Birgitta of the Judgement of Sir Charles her son; and what allegiance our Lady and his good angel made before Christ for his soul; and what the fiend alleged against the soul; and of the sentence that Christ gave for the deliverance of the soul.[66] [VII.13]

[66]Jørgensen 2: 210, 1628 edition; this vision concerning her son Charles is said first to have occurred to Bride in Naples following his death,

Our Lady Saint Mary spoke to Saint Birgitta and said: "I will tell you what I did to the soul of Charles your son. When it was separated from his body, I was like a woman who stands by another woman when she is giving birth, to help the child so that it not die from the flowing blood nor be killed in that narrow place from which it is born; being also careful that the child's enemies that are in the house not kill it. I did the same; for I stood near the said son a little before he gave up his spirit, so that he should not have fleshly love so in his mind that it should cause him to think or say anything against God; nor that he should desire to leave any things which were pleasing to God; nor desire to do the things that might in any way be contrary to God's will and hinder his soul. I helped him also in that narrow place that is in the exiting of the soul from the body[67]; so that he should not suffer such great pain in death that should cause him to be unstable or to despair in any way, nor that he should forget God in his dying. I kept also his soul in such a way from his deadly enemies, that is to say, from fiends, that none of them might touch it. But as soon as it was gone out of the body, I took it into my keeping and defence. And then all the company of fiends hastily fled and went away, who out of malice desired to have worried the soul and everlastingly to have put it to torment. But how the judgement was of the soul of the same Charles after his death, it shall be shown you plainly when it pleases me."

Then, after a few days, our Lady Saint Mary appeared to Saint Birgitta waking in prayer, and said: "Now it is lawful to you, by the goodness of God, to see and to hear how the judgement was done upon the said soul when it departed from the body, and that was done then in a moment of time, that is, in a very short while, before the unspeakable majesty of God shall be shown to you in order and at leisure, by bodily likeness, so that your understanding may conceive it."

Then, soon after, Saint Birgitta was taken into a great and beautiful palace, where she saw our Lord Jesus Christ sitting to judge like a crowned emperor, with an innumerable company of angels and saints serving him. And by him she saw standing his most worthy Mother, listening to the

then on shipboard and in Jerusalem, its consummation in the Church of the Holy Sepulchre. See Vatican MS Ottob. lat. 90, fol. 132.

[67]The folkore of dying is that the soul, like a child, exits from the mouth. Bride describes the act as being similar to the birthing of a baby through the dilated cervix and vagina.

Judgement. It seemed also that a soul stood before the Judge in great fear and dread, and naked as a new-born child, and as if blind in all ways, so that it saw nothing with comprehension. But yet it understood what was said and done in the palace. There stood also an angel on the right side of the Judge by the soul, and a fiend on the left side. But neither of them touched the soul nor came near it.

After this the fiend cried and said: "Hear, almighty Judge. I complain before you that a woman, who is both my Lady and your Mother, whom you loved so much that you have made her mighty above Heaven and earth and above all of us fiends of Hell; for she has done me wrong and incorrectly concerning this soul that now stands here. For I ought of right to have taken this soul to me as soon after it was gone from the body, and with my fellowship to have presented it to your Judgement. And see, rightful Judge, that woman, your Mother, took this soul into her strong keeping before it was fully out of his mouth, and has brought it to your Judgement."

Then the holy Virgin, our Lady Saint Mary, Mother of God, answered: "Hear my answer, you devil. When you were created, you understood that Justice that was in God everlastingly without beginning. You also had free choice to do what you thought best. And though you chose rather to hate God than to love him, yet you always understood well what ought to be done according to justice. Therefore I say to you that it is more appropriate to me than to you to present this soul before God, the true Judge. For while this soul was in the body, it had great charity and love towards me, thinking often in his heart that God vouchsafed to make me his Mother, and that he would enhance me above all things that he made. And for this cause he began to love God with so much charity that he said this in his heart: 'I joy so much that God loves the Virgin Mary his Mother above all things that there is no creature nor bodily delight in this world that I would change for that joy; but I should prefer that joy before all earthly delights. And if it were possible that she might be hindered in the least point from that worthiness that she is in towards God, I should rather chose myself to be allowed to be tormented everlastingly in the deepness of Hell. And therefore endless thanks and everlasting bliss be to almighty God for that blessed grace and great glory which he has given to his most worthy Mother.' Therefore, you devil, see now with that will this knight died. And what does it seem to you; whether it was more correct that his soul should come into my protection before the Judgement of God, or into your hands, wickedly to be tormented?"

The fiend answered: "It is not my right that that soul which loved you more than itself should come to my hands before the Judgement is given. But though you have one right to do this grace with him before the Judgement, yet after the Judgement is given, his works shall judge him to my hands to be punished. Now, Queen, I ask of you why you so drove all us fiends from the presence of his body in the passing of the soul that not one of us might make there any terror, nor bring him into any fear or dread?" The Virgin Mary answered: "That I did for the burning charity and love which he had for my body and for the joy that he had that I was the Mother of God. Therefore I obtained for him that grace of my Son that no evil spirit should come near him wherever he was, nor even where he is now."

After this, the fiend spoke to the Judge and said: "I know well that you are justice and power. You judge no more unjustly to the devil than to an angel. Judge therefore and condemn this soul to me. In that wisdom that I had when you made me, I have written down all his sins. I have also kept all his sins in that malice that I had when I first fell from heaven. For when this soul came first to such an age of discretion that it understood well that it was sin which it did, than his own will drew him more to live in worldly pride and fleshly delight than to withstand such things."

The angel answered: "When his mother understood first that his will was flexible and ready to bow to sin, immediately she saved him with works of mercy and long prayers that God should vouchsafe to have mercy on him, that he feel not far from God. And by these works of his mother he gained the dread of God, so that as often as he fell into sin, immediately he hastened to confess them."

The fiend answered: "I ought to tell his sins." And as soon as he would have begun to tell, he began to cry and wail and to quest busily in himself, both in his head and in all the members that he seemed himself to have. And it seemed that he trembled all over and shook, and of great trouble he cried: "Alas, and woe, to me, wretch. How have I lost my long labour? For not only have I lost the text, but also all the matter is burnt in which all the things were written. The matter meant the times he sinned, of which I have no more memory than of the sins that were written there."

The angel answered: "This has the weeping and long labor of his mother and many prayers done;[68] so that God, having compassion of her wailings, gave her son such grace that for each sin that he did, he obtained contrition and made humble confession of goodly charity. And therefore those sins are forgotten and put out of your mind."

The devil answered, affirming that he had still a sack full of writings of

[68]Augustine, *Confessions* 3.12, concerning the priest telling Monica her tears will save her son's soul.

such sins as the knight had intended to have mended, but to which afterwards he had not paid heed. And, therefore, he must be tormented until he has done satisfaction by pain for such sins as he had not amended during his lifetime.

The angel answered: "Open your sack and ask my judgement of those sins for which you must chastise him."

Then the fiend cried as if he had gone mad, and said: "I am despoiled of my power; for not only my sack is taken away from me, but also the sins that were in it. This sack was sloth, in which I previously put all his sins for which I needed to punish him. Because out of sloth he left many good deeds undone."

The angel answered: "The tears of his mother have despoiled you and broken your sack and destroyed your writing, so much do her tears please God."

The fiend answered: "Yet have I here some things to say against him; that is to say, his venial sins."[69]

The angel answered: "He had a will to go on pilgrimage away from his country, leaving his goods and his friends, visiting holy places with much labor. And these he fulfilled in deed. He dressed him also in such a manner that he was worthy to receive indulgence and pardon from holy Church. And he desired to please God, his Creator, by the amending of his sins. Wherefore all those causes which you said that you had written are forgiven."

The fiend answered: "Yet, at the least, I must punish him for such venial sins that he did, for they are not all done away with by indulgences; for there are thousands of thousands which are written on my tongue."

The angel said: "Put out your tongue and show your writing."

The fiend answered with great yelling, wailing and crying, and said: "Alas and woe is me, for I have not one word to speak; for my tongue is cut away by the roots losing all its strength."

The angel answered: "That has his mother done with her busy prayers and labor. For she loved his soul with all her heart. And therefore, for her charity, it has pleased God to forgive all his venial sins which he did from his childhood until his death. And therefore is your tongue is without strength."

The fiend answered: "Yet have I kept in my heart one thing which may not be removed. And that is that he obtained things unlawfully, not taking

[69]Venial sins are the less grave sins which do not result in the loss of the soul's salvation.

heed to restore them."

The angel answered: "His mother did satisfaction for such things with alms and prayers and deeds of mercy, so that the rigor of justice bowed itself to the softness of mercy. For God gave him a perfect will, without sparing any of his goods, to do full satisfaction after his power to them from whom he had taken anything unrightfully. And this will God accepts for the effect of the deed, because he might live no longer. And therefore his heirs must do satisfaction for such things within their power."

The fiend answered: "Then, if I may not punish him for his sins, yet it is proper for me to chastise him; for he did not do good works and virtuous after his abilities, when he had a full understanding and a whole body. For virtues and good works are that treasure that he should bear with him to such a kingdom; that is the glorious kingdom of God. Suffer me therefore to fulfil with pain that which he lacked in virtuous works."

The angel answered: "It is written that to the asker it shall be given and to the knocker with perseverance it shall be opened. Hear, therefore, fiend. His mother knocked for him at the gate of mercy, perservering with prayers of charity and deeds of pity for more than thirty years, weeping many thousands of tears that God should vouchsafe to give the holy Spirit into his heart, so that he should with glad will give his goods, his body, and his soul to the service of God. And so God did. For this knight was made so fervent in charity and it pleased him to live for no other thing but for to follow and to do the will of God. For God was prayed to for so long that he gave his blessed Spirit into his heart. Also the Virgin Mary, Mother of God, gave him of her virtue all that failed him in spiritual armor and clothing that is proper to knights who shall enter the kingdom of Heaven to the high and sovereign Emperor. Saints also who have been in the kingdom of Heaven, which his knight loved while living in the world, have given him comfort by their merits. For he gathered treasure as those pilgrims who exchange every temporal day temporal goods into everlasting riches. And because he did so, therefore he shall have joy and praise everlasting; and especially because of that fervent desire that he had to go on pilgrimage to the holy city of Jerusalem; and because he desired fervently to have given his life in battle that the holy land might be reduced to the lordship of Christian men, so that the glorious Sepulchre of God might be had in due reverence, if he had been strong enough to have brought it about. And [British Museum, Julius F. II, folio 238^v, line 14 ff.] therefore, devil, you have no right to carry out those things which he personally did not do." Than the devil hearing that cried impatiently and roared: "Woe is me, for all my memory is taken from me. For I have forgotten his name."

The angel answered; "His name is called in Heaven 'The Son of Tears.'"[70]

The devil cried and said: "O cursed is that mother of his who had so large a womb that so much water was in it. And cursed is she by me and all my fellowship."[71]

The angel answered: "Your curse is the Honor of God and the blessing of all his friends."

Then Christ the Judge spoke thus, saying: "Devil, go away." Furthermore, he said to the knight: "Come, my well beloved."

And so immediately the devil fled.

Then the Bride seeing these things, said: "O everlasting virtue and beyond comprehension, my Lord Jesus Christ, you give all good thoughts to hearts with prayers and tears. Therefore honor and grace be to you of all things that you have created. O my sweet God, you are most dear to me and truly dearer to me than my body or my soul."

And then the angel said to the Bride: "You ought to know that this vision is not only shown by God to you for your comfort, but also so that the friends of God may understand what he will do for the prayers, weeping and labors of his friends, who pray charitably for other men and labor with perseverence and good will. You may know that this knight your son should not have had such grace but that he had desired from his youth to love God and his friends and to eschew gladly falling into sin."

[70]Again, Bride is remembering Augustine's Monica, *Confessions* 3.12.

[71]One appreciates Bride's sense of humor. It is how she coped with her son Charles. In 1369 or thereabouts, Bride and her two sons had an audience with Pope Urban V, Birger being sober and being told he was his mother's son, Charles, who was wearing elaborate furs, chains and bells, being called a son of the world. Bride asked the Pope's absolution for her sons, saying she would take care of Charles' ridiculous belt and garb: Jørgensen 2:211-212.

Interpretive Essay: Saint Bride as Sibyl, her Book as Apocalypse

I. Saint Bride as Sibyl and Prophet

 A most exquisite Brigittine manuscript is in Rome. It is Renaissance, written in a most beautiful humanist script upon the best vellum, with fine incipit initials in gold leaf at the opening of each book. It proclaims itself to be the *Revelations* of Saint Birgitta. But it actually begins with the prophecies of the Eritrean Sibyl, before it gives Saint Birgitta's *Revelations*, clearly equating the two women.[1]

The Sibyls of the Hellenic, Greco-Roman world were like the Prophets of the Hebraic, Judaeo-Christian world, people capable of foretelling the future. Christianity believed that the female Sibyls equally with the male Prophets had foretold the coming of Christ. Therefore, medieval Advent dramas included the Sibyl and Virgil (because of his Eclogue IV "*Iam redit Virgo*," "Now the Virgin returns") with the Prophets.[2] Therefore, Abelard writing to Heloise, told her of the Erecthean Sibyl, from Augustine's *City of God* and Lactantius, as prophesying the coming of Christ.[3] Therefore, Michelangelo painted them upon the Sistine Chapel ceiling. Many Sibylline manuscripts contain Brigittine texts.[4]

The Cumaean Sibyl, to be adopted by Christine de Pizan as her teacher in *Le Chemin de Long Estude*, or *Road of Long Learning*, wrote nine books of prophecies concerning Rome. When Tarquinius Superbus, the Etruscan tyrant king, demanded these books of her, she destroyed three. When he insisted, she destroyed three more. Finally, he only obtained one third of the whole. His reign was to end and the Republic be born over Rome's indignation at his rape of the chaste, married Lucretia who killed herself rather than endure the shame. The Cumaean Sibyl had been likewise Virgil's Aeneas' guide to the underworld, a role Virgil would next assume in Dante's poem at the culmination of which Dante speaks of his text, the *Commedia*, as Sibylline (33.65-66). Mingled with the classical material on the Sibyls was also the Swedish version of the legend of the True Cross which Bride knew and in which the name of the Bride, the Queen of Sheba, of

Solomon's Song of Songs, beloved by Cistercian St. Bernard, is "Sibilla."[5] The Sibyls through time would especially be used by women to justify their writing of books.[6]

Bride's credibility was very strong. She had begun her international career by writing to King Edward III of England and King Philip VI of France that they must cease their Hundred Years' War, sending a letter to them and to Pope Clement VI at Avignon, through her emissaries Bishop Hemming of Äbo and Prior Peter of Alvastra in 1347-1348, that letter being preserved in English manuscripts.[7] She had told King Magnus of the Black Death. And it had occurred (pp. 37-38). She had told the Pope that lightning would strike the bells of St. Peters and that he would die. And these events happened. She prophesied that the Pope and the Emperor would come together in Rome in her presence. And so it came to be. It was even thought that she had prophesied the 1452 Fall of Constantinople in her sermon on Cyprus. Perhaps the juxtaposition of these events was assiduously cultivated by her household who were intensely interested in her canonization and who functioned as her public relations experts. But for the success of that endeavor there would have had to have been much truthfulness mixed in with the bending of that truth. Bride's strategy and tactfulness was also highly successful. She did not scold in her own person but had Christ and the Virgin do so while she functioned as their ambassador and *canale* or channel of communication. And quite clearly people wanted to hear her sermons which mixed together terror and laughter, sternness and compassion, justice and mercy.

Much of Bride's writing is Sibylline and Prophetic. It is not fictional nor is it theoretical; instead it foretells and influences history and theology. Sometimes it does so through a theatre of allegory drawing intertextually upon prior texts and experiences, using religion and law to do so. One example, omitted elsewhere in this book, is in the account in Book V of the event which occurred while Birgitta was still in Sweden. One day, while still living the life of a member of the nobility, Birgitta was riding her white horse to the King's castle at Vadstena with her retinue, when an intense vision came to her. She saw a ladder reaching to Heaven, on it a monk. The vision is drawn from the text written by John of Climacus, the monk on Mount Sinai, who in turn was copying, revisioning, Jacob's vision of the ladder.[8] In the dialogue that follows, Bride in her *Revelations*, Book Five, section questions, in the role of the doubting monk, Christ and the Virgin and receives important theological answers settling her doubts. The manuscripts of the scene can illuminate it powerfully[9]; likewise does the woodblock in the 1492 Lübeck *editio princeps*, where Bride is shown with equestrian monumentality.[10] The Middle English text is enchanting, reading as it does like Malory's *Morte Darthur*. Therefore, for once, I shall give no translation.

As she rode on a day towarde a Castel wyth moche meyne that was cleped Watzthen . . . Than as she roode by the wey. She reysed up her mynde and made her prayeres to God. And anoon she was ravisshed yn spyryt and went forthe as she had ben oute of her self reysed from the wyttes of her body and yn a dremyns or a masynes, yn contemplacion yn her mynde. Than she sawe yn spirit a laddre sett on þe erthe wereof the ovyr ende touched heven. She sawe our lorde Ihu Cryst sytt yn a wonder throone as a juge demyns. at whose feete stode mayden mary.

And after this the lady kepte thys hoole booke wel yn mynde and in thys same revelation she reyshed to the Castel. And than they that wer aboute her toke the brydel of her horse and begane to meeve her. And whan she was awaked oute of that ravysshyng she turned to her self and was sory that she was letted of that swetnes that she was yn. Þe whych booke of questyons effectually dwelled stylle yn her herte and in her mynde as though yt had be graven yn stone. Soone aftyr she wrote thys booke yn her owne tonge the whych booke her confessour translated yn to latin as he was wonte to do to thys books of her Revelations.[11]

In this text, as also with Jerome's Paula, with Julian of Norwich, and with Margery Kempe, the vision is given as an inward and mental occurrence, "she sawe yn spirit a laddre." The text also brilliantly describes the creative process of the writer, composer, or artist who first conceives the entirety of the work, then executes it. That act, in the Middle Ages, was considered to be analogous to that of God, who first thought, then wrought, the world.[12]

II. The Texts' Intertexts

Powerless as a woman to change evil to good, Bride, like others, including Hildegard of Bingen and Christine de Pizan, borrowed the male instrument of power, the Book, to do so. Books transcend the earthly temporal body and its dying and being forgotten, by being heavenly, eternal, mental and memorable. Women in the Middle Ages, especially after their exclusion from the newly instituted universities and thus from the world of the Book, the Latin Vulgate Bible, subversively insisted upon their defiant portrayal with books, upon their ownership of exquisite Books of Hours, upon paintings of the Virgin at the Annunciation reading from the Book, and upon the account of St. Anne wilfully teaching her daughter, the Virgin, how to read.[13] Thus flesh and blood, parchment and ink, became intertwined.

The books of the Bible were written by the Prophets and the Gospelers, each in turn as inspired by God. He, as the Word creating the World, was seen as having indeed written two books, the Bible and Creation. Men writing even secular books were as if similarly in that mirror image. So also were women when they wrote books. We see this in the iconography of Hildegard of Bingen, Birgitta of Sweden, and Christine de Pizan, who mandated their author portraits in a deliberate and conscious echoing of their book writing as akin to that by Prophets, by Gospelers, and even by God the Creator. Bride was both female Sibyl and male Prophet. Her opening to the *Revelations* mirrors God's Bible: "I am the Creator of heaven and earth and sea and of all things that are in them" (p. 33). Bride's *persona* and voice therefore is the highest *auctor*, or authority, God. Though an entourage of male scribes carry out her writing, she dictates to them how it will be shaped, specifically stating that her vision in the Holy Sepulchre (pp. 113-119) be placed last in the *Liber Celestis*, the *Heavenly Book*, as its Apocalypse.[14]

What books and what models shaped for her that sense of empowerment? Saint Birgitta, as a pious young noblewoman, was much exposed to books. Let us investigate the stories and books she knew, their words becoming her flesh. One story was clearly the legend of Saint Cecilia of Rome. Another is likely that of Saint Elin, also a daughter of a law man. The *vita* or life was written by Bishop Brynolf of Skara, describing how the Swedish Saint Elin, mirroring the Roman Saint Helena, the mother of Constantine,[15] around 1150, had gone likewise on pilgrimage to Jerusalem, but, upon her return, was killed. A blind man's boy found the finger which the murderers had cut off to snatch at its ring, this ring restoring the blind man's sight. The body was then found and wherever it was laid down a spring gushed forth.[16] For these acts Alexander III, at the entreaty of Archbishop Stefan of Uppsala, made Saint Elin a saint.[17] That story gave to Bride of Sweden the sense that she, too, could be a pilgrim to Jerusalem and that she, too, could be a saint.

These were the powerful *legenda*, the readings of saints' lives, Birgitta heard as a child which shaped her own in turn. She was also exposed to books such as the *Speculum Virginum*, *The Virgin's Mirror*, a work composed in the form of a dialogue between Theodora and Peregrinus (whose names mean "Gift of God" and "Pilgrim"), written around 1100 by a German monk.[18] Prior Peter, during Bride's process or trial for sainthood, told how he had read aloud to her from that book in its Latin version in Sweden.[19] A further book we know of, even still possess, is one she acquired on her pilgrimage to Compostela and which today is in the University Library at Uppsala, supposed to be Saint Bernard's *Liber de modo bene vivendi*, the *Life Well*

Lived, written at the request of his sister, "*Quem composuit ad instanciam sororis sue.*"[20] (In actual fact it was instead by another Cistercian, Thomas de Froidmont, and composed for his sister, Margaret of Jerusalem, and thereby hangs a strange tale. Margaret of Jerusalem had been born to her pilgrim parents in Jerusalem. The family was from Beverley, Yorkshire. Margaret, when adult, decided to return to the place of her birth, was caught in the seige of Jerusalem and fought with a cook pot on her head against the Saracens; then, after many adventures, on her second return, came to stay with her brother at his Cistercian abbey, at which point he cast his sister's adventures into Latin verse. A transcription of the medieval manuscript survives, though the manuscript itself is lost.[21]) Thomas de Froidmont's *Liber de modo bene vivendi*, the *Life Well Lived*, which so attracted Bride, begins:

This book is a mirror in which the soul can see its stains and learn what is pleasing to God and what displeases him. Read this book again and again and you will lean how you must love God and your neighbour, despise what is earthly and transient, striving after the everlasting and heavenly, enduring for Christ's sake the adversities of this world and despising its prosperity and enticements, thanking God in sickness, not taking pride in good health, not becoming presumptious in good fortune nor downcast in trials.[22]

She carried that book with her for the rest of her days. These stories and these books gave powerful patterns for her to follow. Biblical types whom she was observed to mirror were Judith,[23] the *mulier fortis*, "virtuous woman" of Proverbs 31.10-31,[24] Miriam,[25] Ester,[26] Sara.[27] These models prepared her for her life of greatness through their own fame and their sense that one had to compensate for the power and knowledge of God and his Book through the sacrifice of the world, the flesh and the devil, through discipline.

They probably justified and prompted her, in turn, to enter that world of textuality herself and to begin her own *Revelations*, her Visions, her Showings, that *Liber Celestis*, or *Heavenly Book*, which she was to write from the age of forty in Sweden following her husband's death in 1343 until her own death in Rome in 1373 in her seventieth year, and which contained eight books, accompanied by two more, the *Regula*, the *Rule*, and the *Sermo Angelicus*, *Conversation with the Angel*, and its *Cantus Sororum*, or *Sisters' Songs*. With this book of books she created a Swedish and European Bible for the fourteenth century. To reach that greater audience it was essential that she learn the theological *lingua franca* or universal language of Latin, not generally taught to secular women. Nor could women attend universities where theology was taught. Birgitta's Swedish language (called "Gothic" in the Latin texts) was not widespread in Europe.[28] Later, a Spaniard would join their group who knew no Swedish. Ambassadors must be good linguists. Bride learned Latin to a certain extent, the Virgin herself demanding this and St. Agnes teaching her,[29] and, though she dictated her visions to Master Mathias and Prior Peter Olavi in Swedish, they translated them into Latin, Alfonso de Jaen further polishing the texts.[30] Her entourage taught her theology. While she supported them, even later begging for the upkeep of her household who included a Spanish bishop become hermit, a Swedish prior, a daughter, two sons, and several priests and servants. All told, this textual community, centered upon a woman, created a powerful and most effective propaganda machine.

From Bride's central vision of herself being told by Christ, "*Thu skalt wara min brudh*," "You shall be my Bride" (pp. 33-35), Birgitta, or Bride, and her Book, the *Liber Celestis*, became inextricably linked. Her iconography, in paintings and in statuary, of a woman in widow's garb, with the accoutrements of a pilgrim, the hat, staff and scrip, shows her also clutching the Book into which she wrote her pilgrim visions, or as writing it. In some instances she is shown dictating that Book to the two Peter Olavis, the most important such depiction being the great carved tryptich in the Blue Church at Vadstena by her shrine. Her visions, narrated within that book, are in turn filled with images of the Book and of the Virgin.

Here is one. The devil is standing with a trembling soul in his hand. The judge asks for the documents concerning the devil's claim to this man's soul. "It is quite a book," says the devil of the ensuing list, having seven chapters, each of fourteen pages, each page, a thousand words, the title being Disobedience, the first chapter, Pride, the second, Covetousness, the third, Envy, the fourth, Avarice, the fifth, Sloth, the sixth, Anger, the seventh, Lechery.[31] Bride's vision about the death of Nicholas Acciaiuoli had the Virgin take the soul from the devils into the sanctuary of her cloak, Bride writing out that account to send to his widow (pp. 54-62).[32] To the future Cardinal Elzear she gave another letter transcribing a message from the Virgin to him in the form of a parable of a king and his daughter and their castle, God, the soul and the body.[33] These parables are reminiscent of the *Gesta Romanorum* or *Deeds of the Romans'* fabling courtly tales, doubling as theological, allegorical teaching, complete with morals[34]; they also anticipate those of Kierkegaard and Kafka.[35] Most daring of all, she instructed Alfonso of Jaen in 1371 to take two letters to the papal envoys, one sealed, one open. He was to read one to them in which the Virgin orders the Pope to return from Avignon to Rome or be damned. Then, acting on her instructions, he tore apart that open letter, saying that in the same manner were the Pope's

Italian possessions to be torn asunder and given to his enemies if he did not return.[36]

Her household was a very bookish one–and some of its manuscripts survive, making their way from Italy and even Spain and Jerusalem to Sweden. These could be patched and sewn together–much like her ancient mantle. One story is of Alfonso busily packing books to take to Jerusalem. Bride stopped him. "You won't be needing them." Those which he did take were mostly thrown overboard in a storm off Jaffa.[37] We even have Bride's daughter testifying to her mother's scriptural acts. At the canonization trial Catherine states: "*Vidit dictam matrem suam scribentem eandem revelacionem in Jerusalem in hospitali sancti Sepulcri*," "She saw her said mother writing that revelation in Jerusalem in the hostel of the Holy Sepulchre," concerning her mother's vision of the drama of the Crucifixion, witnessed by her on Good Friday.[38] We even have scraps, two pieces of which are sewn together in the same manner as her threadbare mantle, of her own handwriting on Italian watermarked paper in Swedish, giving part of the text of the *Revelations*.[39] Later, her nuns, copying out her liturgy and other writings, would similarly turn to needle and thread as well as pen and ink, combining feminine with masculine activities, where they cut and pasted engravings from printed books of the *Revelations* and other texts onto the pages of their manuscripts, illuminating these and then sewing scraps of red or green silk across the top to protect the gold leaf from being smudged by later readers.[40]

In her Book, her *Revelations*, Bride presented herself as carrying out sacred dialogues, sacred conversations, "theatres of devotion," with Christ and with Mary and other saints, whom she sees on clouds[41]; as with modern comic strips balloons these serve to indicate a physical externalization of an intellectual process. Even at her birth that vision seen by the parish priest had been of the Virgin seated in a shining cloud having a book in her hand (p. 4).[42] Christine de Pizan similarly was to show her allegorical and mythical figures within clouds. Likewise, Renaissance paintings would present figures of saints and Christ standing with their donors and viewers as "Sacred Conversations," the sacred scenes from the past witnessed by present and secular donors included within the paintings. It would be wise to think of her reported visions as such "Sacred Conversations." Her narrations of her visions are almost dramas and to edit these texts one must resort to quotations within quotations, and sometimes, even quotations within these quoted quotations, as if caught up in tailors' mirrors of myriad dialogues within dialogues, similar to those in Plato's *Symposium* and Cicero's *Somnium Scipionis*.[43]

The use of theatrical modes had also been practised in Christianity,

Ephraem the Syrian creating dramatic sermons narrating episodes from the lives of holy women, the Byzantine Romanos continuing this custom with his dramatically sung sermons or *Kontakia*.[44] Paula and Jerome had likewise practised, in their mind's eye, perceiving the sacred dramas that had occurred at Bethelehem and upon Golgotha. A Franciscan friar wrote for a Franciscan nun a popular book which influenced many medieval women, including Margery Kempe, the *Meditations on the Life of Christ*, which further dramatized with feminine details episodes of Jesus' childhood and adulthood.[45] Bride's spiritual advisor was to be the Spanish bishop and Hieronomyte hermit, Alfonso of Jaen, the Hieronomytes being the followers of St. Jerome and continuing his devotional practices. These, eventually, would be taken up in turn by Ignatius Loyola in his *Spiritual Exercises*, practised by members of his Order, the Society of Jesus. Such practices consisted of re-visioning the sacred drama with oneself as witness and participant, transcending both time and space. Rather than as hallucinations, it could be wise to perceive these visions, these texts and these paintings, as spiritual exercises, sacred conversations, and participatory reenactments of the past's sacred drama.

The world of the theatre and the world of law have been related since Greek civilization. Birgitta, daughter of a Lawman, would blend this Christian material with that of the apocalyptic Judgment Day. Bride's visionary accounts (pp. 36,54-62,67-98,102-119) frequently center upon court room dramas, mirroring that of the prophet Ezekiel in the Hebrew Scriptures, which is mirrored in turn in the Apocalypse, of the Christian Scriptures, where God presides as Judge over the destiny of the human soul he has created. These *Revelations* in turn, written by a Sibylline woman, resonate with the Old and New Testament books of prophecies written by men, including those by Isaiah, Ezekiel and Jeremiah, fulminating against a corrupt Jerusalem, and culminating with John's Book of the Apocalypse, Revelation, fulminating against a corrupt Babylon (in actuality, imperial Rome, but now read as medieval, papal Avignon, in the anachronistic encoding of censorship enforced by tyranny). In this book, Birgitta, "Bride," becomes as if the Song of Songs' Queen of Sheba, Sibilla, the bride of King Solomon, and the Apocalypse's "Woman Clothed with the Sun," the Bride of the Lamb, in doing so speaking to her own King Magnus of Sweden, to King Edward III of England and Philip VI of France in October, 1348,[46] to the Emperor Charles of Bohemia (father to Chaucer's Richard II's Queen Anne of Bohemia) and to Popes. Just as the Apocalypse was the last book of the Bible, which went from Alpha to Omega, so would women, taking up that paradigm, themselves be able to have the "last word."

The apocalyptic imaging beyond the text evokes the Reconquista/ Crusade era Romanesque *tympani* sculpture above church doors and the illuminated manuscripts of the Beatus Apocalypse in Spain and those in France and England,[47] the Middle English poem, the *Pearl*,[48] the Wilton Diptych, Fra Angelico's frescoes and paintings, and Jan and Hubert Van Eyck's Ghent Altarpiece. Sweden possesses a wealth of church wall paintings of the Apocalypse, which are sometimes even referred to by Bride in her text. The most compelling image of the Apocalypse, mirrored from Ezekiel, is its use within the book of the book presented within itself in Gödelian self-referentiality. Bride borrowed this powerful self-referentiality. There is, for instance, the vision Bride wrote for her King Magnus, of a vast hall with a book upon a lectern, coloured with rainbow light, red, white and gold, signifying the Trinity. The book "shines like the brightest gold, for every word in the book was not written with ink, but every word in the book was living and spoke of itself" (pp. 71-72)[49] Next she sees King Magnus sitting on his throne, a crown upon his head, within a glass globe, above which is poised a sword which draws nearer and nearer to strike, like the weight in a clock (pp. 72-73).[50] Elsewhere, she spoke of him in the medieval topos and convention, as the "crowned ass." She is harnessing the prophetic mode of the Bible to match the needs of Sweden in her own day. The Apocalypse is her "Distant Mirror."[51]

Of her son Charles' death, Bride again had a vision, and again it centered upon books (pp. 113-119). The devil, about to cite Charles' numerous sins, is suddenly seized with amnesia and cannot remember them, and even the book in which he had written them down suddenly disappears, likewise the sack into which he has placed them turns out to be empty, then, when he starts to speak of the sins, his tongue is as suddenly paralysed–the angel explaining these miracles as due to his mother's tears. With a roar the devil yells: "Woe is me, I cannot even remember what the man had done, nay, I cannot even remember his name. Cursed be that old sow, his mother, and all her tears!" "This revelation was consummated in the Church of the Holy Sepulchre," was written into the *Revelations*.[52] This Revelation ends the Princeton manuscript.

Not included in that manuscript is the other important Revelation. At the same time that Bride, in her seventieth year, visited the Holy Sepulchre, the place of dying, she also visited Bethlehem, the place of birth. There her vision was to deeply influence Europe's iconography, image writing, and dramatic performances, of the Nativity.[53] Indeed in not a few Nativity paintings, Saint Bride is herself to be seen as witness and participant in that drama, participating in its "Sacred Conversation." Here, in her own motherly words, given from the Middle English *Liber Celestis*, or *Heavenly Book*, is her description of the event:[54]

The Bride said thus: "When I was in Bethlehem I saw a maiden with child, the fairest that I ever saw, clad in a white mantle, and one small skirt: and with her a proper old man, and with them an ox and an ass. And he tied the ox and the ass at the stall, and he went and lighted one candle and fastened it on the wall. And then he went out, for it was near her delivery. Then she laid down her mantle and took off the kerchief from her head, and stood in her skirt only, and her hair hung down about her shoulders as fair as gold. And she took two clean napkins of linen and two of cloth that she had brought with her, to wrap the child in when he was born. And she laid them down beside her, in readiness.

And when she was all prepared, she kneeled down with great reverence and prayed, and set her back against the manger, and turned her face to the east and held up her hands and her eyes up to Heaven, and she was raised in contemplation with so great a sweetness that it is hard to write about it. And then I saw in her womb something stir; and suddenly she bore her Son. And there came so great a light and brightness that it passed the brightness of the sun, and the light of the candle that Joseph had set on the wall could not be seen.[55] And it was so sudden, that birth of the child, that I might not perceive the passing forth of the child. Nevertheless I saw that blissful child lying naked on the earth, and he had the fairest skin that I ever saw, without any spot. Also I saw the afterbirth, that is the surrounding that the child was in, lying all white. Then I heard the angels sing wondrously sweetly and pleasingly.

And when the maiden felt that she had born her child, she bowed down her head and held up her hands and worshiped the child, and said to him: "Welcome my God, my Lord, and my Son!"

And the child, weeping and trembling for cold and the hardness of the pavement, stretched himself to seek refreshment. Then his mother took him in her arms, and pressed him to her breast, and with her cheek and her breast she warmed him with great joy and love. Then she sat down on the earth, and laid the child on her knee, and took him and laid him, first in a linen cloth, and then in a woolen one, and swaddled his body, his arms, and his legs with one band; and then she bound the two little linen cloths that she had brought with her, about his head.

And then Joseph came in and fell down on his knees and worshiped him, and he wept for joy. And the mother was neither changed in hue, nor had she any sickness nor feebleness and her womb was as small as it had been before she had conceived. And then she rose up, and Joseph helped her to lay the child in the manger, and they both kneeled down and worshiped him.

Thus Bride conjoined birth to death, bringing consolation to the dying with the hope of a new birth. She re-visioned sacred dramas of flesh and blood, resurrecting the old Latin and Greek texts inscribed by men anew into texts written and then rewritten by women. Paula, friend of the crusty Jerome, had already described her vision of that scene in the fourth century after Christ. Now Bride did so in the fourteenth. That, in turn, would enable Margary Kempe to likewise pilgrimage to the Holy Land and likewise participate in her "ghostly sight" in these events of birth and death.

III. The Book of Saint Bride

The particular manuscript translated here was written in Middle English in the fifteenth century, likely at Syon Abbey or at nearby Sheen and designed either, which was most likely, for a nun at Syon, or, less likely, for a recluse elsewhere, such as Julian of Norwich, or for a noblewoman, such as Cecily, Duchess of York, to read, or for such a bourgeoise as was illiterate Margery Kempe to have read to her. If the manuscript had been a Swedish Brigittine one it would very likely have been written by a nun. The English Brigittines, however, were less productive as scribes of books, than were their Swedish counterparts. What is clear is that two scribes wrote this text, extracting their favorite episodes from the lengthy eight-volume Latin *Revelations*. And that the second scribe deeply empathizes with Brigitta's perceptions as a woman.

The text begins, as does the *Revelations* proper, not in Birgitta's voice, but God's, Christ's, as Creator, proclaiming "I am the Creator of Heaven and earth and sea and of all the things that are in them." Thus a woman from the farthest edge of Christendom assumes not merely a male, but a deific voice, that of Christ as Creator. Next, the marriage of the Author of the Creation with the authoress of this book takes place, further validating her prophetic voice and her text. The text's readers thus become witnesses to that marriage in law in an extraordinary oral/scribal speech act (pp. 33-35). The second chapter buttresses Birgitta's position by having Christ tell her that she is inspired by the Spirit and not the devil or fiend, these two chapters being deeply influenced by her relations with Master Mathias (pp. 9,35-56). The third, largely omitted, chapter describes a law court at which Christ presides as Judge (p.36).

The fourth chapter is Birgitta's powerful prophecy, given in Christ's voice, to King Magnus Eriksson of Sweden, two years prior to the Black Death in which Christ says he will come as the Ploughman (pp. 37-38), a text which may well have influenced William Langland's great English work, written after the Black Death, *Piers the Ploughman*. The fifth chapter discusses Birgitta's special role in preparing people for death and discusses the difference between holy and evil dying (p. 38). The sixth through ninth chapters are largely omitted here; they give a long drawn out allegory on housekeeping and religion, and begin with a statement by the Virgin concerning her sorrows, and include a discussion on the bread become flesh in the Mass (pp. 38-40).

The tenth and eleventh chapters present the lives of Mary (the contemplative life) and Martha (the active life), applying these to the clergy, who could only be male, except in the case of nuns in convents. In the Latin text the gender use is not obvious but in the Middle English it is startling, the text having to use "he," "his," and "himself" in a kind of jarring grammatical transvestism in connection with the two women's names of Mary and Martha (pp. 40-50). One suspects this has occurred because the Middle English scribe of this section of the manuscript is male and could only relate the text to his gender, even though in it Christ is addressing Birgitta as "My daughter." The twelfth and thirteenth chapters are omitted here. The fourteenth discusses the faith of a heathen woman, an analogue to Dante's and Langland's uses of the faith of pagan Trajan, a male (pp. 50-51). The fifteenth chapter discusses the death of a woman close to Birgitta in which St. Peter draws the analogy to the death of his own daughter, Peronell or Petronilla (pp. 52-53). The sixteenth chapter has God address Birgitta in this way, "Stay truly humble; that is, a man to show himself such as he is, and to give praise to God for his life" (p. 53) This again is an instance where the male translator has taken originally unisex language and made it relevant to himself rather than to a woman reader.

The seventeenth through eighteenth chapters give a magnificently theatrical and legal scene in which the soul of Nicholas Acciaiuoli is judged and almost damned for his dealings with Queen Joan and King Lewes of Naples (pp. 54-62). The nineteenth chapter is omitted. The twentieth chapter discusses how Master Mathias or Prior Petrus is requested by Christ to take Birgitta's writings to the archbishop and other clergy and how King Magnus will support Birgitta's mission (pp. 63-64). The twenty-first chapter repeats the second chapter's discussion concerning whether Birgitta is inspired by the good or the evil spirit (pp. 64-65). The twenty-second and twenty-third chapters, like the seventeenth through eighteenth, gives a judgement scene, this time of the King of Sweden, Magnus "Smek" Eriksson and his forebears (pp. 67-97). Chapter twenty four, which the scribe states is the one Birgitta wished to have conclude her writings, though this is not correct, gives a more generalized judgement scene and a warning to the people of the world (pp. 97-98). The scribe ends this section with praises to God (p. 98).

Following a mainly blank folio the second scribe takes up the task of translating from Birgitta's Latin *Revelations*. Unlike the first, this scribe does not awkwardly wrench a woman's text to serve masculine purposes, but carefully selects those chapters that emphasize women and which are the closest to Birgitta's own heart. I believe this scribe to be a woman, likely a Brigittine nun, or a male scribe working directly at the request of a woman, which would be difficult in the enclosed cloistering of Syon. Chapter twenty-five, for instance, opens with the Virgin helping wives, widows and maidens (pp. 98-99). Chapter twenty-six discusses the Virgin's mantle of meekness (mentioned already in the first section, p. 56), copied in reality by Birgitta with the mantle in which she had begged for her Roman household (pp. 99-102). Chapter twenty-seven continues the discussion on humility (p. 102), this time in Christ's voice, rather than the Virgin's.

Chapter twenty-eight has the Virgin give to Birgitta a terrifying vision of three women, one in Hell, one in Purgatory and one still alive (pp. 102-113). These women appear to be Birgitta's own dead mother and daughter and herself. This chapter and the next last present extraordinary autobiographical materials, in this instance unrelenting and unforgiving, and filled with horror and anxiety, on the distaff side; in the next, the capacity to forgive the beloved prodigal son, Charles. This twenty-ninth chapter is the one Birgitta directed should be written last in her *Revelations*. It came to her mostly in the Church of the Holy Sepulchre, following her son Charles' death on their pilgrimage to Jerusalem, while at the court of Naples and in the midst of his torrid love affair with Queen Joan of Naples, with whom Nicholas Acciaiuoli had also had a love affair. Birgitta writes this section of the text with that "laughing cheer" Katherine of Flanders described her as having to Margery Kempe and with which Swedish statues invest her. Death no longer has terror for her, but laughter (pp. 113-119).

The second scribe has skilfully filled in the gaps the first scribe left and has come closer to the essence of Saint Birgitta in the sections she has chosen to translate. Both have stressed political prophecies, religious and ethical teachings, and Swedish Birgitta's visionary stance to all Christendom.

IV. The Texts' Communities

Bride created a textual community centered upon a woman's visions but which reached out to men and to all known nations.[56] Bride's life and her

Revelations were much studied and imitated by women in Italy, where she is known as "Santa Brigida," and in England–where her name became Bride, as in "Bride of Christ," and "Bridget," echoing the name of the Irish saint,[57] and throughout the rest of Europe. Saint Catherine of Siena closely modeled her *acta*, her deeds, upon those of Saint Birgitta of Sweden. Chaucer, perhaps, satirized Bride in his portrait of the Wife of Bath in a patriarchal subversion of her matriarchal liberation. But Margery Kempe and Julian of Norwich followed reverently in her physical and spiritual footsteps in an *imitatio Brigidae*, an imitation of Bride. She gave to women of the later Middle Ages, especially in England, a major paradigm for their access to power.

Besides the *Revelations* or *Liber Celestis*, the *Heavenly Book*, which was copied out, and later printed, again and again, Bride had also written the *Regula Sancti Salvatoris*, the *Rule of the Holy Savior*, for her Order,[58] and the offices for her nuns to sing, the *Sermo Angelicus*, the *Conversation with the Angel*, and the *Cantus Sororum*, the *Sisters' Songs*. These texts were next enacted in flesh and blood by the nuns and monks of her mother house at Vadstena and innumerable daughter houses in Sweden, Finland, Denmark, England, Holland, France, Germany, Bavaria, Italy, Spain, Portugal, even Mexico, who in turn wrote out texts, hers and their own. Brian Stock has spoken of "Textual Communities," Roland Barthes in *Sade, Fourier, Loyola*, has spoken of the importance of texts which are enacted as systems and models by individuals and by groups in flesh and blood reality.[59] Usually it is men who create such written models for men and for women, St. Caesarius for his sister, St. Caesaria,[60] St. Augustine for his sister,[61] St. Benedict for his monks, and also for nuns,[62] St. Francis for his friars, and, unusually, St. Clare for the Poor Clare nuns, and Abelard, at Heloise's request, for her nuns of the Paraclete.[63] Bride's is the first instance (except for St. Clare) where the woman writes the Rule and establishes the Order.[64]

Renaissance, Humanist Florence celebrated Saint Bride–who had had such important contacts with Nicholas Acciaiuoli, Seneschal of Naples, and Lapa Acciaiuoli Buondelmonte, his sister and Bride's great friend. Boccaccio had dedicated his *De mulieribus claris*, *Of Famous Women*, to their sister Andrea Acciaiuoli.[65] Already Acciaiuoli had founded the Carthusian Certosa and been buried there (pp. 54-62). We find Francesca Papazura, Bride's landlady of the Campo dei Fiori, who had had Bride as her tenant from the end of 1354 to 1373, writing to the Acciaiuoli household requesting permission to place paintings in Bride's death room,[66] and we meet Francesca Papazuri in the pages of the canonization trial.[67] She had accompanied Bride to Assisi and Jerusalem and was therefore a most knowledgeable witness.[68] The Acciaiuoli reverence for Bride, in turn, caused

Antonio degli Alberti to give his palace, the Paradiso, for a Brigittine monastery, outside of Florence. Conversations had been held at the Paradiso degli Alberti in which Coluccio Salutati, Francesco Landino, and Marsilio Ficino participated.[69] In Italy, Bride's politico-religious prophecies are to be found in Renaissance manuscripts bound with letters of state penned by Francesco Petrarch, Leonardo Bruni Aretino, and other Humanist statesmen of power and influence and which also include those of her follower, St. Catherine of Siena.[70] Amidst vicissitudes on the part of the Alberti fortunes, and negotiations with Vadstena, the monastery of Paradiso was commenced twice, a daughter monastery being founded in Genoa.[71] Its members included daughters of the Medici, the Machiavelli and many other great Florentine names.

A particularly charming vignette demonstrating Bride's impact in this period is the account by Ser Lapo Mazzei, the Florentine lawyer, written in a letter to Francesco Datini, the merchant of Prato, speaking of his love for Bride's writings, whom he calls "Brisida," and his great desire to possess a codex of her *Revelations*, which he especially loved for saying that the only services Christ wanted were those performed with a free spirit and in the charity of love.[72] One can still read the actual letter the notary wrote from Florence at three o'clock in the morning to his friend in Prato as it is preserved *in situ*, in place, in the house of Francesco Datini.[73] Lapo Mazzei was the notary who cared for the legal matters in connection with Santa Maria Nuova, the Florentine hospital founded by Folco Portinari, the banker father of Dante Alighieri's Beatrice Portinari. That hospital is in use to this day.

Already, by the 1370s, literary traces of Bride's writings were to be found in English texts, their importance being especially stressed in the East Anglian region about Cambridge University, and also centering upon Oxford University.[74] The Carmelite Richard Lavenham, Richard II's confessor and Professor of Theology at Oxford, owned Bride's *Revelations* and was teaching that text at Oxford, likewise the Dominican Thomas Stubbs, around the year 1370.[75] Eric, King of Sweden, Norway and Denmark, in 1406, married Philippa, daughter of Henry IV and sister of Henry V. Her royal party returned to England after visiting Vadstena and Sir Henry Fitzhugh strongly recommended to leprous Henry IV that he found a similar house in penance for his murders of King Richard II and Archbishop Richard le Scrope.[76] Henry V brought the body of Richard II for burial in Westminster Abbey and founded Syon Abbey, in April, 1415, simultaneously with the Charterhouse of Jesus of Bethlehem at Sheen, ordering prayers for his father, " . . . for the souls of John, late Duke of Lancaster, our grandfather, and Blanche, his late wife, our grandmother," (who was elegized in Chaucer's *Book of the Duchess*). Henry declared before Agincourt, according to Shakespeare, "I have built/ Two chantries, where the sad and solemn priests/ Sing still for Richard's soul" (*Henry V*, 4. 1. 317-319). In the King's Charter for Syon it is stated that whichever kingdom has within it a Brigittine monastery, "there peace and tranquillity, by meditation of the same, should be perpetually established."[77] Pope Martin V approved the English Brigittine Rule in 1419,[78] Brentford's Syon Monastery had a magnificent library for its monks, filled with Humanist texts. This was, in the manner of these double monasteries, unavailable to the nuns. However, its contents were appreciated by such men as Thomas More.[79] Thomas Gascoigne, who had accompanied Sir Henry Fitzhugh to Sweden as his chaplain and who became Chancellor of Oxford University, supported the Brigittines, seeing to it that a copy of the process for her canonization was available at Oxford[80] and himself translating her life into Middle English. Similarly the Carthusians, at Sheen and at Mount Grace Priory, were interested in the Brigittine texts.[81] Numerous references are made to Magaret, Duchess of Clarence, in the manuscripts, Symon Wynter of Syon having been her personal minister.[82] Cecily, Duchess of York, Richard III's mother, had Bride's *Revelations* read to her.[83] Then, in 1430, Queen Philippa, sister to Henry V, died and was buried at Vadstena.

To the introduction of the Brigittine Order to England are due important manuscripts and printed books in Middle English written down by English men and women in these severe and literate women-centered monastic houses and also beyond their walls.[84] These manuscripts and books are beautiful, both their script and their illuminations, their type and their engravings, their illuminations strongly reminding one of the Franciscan Pseudo Bonaventura *Meditations on the Life of Christ*, except here the figures are more courtly and more Gothic.[85] The groundwork had already been laid with Anselm's writings to Anchoresses, women recluses and hermits, and those of the *Ancrene Wisse*, or *Rule for Anchoresses*, centered upon the imagery of the woman recluse, like the nun, as the "bride of Christ."[86] Had Martin Luther and Henry VIII's Reformation not dissolved such establishments in Sweden, Germany and England, these Brigittine houses could have provided for women, both in monastic orders and in the world, a paradigm for their education and their empowerment.[87]

What especially drew women to Bride was that she was a mother. Thus she appealed not only to celibate clergy but also to lay and especially married women. They stressed her linking of the body and the book, defying the requirement that for access to Latin one had to be virgin and/or celibate, giving up the body for the book. We have already read of the vision of the Virgin helping Bride in her childbirth with Cecilia.[88] One later story is of a woman in Rome whose seven previous pregnancies had all miscarried. She requested that Catherine give her something of Bride's clothing, wearing this for the rest of the pregnancy. The living child who was born was named "Brigida."[89] Another has already been given in the life of Saint Bride, the story of Elsebi Snara of Linköping and her dead child. St. Margaret was the patron saint of childbirth, because she had been swallowed by the devil as a dragon and had burst it, emerging free and safe from its womb. Women named Margaret particularly cultivated Saints Margaret and Birgitta, Margery Kempe of Lynn among them.[90] We learn of a woman in Trondheim in Norway named Margaret who had been paralysed and mute but to whom came a vision of a lady who said, "I am Birgitta of Vadstena who will cure you of your terminal illness, and you will go healed to my place and proclaim publically what grace has been done to you." Which she did.[91] It is likely that the miracles of healing given in the life and the canonization process, which generally occur with women, are an endorsement by these women concerning the empowerment they felt Bride had given to them.

Bride's women's textual community not only involved strictly enclosed nuns and aristocrats but lay women of humble origins as well. In the process for canonization it is clearly stated that Catherine of Flanders, Bride's maid servant fell gravely ill while they were returning from Bari, likely with appendicitis, and was given extreme unction, the others asking Peter Olavi to ask Bride to pray for her, believing that her prayers would cure Catherine. Bride prostrated herself on the floor and prayed, and Catherine of Flanders was freed from the illness and rose up cured and was able to journey on horseback quickly to Rome.[92] The passport for the journey to Bari was written out in 1369. In 1415, Margery Kempe, the mother of not eight but fourteen children, on her pilgrimage modeled on that of Saint Bride, stopped in Rome, staying at the English College, adjacent to the Casa di Santa Brigida, and talked with Bride's now very elderly servant, Catherine of Flanders, about her mistress, and was told that she was "Seynt Brydys mayden," Saint Bride's maid, and that Bride *"was goodly and meke to euery creatur and þat sche had a lawhyng cher,"* "had been gentle and kind to everyone and always shown a smiling face."[93] The host agreed with the maid, saying that Saint Bride was so humble he did not even realize that she was a great saint. Dame Margery visited the chamber in which Saint Bride had died and heard a Dutch priest preach there concerning her.[94] In turn, she kneeled upon the stone upon which Saint Bride was said to have kneeled when she had her vision of Christ telling her of her death.[95]

Dame Margery of Lynn and Norwich also was to have her Revelations written down as the 1436 *Book of Margery Kempe*, imitating that of Bride's 1372 *Revelations*. Then Margery visited the English Brigittine Monastery, Syon, at Sheen, in the 1430s,[96] and also Julian of Norwich, with whom she enjoyed many days of "holy dalyawns" and "comoyning in þe lofe of owyr Lord Ihesu Crist," of holy conversation and communion in the love of Christ.[97] The anchoress, Julian of Norwich, likewise wrote down her Revelations, her *Showings*, of her vision which came to her on May 13, at four in the morning, in 1373, and there is evidence she had already written such *Revelations* out as early as 1368. Birgitta's *Revelations* was already available in England and lectured on at Oxford University by 1370, three years before her death. We know that the influence of Bride was particularly strong in the area about Lynn and Norwich in East Anglia, influencing as well Ely and Cambridge, Lynn and Norwich being ports giving on to the North Sea and Scandinavia.[98] Thus Bride gave to these two other very disparate women, the hysterical Margery of Lynn and quiet Julian of Norwich, the same pattern for their lives, of women who could attain praise and respect—what Bride's text call "worship"— through their visions and their writings. Margery, who was illiterate, speaks of the books read to her, which include Hilton's book, "St. Bride's Book," the *Stimulus Amoris*, the *Prick of Love*, and the *Incendium Amoris*, the *Fire of Love*.[99]

Several scholars have discussed the interrelationships between Syon Monastery and the Charterhouses of Sheen in London and Mount Grace in Yorkshire, some observing that the sole surviving manuscript of the *Book of Margery Kempe*, modeled on that of Bride, came from Carthusian Mount Grace (the manuscript itself states that it is "Liber Montis Gracie. This boke is of Mountegrace").[100] Similarly were there ties betwen Carthusian Certosa, founded by Nicholas Acciaiuoli, and Brigittine Paradiso, founded by Antonio degli Alberti, in Florence. Similarly were there ties between German Carthusian monasteries and Brigittine houses. What is especially interesting is that not only is Margery's manuscript associated with the Charterhouse of Mount Grace but that the earliest manuscript of Julian's *Showings* is written out in 1413, noting that Julian of Norwich at that date was still alive, and which was to be annotated around 1500 by a scribe, James Grenehalgh, who was himself a Carthusian monk residing at Sheen, then Coventry and possibly Mount Grace. That manuscript, British Library, Add. 37,790, gives the Short Text of Julian's *Showings*, extracts of Birgitta's *Revelations* and the story of St. Cecilia. James Grenehalgh of Sheen usually annotated such texts for Joan Sewell, the Brigittine nun of Syon, constructing elaborate monograms with the initials of their two names.[101] Another manuscript, written around 1500, but giving as its original date of writing, 1368, at Westminster Cathedral, gives a First Text of Julian's *Showings*, which is clearly written on the model of Birgitta's *Revelations*, yet without including any of the material in connection with Julian's near-death vision of May 13, 1373.[102] The Long Text manuscripts are all much later.

The Middle English manuscript text which this book translates is the kind of text which could have been heard and read by Margery and Julian. It could have been known to the textual communities fostered by Carthusians and Brigittines in England. It most likely originated in Syon Monastery before 1450. It would either have been compiled from the official text such as British Library Harley 612, formerly Syon Monastery Library 64, copied out in Latin from the original manuscript at Vadstena Monastery, today in the Uppsala University Library, C621, or it may–more likely–even represent an earlier original ordering of Saint Bride's Book. That it is not listed in the Syon Monastery Catalogue is plausible because this Catalogue listed only the Latin texts belonging to the men's library, which therefore allows us to consider this as a vernacular book for Syon's nuns' library.[103] Brigittine monasteries, like the later American Shaker establishments, kept the two sexes rigorously apart while they co-existed in the same establishment.[104] Two scribes shaped this text in the fifteenth century. The male editor of the Early English Text Society volume, William Patterson Cummings, spoke of the scribes as male, but the second could have been a women scribe. Rubrication in red and blue capitals divide the black ink body of the text. The parchment in some places is patched together. It was acquired from the Thomas Phillips Collection by Robert Garrett in 1906 and placed on deposit at Princeton the following year where it came to join the will of Aethelgifu, an Anglo-Saxon noblewoman, in which she divided up her worldly goods shortly before the supposed Apocalypse of the year 1000.[105]

The 1492 printed edition of her Sibylline and Apocalyptic writings shows Saint Bride distributing God's words, her Book, to popes and emperors and kneeling women and men (p. 31).[106] Similarly did the printed edition of Hrotswitha's writings show her presenting her book, prompted by her abbess, to her emperor.[107] Thus the shift from manuscript to print still preserved the record of the power book-writing women could wield.[108] Emily Dickinson, centuries later, would shadowily evoke that dream women have had through time, of making emperors stop their destructive worldliness and lust after power and listen to women's silenced wisdom.[109]

Notes

1 Biblioteca Apostolica Vaticana, Urb. lat. 104.

2 Karl Young, "The Procession of the Prophets," *The Drama of the Medieval Church* (Oxford: Clarendon Press, 1953) 1: 125-171. The Salerno Play specifies that the Sibyl is the Eritrean one, "Sibilla Erythraea," p. 136.

3 *The Letters of Abelard and Heloise*, p. 181.

4 For example, Florence, Biblioteca Nazionale, Magl. II.I.249; Siena, Biblioteca Communale, I.V.25/26 (text written by St. Catherine of Siena's secretary, Christopher Di Ganno); British Library, Arundel 66, which also includes Merlin's prophecies; Cotton Vespasian E. VII, linking Bride, fols 116ᵛ-117, Sibyl, Merlin, Richard le Scrope; Royal 13 E X, Scottish Black Book of Paisley; Bodleian Library, Laud 588 (Archbishop Laud's compilation of prophetic writings from the Sibyls, Merlin, Hildegard of Bingen, Joachim of Flora, etc.); Ashmole Roll 27, linking Bride, Merlin, Sibyl, Henry of Derby, Richard le Scrope; Cotton Vespasian E. VIII, fols. 116ᵛ-117 on Bride's Revelation to Kings of France and England about peace, following upon prophecies of the Sibyl and Merlin and contemporary events concerning Archbishop Richard le Scrope; Nostradamus. Two late texts in the British Library are a Black Letter printed German book, anthologizing the Sibyl, Bride and Joachim, and a printed indulgence to protect a house from plague, purporting to have been found in a tomb in Jerusalem and given by Christ to St. Bride, Widow, Queen of Hungary (*sic*). See Eric Colledge, "*Epistola Solitarii ad reges:* Alphonse of Pecha as Organizer of Birgittine and Urbanist Propaganda," *Medieval Studies* 18 (1956), 19-40, esp. p. 20.

5 Jørgensen 2: 255.

6 Natalie Zemon Davis observed that seventeenth and eighteenth century French women writers had themselves portrayed as the female Muses, in frontispieces of their books, resonant with the Sibyls. Elizabeth Barrett Browning wrote her woman's epic poem, *Aurora Leigh*, in the Sibylline numbering of nine books. For the medieval reader Boethius' *Consolation of Philosophy* gave the paradigm of a learned woman, Wisdom, teaching truth to men.

7 British Libary, Harley 612; Cambridge, Corpus Christi College 404; Oxford, Bodleian, Ashmole Roll 27.

8 Uppsala University Library MS C86, written by Alfonso giving Bride's pilgrimage to Jerusalem, is prefaced by *Scala Virtutum*.

9 Carl Nordenfalk, "Saint Bridget of Sweden as Represented in Illuminated Manuscripts," in *De artibus opuscula XL: Essays in Honor of Erwin Panofsky*, ed. Millard Meiss (New York: New York University Press, 1961), pp. 371-393, esp. 376-8, figures 3-4, Palermo, Biblioteca Nazionale MS IV. G. 2. and New York, Pierpont Morgan Library MS M. 498; artist of the latter could be Robert di Oderisio of Naples in 1375-1377; manuscript was originally owned by Alfonso's Hieronomyte Order in Genoa; was used at the 1391 canonization; at Vadstena in 1417; may next have been at the Council of Constance, 1417-18, when Jean Gerson was attacking Bride of Sweden's veracity. Nordenfalk, p. 376, notes unique use in this manuscript of Virgil in mandorla appearing to Bride.

10 Foliation not given in volume, woodblock appears on the folio before the *Prologus libri questionum. Liber quintus.* We know that two monks came from Vadstena to Lübeck with manuscripts to oversee the production and editing of the *Revelations.* It is possible they brought this manuscript with them.

[11] British Library, Harley 4800, fol. 107. See complete translation of *Revelations*V in *Birgitta of Sweden: Life and Selected Writings,*ed. Marguerite Tjader Harris, Albert Ryle Kezel, Tore Nyberg (New York: Paulist Press, 1990), pp. 99-156.

[12] Erwin Panofsky, *Idea: A Concept in Art Theory*, trans. Joseph J.S. Peake (New York: Harper and Row, 1968).

[13] Susan Groag Bell, "Medieval Women Book Owners: Arbiters of Lay Piety and Ambassadors of Culture," *Signs* 7 (1982): 742-68, republished in *Women and Power in the Middle Ages*, ed. Mary Erler and Maryanne Kowaleski (Athens: University of Georgia Press, 1988), pp. 149-187; Gail McMurray Gibson, "The Thread of Life in the Hand of the Virgin," republished in *Equally in God's Image: Women in the Middle Ages*, ed. Julia Bolton Holloway, Joan Bechtold, Constance Wright (New York: Peter Lang, 1990), pp. 46-54.

[14] *SRSMA*, 227; *Revelationes* texts: British Library, Harley 612; *Revelationes Sancte Birgitte* (Lübeck: Ghotan, 1492); Sancta Birgitta, *Revelacions* I, ed. Undhagen (Uppsala: Almquist and Wiksell, 1977), V, ed. Birger Bergh (1971), VII, ed. Bergh (1967).

[15] Jacobus de Voragine, *The Golden Legend*, trans. Granger Ryan and Helmut Ripperger (New York: Arno Press, 1969), pp. 269-276.

[16] The legend is a prototype for Ingmar Bergman's film, *Virgin Spring*.

[17] Jørgensen 1: 30-31.

[18] Comtesse de Flavigny, *Sainte Brigitte de Suéde, sa vie, ses révélations et son oeuvre* (Paris: Leday, 1892), p. 30, notes that it would be translated into Swedish by a Brigittine monk in the fifteenth century who was chaplain to Charles VIII.

[19] *ASS* Oct 4: 507F; Jørgensen 1: 31.

[20] Jørgensen 1: 117, 279; Uppsala, University Library, MS. C240, formerly in the Vadstena convent library, with faded inscription: "*Hunc librum qui intitulatur doctrina Bernardi ad sororem portavit beata mater nostra sancta Birgitta continue in sinu suo, ideo inter reliquas suas asservandus est,*" "This book of Bernard's teaching to his sister, our blessed mother, Saint Bride, carried always in her pocket, therefore it is to be kept amongst her relics," followed by Spanish writing concerning its contents; photograph of its binding, which is like an envelope with a flap to close it, upon that a Swedish button, similar to those found on other Brigittine manuscripts: Aron Andersson and Anne Marie Franzén, *Birgittareliker* (Stockholm: Almquist and Wiksells, 1975), pp. 54-55.

[21] Anthony Luttrell, "Englishwomen as Pilgrims to Jerusalem: Isolda of Parewastell, 1365," in *Equally in God's Image*, pp. 184-197, esp. 185, 193, discussing Joseph F. Michaud, *Bibliothèque des Croisades* (Paris: Ducollet, 1829), III, 369-375; M. de Florival, "Un Pèlerinage au XIIᵉ Siècle: Marguerite de Jérusalem et Thomas de Froidmont," *Bulletin de la Societé académique de Laon*, 26 (1887).

[22] Jørgensen 1: 117.

[23] *ASS*, Oct IV, 403D, 490D. Especially inspiring at the Brigittine Congress in Rome, 1991, was hearing the lesson of Judith read by a woman in Swedish at the Papal Mass in the Piazza Farnese, by the Church of St. Birgitta.

[24] *ASS* Oct 4: 393A.

[25] *ASS* Oct 4:403D; *Myroure of oure Lady*, pp. 36,59.

[26] Margaret Clausdotter making this comparison, *SRSMA*, 208.

[27] Jørgensen 1: 48.

[28] *ASS* Oct 4: 406D.

[29] *ASS* Oct 4: 435E,F; *SRSMA*, p. 223, however, recounts Count Nicholas of Orsini noting, during the canonization trial, that Bride did not know sufficient Latin to speak with Urban V face to face.

[30] See, for instance, *Mirroure of oure Lady*, pp. 18-20.

[31] Jørgensen 2: 172-173.

[32] Pp. 75-84; Jørgensen 2: 184-185. The documents concerning Bride's relationship with the Acciaiuoli household are numerous and can be traced in the Florentine State Archives.

[33] Jørgensen 2: 193-194.

[34] *Gesta Romanorum: Entertaining Moral Stories; Invented by the Monks as a Fireside Recreation, and Commonly Applied in Their Discourses from the Pulpit: Whence the Most Celebrated of Our Own Poets and Others, from the Earliest Times, have Extracted their Plots*, trans. and ed. Charles Swan and Wynnard Hooper (New York: Dover, 1959).

[35] Franz Kafka, *Parables and Paradoxes* (New York: Schocken Books, 1961); Paul Gordon, "Kafka's Parable "On Parables,'" *Cithara*, 27 (1988), 11-19. One appreciates Saint Bride's laughter, especially hearing it in these stories.

[36] *Revelations* 4:140; Jørgensen 2:226.

[37] Jørgensen 2: 236,240-41.

[38] Jørgensen 2: 330.

[39] Stockholm, Kungl Biblioteket MS A65.

[40] See especially Stockholm, Kungl Biblioteket MS A12.

[41] *ASS* Oct 4: 406A, "*ubi de Christo in nube lucida S. Birgittae apparente . . . cum primo hujus modi revelationes inciperet habere et vidisset nubem lucidam, audissetque vocem quasi hominis dicentem: 'Mulier, audi me.'*" "Where Christ appeared to St. Bride in a shining cloud . . . when she first began to have these revelations in this manner and would see the shining cloud, hearing a voice as of a man, saying, 'Woman, hear me.'"

[42] *ASS* Oct 4: 486A, "*vidit inter orationes suas nocte nubem lucidavi, et in nube sedentem virginem, habentem librum in manus sua,*" "he saw between his nocturnal prayers a shining cloud and in the cloud sitting the Virgin, having a book in her hand."

[43] Plato, *Symposium*, trans. W. Hamilton (Harmondsworth: Penguin, 1957); Cicero, *Somnium Scipionis*, ed. James A. Kleist (New York: Schwarz, 1915).

[44] Ephraem Syri, *Hymni et Sermones* (Mechlin: Archiepiscopal Press, 1882); *The Kontakia of Romanos*, trans. Marjorie Carpenter (Columbia: University of Missouri Press, 1970).

[45] Pseudo-Bonaventure, *Meditations on the Life of Christ*, trans. Isa Ragusa and Rosalie Green (Princeton: Princeton University Press, 1961).

[46] The letter she sent to these kings by Bishop Hemming of Äbo and Prior Peter Olavi of Alvastra survives in Cambridge, Corpus Christi College 404, and elsewhere, Edmund Colledge, "Epistola solitarii," p. 32.

[47] See John Williams, *Early Spanish Manuscript Illuminations* (New York: Brazillier, 1977); Florens Deuchler, Jeffrey M. Hoffeld, Helmut Nickel, *The Cloisters Apocalypse* (New York: Metropolitan Museum of Art, 1971), 2 vols; Barbara Nolan, *The Gothic Visionary Perspective* (Princeton: Princeton University Press, 1977); Jesse M. Gelrich, *The Idea of the Book in the Middle Ages: Language Theory, Mythology, and Fiction* (Ithaca: Cornell University Press, 1985).

[48] *Pearl*, ed. E.V. Gordon (Oxford: Clarendon Press, 1953).

[49] Pp. 92-93; Jørgensen 2:133.

[50] Jørgensen 2: 134, suggests the glass globe is evoked by the shape of the royal seal.

[51] I borrow Barbara Tuchman's title for her book, *A Distant Mirror: The Calamitous Fourteenth Century* (New York: Knopf, 1978), in which she draws the analogy between the Black Death and nuclear holocaust. In our own time the film director, Ingmar Bergman, has used much Brigittine material, for instance in his *Wild Strawberries* and in the scene in *The Seventh Seal* where Mia, Jof and the Knight eat wild strawberries, in recollection of the story where a little great granddaughter, likewise named Bride, when dying, and pleading for strawberries in the dead of winter, was told by Saint Bride's spirit where they could be found, under her cloak: *ASS* Oct 4:389B; Jørgensen 2:154-55; in *Seventh Seal* when the Knight returns to his castle at the time of the Black Death after many futile years upon the Crusades, it is to hear his wife Karin (the Swedish form of Bride's daughter, Catherine) reading from the vast manuscript of the Apocalypse, the film title referring to the seven seals upon the book, within the book of the Apocalypse, which are each opened in turn at the ending of the world. Vadstena Apocalypse commentary manuscripts include Stockholm A7, Uppsala, C104.

[52] Pp. 132-137; Jørgensen 2: 246-247.

[53] J.W. Robinson, "The York Play of the Nativity," *Studies in Fifteenth-Century Stagecraft* (Kalamazoo: Medieval Institute Publications, 1991), pp. 64-65,80.

[54] *Rev.* 7:24; *Processus*, pp. 385-6; British Library MS Claudius B1, ed. Roger Ellis, EETS 291, pp. 485-487. The manuscript illuminates the scene exquisitely at fol. 269, showing the Virgin in regal ermine robes, Saint Bride in her simple widow's garb, both worshiping the Child laid upon the ground beside the manger and the ox and ass. One can see this scene frescoed on the wall as one enters Santa Maria Novella in Florence. See also Florence, Biblioteca Nazionale MS, Magl. II.II.393, illuminations.

[55] Panofsky, *Early Netherlandish Painting*, p. 158.

[56] For the term, "textual community," Brian Stock, *Implications of Literacy: Written Language and Models of Interpretation in the Eleventh and Twelfth Centuries* (Princeton: Princeton University Press, 1983), who sees the importance of a group of people brought together through a shared knowledge of a written text.

[57] William Patterson Cummings, in *The Revelations of Saint Birgitta, Edited from the Fifteenth-Century Manuscript in the Garrett Collection in the Library of Princeton University*, p. xxiii, notes that the Irish *brighid* derives from *brigh*, virtue, strength.

[58] Roger Ellis, *Viderunt eam filie Syon: The Spirituality of the English House of a Medieval Contemplative Order from its Beginnings to the Present Day* (Salzburg: Institut für Anglistik, 1984), Analecta Cartusiana, 68, ed. James Hogg, presents a close study in English of the Brigittine Rule.

[59] Roland Barthes, *Loyola, Sade, Fourier* (Paris: Seuil, 1971).

[60] A.D. 501-573: Maria C. McCarthy, *The Rule for Nuns of St. Caesarius of Arles* (Washington: Catholic University Press, 1960).

[61] Augustine, Epistola 211, *Patrologia Latina*, ed. J.P. Migne, 33:958-67.

[62] *The Rule of St. Benedict in English*, ed. Timothy Fry, O.S.B. (Collegeville: Liturgical Press, 1982).

[63] "Abelard's Rule for Religious Women," ed. T.P. McLaughlin, C.S.B., *Mediaeval Studies* 18 (1956):241-292; *The Letters of Abelard and Heloise*, trans. Betty Radice (Harmondsworth: Penguin, 1974).

[64] Manuscripts produced by her Order and her circle contain many women's texts, Mechtild, Hildegard, Julian and Margery's among them. Mary Bateson, *Catalogue of the Library of Syon Monastery, Isleworth* (Cambridge: Cambridge University Press, 1898), p. 120, notes Syon had five Mechtild manuscripts, M22,47,59,94,98, in the men's library.

[65] Jørgensen 2: 169.

[66] Letter in Florentine State Archives, written by her in 1374 to Madonna Lapa, Carte Strozziane, serie prima, CCCLII. e.4,352, serie secunda, CXVIII, fol. 65; transcribed, Isak Collijn, p. 20, speaking of Francesca Papazura's desire to place a painting of the Crucifixion of Christ and his Mother and St. John the Evangelist, Saint James and Saints Catherine of Alexandria and Mary Magdalen, and then also Saints Peter and Paul and Saints Agnes and John the Baptist, in that chamber. The request reflects the favorite saints of the Brigittine household. It is also a "Holy Conversation" painting. Paul Riant noted that a Casa di Santa Brigida painting of Bride, Catherine, Madonna and Child, and two sainted queens came to be at the University of Notre Dame, Indiana, is now in Darien, Connecticut.

[67] Vatican Library, Ottob. lat. 90, fol. 99, "Domina Francescha Papaçura"; Nicholas Acciaiuoli being discussed there, fol. 120; Uppsala University Library, MS C251, fol. 16; A. Jefferies Collins, *The Bridgettine Breviary of Syon Abbey from the Manuscript with the English Rubrics F.4.11 at Magdalene College, Cambridge* (Worcester: Stanbrook Abbey Press, 1969), Henry Bradshaw Society, 96, p. xxviii; the *Liber de Miraculis Beate Brigide de Suecia*, Codex San Lorenzo in Panisperna, 1374, now in the archives of the Franciscan Curia Generale, Rome, notes that she gave the Casa di Santa Brigida to Vadstena in 1383; Monasterio di Santa Brigida detto del Paradiso 322, 4, fol 17, transcription of request from Francesca Papazuri and the Church of St. Bridget in Rome to the Pope.

[68] Jørgensen 2: 107-108.

[69] *Il Paradiso degli Alberti*, ed. Wesselofsky.

[70] Francesco Petrarch, 1304-1374; Leonardo Bruni, 1369-1444, Colluccio Salutati, 1331-1406, Nicholas Acciaiuoli 1310-1365, were all letter writers and statesmen who shaped the Italian Renaissance. See, for instance, Florence, Biblioteca Nazionale, Magliabechiano II.II.90, fol. 47.

[71] Hans Cnattingius, *Studies in the Order of St. Bridget of Sweden* (Uppsala: Almquist and Wiksells, 1963), pp. 29-39.

[72] Iris Origo, *The Merchant of Prato* (Harmondsworth: Penguin, 1963), p. 220.

[73] Lapo Mazzei to Francesco Datini, 1096, 13 November, 1395, Archivio di Stato di Prato; published in Cesare Guasti, *Lettere di un Notaro a un Mercante del Secolo XIV* (Florence: Le Monnier, 1880), pp. 118-123, in which he notes her likeness to St. Francis, especially in connection with the five wounds, the stigmata, and terming her "*quello ambasciadore che Cristo ci manda*," "this ambassador sent by Christ." Magl. II.III.270, fols. 147-148[v], records miracle of Ser Piero di Ser Mino da Montevarchi, elected Chancellor, became deathly ill, saw devil and Bride, joined Paradiso and became its Prior.

[74] *Liber Celestis*, ed. Ellis, p. xii.

[75] *ASS* Oct 4:409A, "*revelationes in scholis Oxoniensibus et in cathedris publicis magistralibus exposuerunt magni sua aetate doctores Thomas Stubbes, Dominicanus, Ricardus Lavynham, Carmelita, et adhunc alii ejus generis multi circa annum domino MCCCLXX*" "The *Revelations* were being much taught at that time in the schools at Oxford and from public lectures, the Dominican Thomas Stubbes, the Carmelite

Richard Lavenham and others reaching many people around the year 1370"; British Library MS Royal 7 C IX; EETS 178, ed. Cummings, p. xxix; Bodleian MS. 169. Later, Hoccleve, Audelay and Gascoigne wrote about Bride. In wills we find Elizabeth Sywardby, 1468, Margaret Purdawnce, 1481, Cecily, Duchess of York, 1495, leaving copies in English of St. Bridget's *Revelations*, ed. Cummings, p. xxxviii; see also Gail McMurray Gibson, *Theater of Devotion*, pp. 21,78.

[76] Richard le Scrope had connections to both Henry Lord Fitzhugh and to Thomas Gascoigne. Lord Fitzhugh sought to donate Cherry Hinton in East Anglia for the Brigittines, that letter of donation dated 1406 being at Uppsala. Thomas Gascoigne, whose uncle William Gascoigne refused to preside over Bishop le Scrope's trial, traveled to both Sweden and Rome visiting Brigittine houses.

[77] *Myroure of oure Lady*, p. 61.

[78] *ASS* Oct 4:477C,E, Martin V's Bull dated Florence, April 7, 1419; Sargent, p. 228.

[79] Bateson, *Catalogue of Syon*, pp. 80-102. It contained such texts as Aulus Gellius, the Sibylline Prophecies, Bernard on the Song of Songs, Ficino, Plato, Erasmus, Ysidore, Josephus, Bede, the *Gesta Romanorum*, John of Salisbury on Thomas Becket, Walter Hilton, Richard Hampole, Lives of Mary Magdalen, Martha, Lazarus, Margaret and Catherine, Cicero, Plotinus, Iamblichus, Aristotle, Boethius, Aquinas, Psellus, Gregory, Zosimus on Mary of Egypt, Jerome on Saints Paul and Anthony, Bessarion, treatises against Wyclif, and many more.

[80] "*ego, Thomas Gascoigne . . . feci scribi . . . in vitulinus Oxoniae, secundum copiam illius libri attestacionum pro canonizacione beate Birgittae*," having these copied from the papal register of Martin V, *Acta et Processus*, ed. Isak Collijn, p. xx.

[81] James Hogg, "Mount Grace Charterhouse and Late Medieval English Spirituality," *Analecta Cartusiana* 82 (1980):1-53; M. Sargent, "The Transmission by the English Carthusians of Some Late Medieval Spiritual Writings," *Journal of Ecclesiastical History* 27 (1976):225-240; E. Margaret Thompson, *The Carthusian Order in England* (London: SPCK, 1930).

[82] Lambeth Palace Library MS 432; British Library Add. MS 40006; St. John's College, Cambridge, MS 250; A.J. Collins, p. xxxix.

[83] *Book of Margery Kempe*, p. lxvi, citing *Ordinances of Royal Household*, p. 37.

[84] David Knowles, and R. Neville Hadcock, *Medieval Religous Houses: England and Wales* (New York: St. Martin's Press, 1972), pp. 202; Colin Platt, *The Abbeys and Priories of Medieval England* (New York: Fordham University Press, 1984), pp. 177-184.

[85] Pseudo-Bonaventure, *Meditations on the Life of Christ*, were written for women, and therefore form part of the women's textual community spreading throughout Europe.

[86] Elizabeth Robertson, "An Anchorhold of her Own: Female Anchoritic Literature in Thirteenth-Century England," in *Equally in God's Image*, pp. 170-183; *Ancrene Wisse*, ed. C. D'Evelyn Francis (Oxford: EETS, 1962); ed. Geoffrey Shepherd (London: Nelson, 1959).

[87] David Knowles, *Bare Ruined Choirs: The Dissolution of English Monasteries* (Cambridge: Cambridge University Press, 1976), pp. 96-108, p. 99, telling of Queen Ann Boleyn distributing English Prayer Books in choir for the Latin psalters and antiphonaries; Cnattingius, p. 21, noting that at Henry VIII's Dissolution of the Monasteries this was the largest convent for nuns in England. Evidence of the sisters'

bookishness, a budget item for 23 new pairs of spectacles, plus mending of old ones, *Myroure of oure Lady*, p. xxvi.

[88] *ASS* Oct 4: 469E; *SRSMA*, 192.

[89] *ASS* Mar 3: 515C.

[90] Lynn's church is St. Margaret's Church, Norwich Cathedral has a most beutiful fifteenth-century painting of St. Margaret in one of its chapels.

[91] *Acta et Processus Cananizaciones Beate Birgitte*, ed Isak Collijn (Uppsala: Almquist and Wiksells, 1924-1931), p. 117. Bride had pilgrimaged to Trondheim on foot from the region around Vadstena. It took me a night and half a day to travel from Stockholm to Trondheim by train, the distance being so great.

[92] *SRSMA*, 226, "*quod Katerina de Flandria, ancilla dicte domine Brigide infirmata fuit graviter ad morten de febribus et de punctura lateris sinistri taliter, quod tractabant et facere extremam unccionem . . . supplicavit eidem domine Brigide matri sue, quod oraret pro illa infirma credens quod oracionibus illius curaretur et fieret sana, et tunc dominus Petrus confessor predictus eidem mandavit, et tunc ipsa extendit se totam in pavimento et ibi oravit pro illa, et statim in momento liberata fuit illa infirma et surrexit illico sana et equitavit et arriuit iter versus Romam.*" Also, Vatican MS, Ottob. lat. 90, fol. 4^v.

[93] Jørgensen 2: 299; *The Book of Margery Kempe*, ed. Sanford B. Meech and Hope Emily Allen, EETS 212 (London: Oxford University Press, 1940), p. 95, which notes that "S. bridis madyn" is rubricated, noted, in red, in the margin of the text.

[94] Margery Kempe stayed at the English College while in Rome, adjacent to the Casa di Santa Brigida: Helen M.D. Redpath, *God's Ambassadress: St. Bridget of Sweden* (Milwaukee: Bruce, 1947), pp. 90-91.

[95] P. 95; Gibson, pp. 47-65, especially discusses Margery's identification with Bride.

[96] *Book of Margery Kempe*, pp. 245-6, the unique manuscript noting in red in margin, beside "Schene" in text, "syon"; Redpath, p. 178.

[97] *Book of Margery Kempe*, pp. 42-43.

[98] Tore Nyberg, *Klostergründungen des Mittelalters* (Leiden: C.W.K. Gleerup, 1965), p. 74. See also Lambeth Palace MS 432, with Brigittine material, fol. 87, on 1350, Norwich, miracle. Cardinal Adam Easton who so strongly advocated Bride's canonization was a monk from Norwich Priory. The initial English Brigittine house was at Cherry Hinton, near Cambridge.

[99] *Book of Margery Kempe*, chapters 17, 58. B.A. Windeatt (*The Book of Margery Kempe* [Harmondsworth: Penguin, 1985]), p. 17, notes that Margery's friend, the Carthusian Alan of Lynn, indexed the *Revelations* of Bridget of Sweden. Such indices are common among the manuscripts. In chapter 20 Christ tells Margery that Bride never saw him this way, so she will also be famous. Hilton and Rolle's writings frequently occur in Brigittine MSS, including those in Sweden.

[100] Michael G. Sargent, *James Grenehalgh as Textual Critic* (Salzburg: Institut für Anglistik, 1984), 2 vols; S.S. Hussey, "The Audience for the Middle English Mystics," pp. 117-118, and Ann M. Hutchison, "Devotional Reading in the Monastery and in the Late Medieval Household," p. 215, both in *De Cella in Seculum: Religion and Secular Life and Devotion in Late Medieval England*, ed. Michael G. Sargent (Cambridge: Brewer, 1989); Edmund Colledge and James Walsh, "Editing Julian of Norwich's Revelations: A Progress Report," *Medieval Studies*, 38 (1976), 404.

[101] Michael Sargent, *James Grenehalgh as Textual Critic* (Salzburg: Institut für Anglistik and Amerikanistik, 1984), 1:75-109.

[102] I shall publish this text shortly.

[103] Bateson, *Catalogue of Syon*, pp. xiii-xiv, Mary Carpenter Erler, "Syon Abbey's Care for Books: Its Sacristan's Account Rolls, 1506/7-1535/6, *Scriptorium*, 39 (1985), 293-307.

[104] Personal observations of architectural structures of the Bavarian Brigittine cloister, Altomünster, and of Kentucky's Shaker Pleasant Hill. Amy Stechler Burns and Ken Burns, *The Shakers: Hands to Work and Hearts to God: The History and Visions of the United Society of Believers in Christ's Second Appearing from 1774 to the Present* (Hong Kong: Aperture, 1987).

[105] Ed. Cummings, pp. xi-xvi, xxi-xxii.

[106] *ASS* Oct IV 407B, noting that of this edition 80 copies were printed on paper, 16 on parchment; two Vadstena monks oversaw its production; British Library copy was owned by a relative of Ann Boleyn.

[107] Roswitha presenting her book, with Abbess Gerberga, Emperor Otto II, Düreer, 1501; reproduced in *The Plays of Roswitha*, trans. Christopher St. John (London: Chatto and Windus, 1923; Salem, New Hampshire: Ayer, 1989, rprt.), frontispiece.

[108] For Brigittine publications in England, see Martha W. Driver, "Pictures in Print: Late Fifteenth- and Early Sixteenth-Century English Religious Books for Lay Readers," in *De Cella*, ed. Michael G. Sargent, pp. 229-244.

[109] Julia Bolton Holloway, "Death and the Emperor in Dante, Browning, Dickinson and Stevens," *Studies in Medievalism* 2:3 (1983): 67-72.

Suggestions for Further Reading

I. St. Birgitta of Sweden

Andersson, Aron. *St. Birgitta and the Holy Land*. Trans. Louise Setterwall. Stockholm: Museum of National Antiquities, 1973.

_____ and Anne Marie Franzén. *Birgittareliker*. Stockholm: Alquist and Wiksells, 1975.

Bechtold, Joan. "St. Birgitta: The Disjunction between Women and Ecclesiastical Male Power." In *Equally in God's Image: Women in the Middle Ages*. Ed. Julia Bolton Holloway, Joan Bechtold and Constance Wright. New York: Peter Lang, 1990. Pp. 88-102.

Birgitta of Sweden. *Doom of Kings*. Trans. Patrick O'Moore. Toledo, Ohio: Clarino Press, 1982.

_____. *The Liber Celestis of St. Bridget of Sweden: The Middle English Version in British Library MS Claudius BI, Together with a Life of the Saint from the Same Manuscript*. Ed. Roger Ellis. London: EETS, 1987. EETS 291.

_____. *Life and Selected Writings*. Ed. Marguerit Tjader Harris, Albert Ryle Kezel and Tore Nyberg. New York: Paulist Press, 1990.

_____. *The Revelations of Saint Birgitta, Edited from the Fifteenth-Century Manuscript in the Garrett Collection in the Library of Princeton University*. Ed. William Patterson Cumming. London: EETS, 1929.

Butkovich, Anthony. *Iconography: St. Birgitta of Sweden*. Los Angeles: Ecumenical Foundation of America, 1969.

_____. *Revelations: Saint Birgitta of Sweden*. Los Angeles: Ecumenical Foundation of America, 1972.

Colledge, Edmund. "*Epistola Solitarii ad Reges*: Alphonse of Pecha as Organizer of Birgittine and Urbanist Propaganda." *Mediaeval Studies* 18 (1956): 19-49.

Ellis, Roger. "A Revelation and its Editions: The *Epistola Solitarii* of Alphonse of Jaen and Book VI, ch. 52, of the *Liber Celestis* of St. Bridget of Sweden." *Vision et Perception Fondamentales, Actes du Colloque 20 et 21 juin, 1981*. Ed. R. Maisonneuve, I.R.I.S. Association Internationale (Lyon, 1982), 78-81.

Jönsson, Arne. *Alfonso of Jaén: His Life and Works with Critical Editions of the Epistolaria Solitarii, the Informaciones and the Epistola Servi Christi* (Lund: Lund University Press, 1989).

Jørgensen, Johannes. *Saint Bridget of Sweden*. Trans. Ingeborg Lund. London: Longmans, Green, 1954. 2 vols.

_____. *Saint Catherine of Siena*. Trans. Ingeborg Lund. New York: Longmans, Green, 1938.

Messenius, Johannes. *Chronologia Sanctae Birgittae: A Critical Edition with Introduction and Commentary*. Ed. Ann-Mari Jönson. Lund: Lund University Press, 1988.

Nordenfalk, Carl. "Saint Bridget of Sweden as Represented in Illuminated Manuscripts." In *De artibus opuscula XL: Essays in Honor of Erwin Panofsky*. Ed. Millard Meiss. New York: New York University Press, 1961. Pp. 371-393 and 38 figures.

Redpath, Helen M.D. *God's Ambassadress: St. Bridget of Sweden*. Milwaukee: Bruce, 1947.

II. Saints, Nuns, Widows, Pilgrims

Abelard and Heloise. *The Letters of Abelard and Heloise*. Harmondsworth: Penguin, 1974.

Augustine. Letter 211. In *Letters*. Trans. Sr. Wilfrid Parsons. New York: Fathers of the Church, 1956.

Bell, Rudulph. *Holy Anorexia*. Chicago: University of Chicago Press, 1985.

Bell, Susan Groag. "Medieval Women Book Owners: Arbiters of Lay Piety and Ambassadors of Culture." *Signs* 7 (1982): 742-68, republished in *Women and Power in the Middle Ages*. ed. Mary Erler and Maryanne Kowaleski (Athens: University of Georgia Press, 1988), pp. 149-187.

Benedict. *The Rule of St. Benedict in English*. Ed. Timothy Fry, O.S.B. Collegeville: The Liturgical Press, 1982.

Brown, Judith C. *Immodest Acts: The Life of a Lesbian Nun in Renaissance Italy*. New York: Oxford University Press, 1986.

Brown, Peter. *The Cult of the Saints: Its Rise and Function in Latin Christianity*. Chicago: University of Chicago Press, 1982.

Bugge, John. *Virginitas: An Essay in the History of a Medieval Ideal*. The Hague: Nijhoff, 1975.

Bynum, Caroline Walker. *Holy Feast and Holy Fast: The Religious Significance of Food to Medieval Women*. Berkeley: University of California Press, 1987.

_____. *Jesus as Mother: Studies in the Spirituality of the High Middle Ages*. Berkeley: University of California Press, 1982.

Christina of Markyate. *The Life of Christina of Markyate*. Ed. C. H. Talbot. Oxford: Clarendon Press, 1959.

Clay, Rotha M. *Hermits and Anchorites of England*. London: Methuen, 1914.

Cutts, Edward L. "Consecrated Widows of the Middle Ages." In *Scenes and Characters of the Middle Ages*. London: Virtue, 1902. Pp. 21-22, 120-194.

Daichman, Graciela S. *Wayward Nuns in Medieval Literature*. Syracuse:

Syracuse University Press, 1986.

Duff, Nora. *Matilda of Tuscany: La Gran Donna d'Italia*. London: Methuen, 1909.

Eckenstein, Lina. *Woman Under Monasticism: Chapters on Saint-Lore and Convent Life Between A.D. 500 and A.D. 1500*. New York: Russell and Russell, 1963.

Egeria. *"Peregrinatio Aetheriae." Egeria: Diary of a Pilgrimage*. Trans. George E. Gingras. New York: Newman Press, 1970.

Equally in God's Image: Women in the Middle Ages. Ed. Julia Bolton Holloway, Joan Bechtold and Constance Wright. Berne: Peter Lang, 1990.

Ferrante, Joan M. "The Education of Women in the Middle Ages in Theory, Fact and Fantasy." In *Beyond their Sex: Learned Women of the European Past*. Ed. Patricia H. Labalme. New York: New York University Press, 1984. Pp. 9-42.

Finucane, Ronald C. *Miracles and Pilgrims: Popular Beliefs in Medieval England*. London: Book Club Associates, 1977.

Graham, Stephen. *With the Russian Pilgrims to Jerusalem*. London: Macmillan, 1913.

Harley, Marta Powell. *A Revelation of Purgatory by an Unknown Fifteenth-Century Woman Visionary: Introduction, Critical Text and Translation*. Lewiston: Edwin Mellen Press, 1985.

Hell, Vera and Hellmut. *The Great Pilgrimage of the Middle Ages: The Road to St. James of Compostela*. Trans. Alisa Jaffa. New York: Clarkson N. Potter, 1966.

Hildegard of Bingen. *Scivias*. trans. Bruce Hozeski. Santa Fe: Bear and Company, 1986.

Holloway, Julia Bolton. *The Pilgrim and the Book: A Study of Dante, Langland and Chaucer*. Berne: Peter Lang, 1987.

Hrotswitha of Gandersheim. *Plays*. Trans. Larissa Bonfante. New York: New York University Press, 1979.

Jacobus de Voragine. *The Golden Legend*. Trans. Granger Ryan and Helmut Ripperger. New York: Longmans, Green, 1941.

Jerome. *Select Letters of St. Jerome*. Trans. F.A. Wright. Cambridge, Mass.: Harvard University Press, 1963. Loeb Classical Library, 262.

Krochalis, Jeanne. "The Benedictine Rule for Nuns: Library of Congress MS 4." *Manuscripta* 30 (1986): 21-34.

Langland, William. *Piers the Ploughman*. Trans. J.F. Goodrich. Harmonsdworth: Penguin, 1959.

Luttrell, Anthony. "Englishwomen as Pilgrims to Jerusalem: Isolda of Parewastell, 1365." In *Equally in God's Image: Women in the Middle Ages*.

Ed. Julia Bolton Holloway, Joan Bechtold, Constance Wright. New York: Peter Lang, 1990. Pp. 184-197.

Makowski, Elizabeth. "Canon Law and Medieval Conjugal Rights." *Journal of Medieval History* 3 (1977): 99-114. Reprinted, in *Equally in God's Image: Women in the Middle Ages*, ed. Julia Bolton Holloway, Joan Bechtold, Constance Wright. New York: Peter Lang, 1990. Pp. 129-143.

Mayvaert, Paul. "The Medieval Monastic Claustrum." *Gesta* 12 (1973): 53-59.

McCarthy, Maria C. *The Rule for Nuns of St. Caesarius of Arles.* Washington: Catholic University Press, 1960.

Medieval Women's Visionary Literature. Ed. Elizabeth Alvida Petroff. New York: Oxford University Press, 1986.

McNamara, Jo Ann. "Cornelia's Daughters: Paula and Eustochium." *Women's Studies* 11 (1984):9-27.

_____ and Suzanne Wemple. "Sanctity and Power: The Dual Pursuit of Medieval Women." In *Becoming Visible: Women in European History.* Ed. Renata Bridenthal, and Claudia Koonz. Boston: Houghton-Mifflin, 1977.

Mustanoja, Tauno, ed. *The Good Wife Taught her Daughter. The Good Wyfe Wold a Pilgrimage. The Thewis of Gud Women.* Helsinki, 1948.

Newman, Barbara J. *Sister of Wisdom: St. Hildegard's Theology of the Feminine.* Berkeley: University of California Press, 1955.

Power, Eileen. *Medieval English Nunneries.* Cambridge: Cambridge University Press, 1922.

Pseudo-Bonaventure. *Meditations on the Life of Christ: An Illustrated Manuscript of the Fourteenth Century.* Ed. Isa Ragusa and Rosalie B. Green. Princeton, Princeton University Press, 1967.

Regularis Concordia: Anglicae Nationis Monachorum Sanctimonialumque. Trans. Thomas Symons. London: Nelson, 1953.

Schulenberg, Jane Tibbetts. "The Heroes of Virginity: Bride of Christ and Sacrificial Mutililation." In *Women in the Middle Ages and Renaissance.* Ed. Mary Beth Rose. Pp. 29-72.

Sumption, Jonathan. *Pilgrimage: An Image of Mediaeval Religon.* London: Faber and Faber, 1975.

Theresa of Avila. *The Life of Saint Theresa of Avila by Herself.* Harmondsworth: Penguin, 1957.

Underhill, Evelyn. *Mysticism: A Study in the Nature and Development of Man's Spiritual Consciousness.* New York: Dutton, 1961.

Woman and Power in the Middle Ages. Ed. Mary Erler and Maryanne Kowaleski. Athens: University of Georgia Press, 1988.

III. Brigittine Syon, Carthusian Sheen and Mount Grace

Bateson, Mary. *Catalogue of the Library of Syon Monastery, Isleworth.* Cambridge: Cambridge University Press, 1898.

Collins, A. Jefferies. *The Bridgettine Breviary of Syon Abbey from the Manuscript with the English Rubrics F.4.11 at Magdalene College, Cambridge.* Worcester: Stanbrook Abbey Press, 1969. Henry Bradsaw Society, 96.

Deanesly, Margaret. *The "Incendium Amoris" of Richard Rolle of Hampole.* London: Longmans, Green and Co., 1915.

Denise, Sr. Mary, R.S.M. *"The Orchard of Syon:* An Introduction." *Traditio,* 14 (1958), 269-293.

Driver, Martha W. "Pictures in Print: Late Fifteenth- and Early Sixteenth-Century English Religious Books for Lay Readers." In *De Cella in Seculum: Religious and Secular Life and Devotion in Late Medieval England.* Ed. Michael G. Sargent. Cambridge: Brewer, 1989. Pp. 229-244.

Ellis, Roger. *"Flores ad fabricandam . . . coronam:* An Investigation into the Uses of the Revelations of St. Bridget of Sweden in Fifteenth-Century England." *Medium Aevum* 51 (1982): 163-86.

_____. *Viderunt eam filie Syon: The Spirituality of the English House of a Medieval Contemplative Order from its Beginnings to the Present Day.* Salzburg: Institut für Anglistik und Amerikanistik Universität Salzburg, 1984). *Analecta Cartusiana,* 68. The Contemplative Life in Great Britain: Carthusians, Benedictines, Bridgettines, 2, ed. James Hogg.

Erler, Mary Carpenter. "Syon Abbey's Care for Books: Its Sacristan's Account Books, 1506/7-1535/6." *Scriptorium,* 39 (1985), 293-307.

Fletcher, John Rory. *The Story of the English Bridgettines of Syon Abbey.* South Brent, Devon: Syon Abbey, 1933.

Hodgson, Phyllis. *"The Orcherd of Syon* and the English Mystical Traditon." *Proceedings of the British Academy,* 50 (1964), 229-249.

Hogg, James. "The Contribution of the Brigittine Order to Late Medieval English Spirituality," *Spiritualität Heute und Gestern, Internationaler Kongres vom 4 bis 7 August 1982.* In *Analecta Cartusiana* 35:3 (1983): 4-164.

_____. "Mount Grace Charterhouse and Late Medieval English Spirituality." *Analecta Cartusiana* 82 (1980): 1-53.

Holloway, Julia Bolton. *The Life of Saint Birgitta by Birger Gregersson and Thomas Gascoigne.* Toronto: Peregrina Publishing Co, 1991. Peregrina Translations Series, 17 (Matrologia Svecica).

Horsfield, Robert A. "The Pomander of Prayer: Aspects of Late Medieval English Carthusian Spirituality and its Lay Audience." In *De Cella in Seculum: Religious and Secular Life and Devotion in Late Medieval England.* Ed. Michael G. Sargent. Cambridge: Brewer, 1989. Pp. 205-213.

Hussey, S.S. "The Audience for the Middle English Mystics." In *De Cella in Seculum: Religious and Secular Life and Devotion in Late Medieval England*. Ed. Michael G. Sargent. Cambridge: Brewer, 1989. Pp. 109-122.

Hutchison, Ann M. "Devotional Reading in the Monastery and in the Late Medieval Household." In *De Cella in Seculum: Religious and Secular Life and Devotion in Late Medieval England*. Ed. Michael G. Sargent. Cambridge: Brewer, 1989. Pp. 215-227.

Ker, N.R. *Medieval Libraries of Great Britain: A List of Surviving Books*. London: Offices of the Royal Historical Society, 1964.

Knowles, David. *Bare Ruined Choirs: The Dissolution of English Monasteries*. Cambridge: Cambridge University Press, 1976.

_____. *The Religious Orders in England*. Volume 3. *The Tudor Age*. Cambridge: Cambridge University Press, 1959.

_____ and R. Neville Hadcock. *Medieval Religious Houses: England and Wales*. New York: St. Martin's, 1971.

Myroure of Oure Ladye containing a Devotional Treatise on Divine Service with a Translation of the Offices used by the Sisters of the Brigittine Monastery of Syon at Isleworth, During the Fifteenth and Sixteenth Centuries. Ed. from the original Black Letter of 1530 A.D., J.H. Blunt. London: Trübner, EETS, 1873. EETS.ES 29.

The Orcherd of Syon. Ed. Phyllis Hodgson and Gabriel M. Liegey. Oxford: EETS, 1966. EETS 258.

Sargent, Michael. James Grenehalgh as Textual Critic. Salzburg: Institut für Anglistik und Amerikanistik, 1984). 2 vols.

_____. "The Transmission by the English Carthusians of Some Late Medieval Spiritual Writings." *Journal of Ecclesiastical History* 27 (1976): 225-240.

Thompson, E. Margaret. *The Carthusian Order in England*. London: SPCK, 1930.

Yorkshire Writers: Richard Rolle of Hampole and His Followers. Ed. C. Horstman. London: Swan Sonnenschein, 1895-96.

IV. Julian of Norwich and Margery Kempe

Atkinson, Clarissa. *Mystic and Pilgrim: The Book and the World of Margery Kempe*. Ithaca: Cornell University Press, 1983.

Beckwith, Sarah. "A Very Material Mysticism: The Medieval Mysticism of Margery Kempe." In *Medieval Literature: Criticism, Ideology and History*. Ed. David Aers. New York: St. Martin's Press, 1986. Pp. 34-57.

Collis, Louise. *Memoirs of a Medieval Woman: The Life and Times of Margery Kempe*. New York: Harper, 1983.

Delany, Sheila. "Sexual Economics: Chaucer's Wife of Bath and the *Book of Margery Kempe*." *Minnesota Review* 5 (1975): 104-115.

Dickman, Susan. "Margery Kempe and the English Devotional Tradition." In *The Medieval Mystical Tradition in England: Papers Read at the Exeter Symposium, July, 1980*. Ed. Marion Glasscoe. Exeter: University of Exeter, 1980.

_____. "Margery Kempe and the Continental Tradition of the Pious Woman." In *The Medieval Mystical Tradition in England: Papers Read at Dartington Hall, July, 1984*. Ed. Marion Glasscoe. Cambridge: D.S. Brewer, 1984.

Ellis, Deborah S. "Margery Kempe and the Virgin's Hot Caudle." *Essays in Arts and Sciences* 14 (1985): 1-11.

Gibson, Gail McMurray. *The Theater of Devotion: East Anglian Drama and Society in the Late Middle Ages*. Chicago: University of Chicago Press, 1989.

Jantzen, Grace. *Julian of Norwich*. London: SPCK, 1987.

Julian of Norwich. *A Book of Showings to the Anchoress Julian of Norwich*. Ed. Edmund Colledge, O.S.A., and James Walsh, S.J. Toronto: Pontifical Institute of Mediaeval Studies, 1978. 2 vols.

_____. *Revelations of Divine Love*. Trans. Clifton Wolters. Harmondsworth: Penguin, 1966.

Lochrie, Karma. "*The Book of Margery Kempe*: The Marginal Woman's Quest for Literary Authority." *Journal of Medieval and Renaissance Studies* 16 (1986): 33-55.

[Margery Kempe.] *The Book of Margery Kempe*. Trans. B.A. Windeatt. Harmonsdworth: Penguin, 1985.

McIlwain, James T. "The 'bodeley sycknes' of Julian of Norwich." *Journal of Medieval History* 10 (1984): 167-168.

Molinari, Paul. *Julian of Norwich: The Teaching of a Fourteenth Century English Mystic*. London: Longmans, Green and Co., 1959.

Reynolds, Anna Maria. "Some Literary Influences in the Devotions of Julian of Norwich." *Leeds Studies in English*, 1952. Pp. 18-28.

Stone, Robert Karl. *Middle English Prose Style: Margery Kempe and Julian of Norwich*. The Hague: Mouton, 1970.

Upjohn, Sheila. *In Search of Julian of Norwich*. London: Darton, Longman, and Todd, 1989.

Weissman, Hope Phyllis. "Margery Kempe in Jerusalem: *Hysterico Compassio* in the Late Middle Ages." In *Acts of Interpretation: The Text in its Contexts, 700-1600: Essays on Medieval and Renaissance Literature in Honor of E. Talbot Donaldson*. Ed. Mary J. Carruthers and Elizabeth D. Kirk. Norman: Pilgrim Books, 1982. Pp. 201-217.

INDEX

I: Primary